Virginia, Maryland & Delaware
& Delaware
BREWERIES

VIRGINIA, MARYLAND & DELAWARE BREWERIES

LEW BRYSON

STACKPOLE
BOOKS

To my parents,

Lewis and Ruth Bryson,

*in appreciation of many vacations spent in Williamsburg and Washington
and along the Blue Ridge and Chesapeake Bay, as well as one very
special trip with my father to Busch Gardens*

Copyright © 2005 by Stackpole Books

Published by
STACKPOLE BOOKS
5067 Ritter Road
Mechanicsburg, PA 17055
www.stackpolebooks.com

The author and publisher encourage all readers to visit the breweries and sample
their beers, but recommend that those who consume alcoholic beverages travel
with a nondrinking driver.

Printed the United States

10 9 8 7 6 5 4 3 2 1

FIRST EDITION

Cover design by Caroline Stover

Labels and logos used with the permission of the breweries

Library of Congress Cataloging-in-Publication Data

Bryson, Lew.
    Virginia, Maryland, & Delaware breweries / Lew Bryson.
        p.   cm.
    Includes index.
    ISBN 0-8117-3215-0 (pbk.)
    1. Bars (Drinking establishments)–Virginia–Guidebooks.   2. Bars (Drinking
establishments)–Maryland–Guidebooks.   3. Bars (Drinking establishments)–
Delaware–Guidebooks.   4. Microbreweries–Virginia–Guidebooks.   5. Microbreweries–Maryland–Guidebooks.   6. Microbreweries–Delaware–Guidebooks.   7. Breweries–Virginia–Guidebooks.   8. Breweries–Maryland–Guidebooks.   9. Breweries–
Delaware–Guidebooks.   I. Title.
TX950.57.V8B79   2005
647.9575–dc22
                                                                              2004025657

ISBN 978-0-8117-3215-4

CONTENTS

FOREWORD

I first got to know Lew Bryson almost a year after we opened Dogfish Head in 1995. From the planning stages forward, I knew I wanted to focus on brewing big and flavorful beers. I was looking for feedback when I sent my first samples of Immort Ale and Chicory Stout off to *Malt Advocate* magazine. I got more than that when Lew returned my call upon tasting the samples. I got encouragement. While I believed wholeheartedly in what we were doing at the brewery, this encouragement was critical. This was the mid-1990s, and there wasn't a lot of experimenting going on in the beer world.

It's easy to forget that the whole craft-brewing segment of the American beer industry is still only twenty-something years old. The Mid-Atlantic was blessed with some great breweries very early in this nascent industry. Some survived and thrived, such as Old Dominion and DeGroens. Some never really made it out of the shakeout fog of the late nineties.

All through this period, Lew was championing not just the beers he liked, but also the places and people who were making them. Regardless of the subject matter, the stature, or history of the brewery he was reporting on, you always got a sense of his pure passion for the world of beer.

I first got to meet Lew in 1998 during a beer festival at Henry Ortlieb's revived brewery in downtown Philadelphia. He approached my booth and asked me what I was serving. I told him it was an IPA made with pureed dried apricots. He thought about that for a second and made a simple statement in a quiet voice: "That sounds horrible." He followed this pronouncement with the cannonball of his trademark laugh, which shook the rafters of the historic brewery. Then he took a breath, extended his glass, and said, "I can't wait to try it."

I'm proud to say that Lew liked the beer and wrote nice things about it in *Ale Street News,* but what I remember being most impressed with at the time is both the honesty and the excitement he conveyed within the first moments I met him: "That sounds horrible . . . I can't wait to try it." There wasn't a doubt in my mind that I was going to get a genuine opinion. Over the last nine years, as I've gotten to really know Lew, I've expected and received nothing less than that genuine opinion, as he goes happily about his job of educating budding beer enthusiasts.

In this day and age, our economy is truly based upon communication. As potential beer consumers, we receive our daily pummeling of communication from the major breweries via radio, billboards, television, and magazines. But often these giant companies are not communicating *with* us so much as they are communicating *to* us. More than 80 percent of the beer being drunk in this country is made by three breweries, and all three focus their production on very similar interpretations of a pilsner-style beer.

The communication we encounter from these breweries boils down to a sweeping branding exercise. In many beer advertisements, you are not asked to think about why you should choose a particular beer based on some quality distinction. You are told that you are uncool if you don't conform to the status quo and have "what he's having." In short, you're being given a directive: "Why ask why," life is short, just do what your television tells you to and buy our beer. This is a form of communication; it's pretty unidirectional, but in the world of billion-dollar advertising campaigns, it's still communication.

This is not the world that Lew Bryson lives in. And if you're buying this book, it's probably not the world you live in either. God bless you. Little breweries like ours might actually stand a chance. One reason that I'm so hopeful is that our community is based not on unidirectional communication, but on education that flows in every direction.

As you read Lew's suggestions for beer recommendations, side trips, and local attractions, you sense the respect that he has for his reader. He might share his opinions on some favorite beers, but he does not assume that they will immediately become your favorites as well. Lew doesn't grade on the curve or give mediocrity the benefit of the doubt, but he also doesn't pretend to be the final authority on what you should be drinking. That authority, of course, should be you. When it comes to your refrigerator, your vacation, or your road trip, you are not the pawn of beers—you are the king.

Somewhere along the way, the dynamic of our young industry has morphed from a renaissance into a revolution. When good beer started being made in small batches throughout the Mid-Atlantic, the styles that were brewed closely mirrored those made by our continental brewing brethren: pale ale, bock, amber, lager, porter. Some great interpretations of these styles are still being brewed throughout our region, but the breadth of new styles and interpretations has truly exploded.

As this book hits the shelf, we are in the midst of this revolution. Regional breweries are growing faster than giant breweries. The great thing about living during a revolution is not knowing where it is going. That in itself can be exhilarating. But it becomes even more exciting if you actually pick a side. It's easy to choose a team. On one side are the people who want to be told what beer to drink. On the other side are the people who look forward to figuring it out for themselves. More people are defecting from the former team to the latter every day. Lew has been instrumental in growing our ranks through communicating the message of better beer.

One of the events I most look forward to each year is the Christmas beer tasting at the Brickskeller in Washington, D.C. This place is a Mid-Atlantic beer mecca and worthy of its reputation for maintaining a stellar selection and beer-friendly environment. Every holiday season, the owners invite the brewers to come down with a keg of something special and take a turn on the stage telling the enthusiastic audience all about the beer that they brought.

I always know that I'm going to try some great beers as I make the drive from Delaware into the capital on that day. I can almost taste Bill Madden's Wee Heavy or the newest Belgian seasonal from The Brewer's Art. I also look forward to sitting down at the brewers' table with the rest of the gang. We tell war stories, catch up on gossip, and try each other's beers. We give and receive a lot of encouragement and positive feedback, and indulge in more than a little goading and carrying on. I've enjoyed getting to know each of the brewers who make it to this event, and I'm sure you will too. Its always fun to meet people who love their jobs and do them well.

Most of these brewers are people like me who took their hobby and devoted their lives to making a career of it. Sometimes a hobby becomes so important to you that it becomes your life. Sometimes it doesn't. I used to have one of those metal detector things that people wander around the beach with in search of lost change. To use these things, you wear a pair of headphones and wave the machine out before you. As you get closer to the treasure you've been searching for, the machine beeps louder and more frequently. I got really bored with this hobby and gave the metal detector away to a relative.

But the experience of using one of these things is sort of what it's like to attend a beer festival with Lew Bryson. As he moves around the room, the closer he comes to the brewers he respects and the beers he looks forward to sampling, the louder and more frequent his signature laugh. I'm sure Lew is going to keep searching for the ultimate beer experiences. There are some real treasures out there, and with Lew's guidance, you can discover them for yourself. Enjoy the trip. Cheers.

Sam Calagione
President, Dogfish Head Craft Brewery

ACKNOWLEDGMENTS

I didn't think this book would ever get done, but it did, and thanks are due. First and always, thanks go to Kyle Weaver, my editor at Stackpole Books, who gave me enough rope on this one, and then gave me a little more when I really needed it.

A bunch of people out there have taught me about beer. Writers like Michael Jackson, John Hansell, Chris Brooks, and Jim Dorsch. Brewers like Bill Covaleski and Ron Barchet of Victory (who both started brewing in Mid-Atlantic breweries), Jaime Jurado and Karl Ockert of The Gambrinus Corporation, and Sam Calagione of Dogfish Head. And Bob and Ellie Tupper, who talk about beer at the Brickskeller and taught me much by example.

To the people who supply me with excellent beer: first and always, Dave Alexander, for many years of education at the Brickskeller; the gang at State Line Liquors in Elkton, Maryland; Jim Dickerson at the Commercial Taphouse and Matt Simmons at the Capital Ale Houses in Richmond; Volker Stewart for the great guest beer selection at The Brewer's Art; and Tom Cizauskas of Clipper City, a good friend for years.

The Internet becomes more and more important in finding good beer and people to drink it with. I've been drinking at the No Bull Inn on Friday nights at www.StarChat.net for more years than you'd believe: thanks to Okie Bob, RP, Mr. Lloyd, BlueBlazer, and Mike the Sextuplet for plenty of advice. Thanks to www.Pubcrawler.com for excellent direction on finding bars and breweries—still the best site on the net for it. Coming on strong is www.BeerAdvocate.com: tip of the hat to the gang for help finding bars in D.C. and Baltimore.

My hearty thanks, of course, to the brewers. Hugh Sisson got the whole thing started in Maryland and has always been a source of interesting ideas and views on the industry. Jerry Bailey has always had time for talk (and some good fresh gossip) and usually leaves me laughing. Mike McDonald is a great source of information on his good friend, Ringwood. Special thanks to Sam Calagione for writing the foreword; he's been a good friend, even when I've been rough on his beers. Bill Madden has been a lot of help untangling the complications of the D.C.-area brewing scene, including the ones he's created. Joe Kalish has always been a solid guy to go to when I need information and a laugh. Thanks to Dave Brockner for the tour at Kegler's; you made my dad's day. Mark Edelson and Kevin Finn taught me a lot about the brewpub business.

Thanks to some friendly beer geeks for their help and accompaniment on the research tours, especially an enjoyable cold and rainy night in Ellicott City with Nick Nichols and his dad, Nick Nichols Sr., and a windy tramp through Fells Point and Federal Hill with the incomparable Sandy Mitchell. Steve Deason showed me Richmond in a way that finally brought it all together for me; he's a sophisticated champion of good beer in the River City. Thanks also to Steve Frank, Lloyd Dolan, Gregg Wiggins, and Martin Wooster for valuable bar suggestions in the D.C. Metro area: I owe you guys a beer.

Special thanks to my old friend and drinking buddy Steve Van Albert and his family, who opened their home to me when I did my D.C. research, and many other times in the past. My brother-in-law Carl Childs, his wife, Joan, and the kids put up with me when I canvassed Richmond and Tidewater; good hanging out with you guys, and thanks!

A special thank-you to my doctor, Arlene Imber, for fixing me up when I caught a wicked string of flu and bronchial infections right in the middle of research for this book, and to Shane Speal Sr. and his band, Jug Fusion, whose CD *Box Set* provided my soundtrack for writing this book: Keep fightin' with the catfish.

Thanks, as always, to my father, Lew, for unfailing map support and for hanging in there on the marathon Blue Ridge trip, which took us all the way to the Jack Daniel distillery . . . a long way to go for a shot and a beer, Sir! To my mother, Ruth, for proofing the manuscript and for always being with my family while I was on the road.

But most of all, thanks go to my family. My children, Thomas and Nora, who are sure that their father is famous, are the best thing to find at the end of a journey. And my wife, Catherine, makes all of this possible. She supports me, she encourages me, she believes in me. I can never thank her enough.

To all of you: Cheers!

INTRODUCTION

Welcome to the malty heart of the lower Mid-Atlantic region: the breweries of Virginia, Maryland, Delaware, and the District of Columbia. It's a great area, stretching from the brewpubs of the Shenandoah Valley to the small breweries around Washington, Baltimore, and Richmond, and on to the coast, where one very big brewery anchors the Tidewater and a couple small breweries with very big ambitions are looking to burst out of Delaware.

This broad area has fifty-seven breweries, with still more on the way. Some were in the first wave of new breweries through this area, and others are just opening. All but one, the Anheuser-Busch brewery in Williamsburg, are less than twenty years old. They are what have been called microbreweries or craft breweries, and they are notable mainly not for their size, but for the broad variety of beer they make. But this is not really a new thing; this is a return to the way beer used to be in America.

To understand where these new breweries came from, and what they represent, we need to take a look back at our country's history, when American brewing went from a vibrant, broad industry to a fossilized oligopoly of brewers making one style of beer, take it or leave it. What happened?

The Rise and Fall of American Brewing
The history of the Europeans in America goes like much of human history since the discovery of alcohol: As soon as they got ashore, most of the early settlers, the colonists, started looking for something to ferment and distill—pumpkins, corn, pine needles, anything for a jolt. The most popular alcoholic drink in early America was cider, followed closely by rum brought in from the West Indies. Americans drank a lot of these beverages, and a lot of alcohol in general. Per capita annual consumption of alcohol was more than ten gallons by the 1840s. That's gallons of pure alcohol, not gallons of rum at 40 percent alcohol or cider at 7 percent. Americans drank pretty much all the time.

When Americans did drink beer, they mostly drank imported British ales. And when Americans began brewing, they mimicked the English by producing similar unfiltered ales. Cider was still the most popular drink through Andrew Jackson's presidency, but things changed rapidly in the 1840s.

There were three complementary components to this change. German-style lager beers are believed to have first been brewed in America in Philadelphia, in 1840, by a brewer named John Wagner. This refreshing beer became very popular with laborers because it could be drunk quickly to quench a thirst.

Paradoxically, the temperance movements that swept the nation in the 1840s accelerated the rise of lager beer. Temperance had strong effects on many suppliers, retailers, and drinkers. One of its major "successes" was wiping out America's cider-producing orchards almost entirely. The 1840s saw fields of stumps on many farms; woodcut illustrations of the devastated orchards are a bemusing legacy. The demand for drink did not go away, of course, and lager brewers picked up the shifting market.

The third thing that drove lager's popularity was the rise in immigration to America after the squashed European rebellions of 1848. Germans and other beer-drinking Europeans came to America by the thousands, and they wanted their beer. America was happy to supply it.

The lower Mid-Atlantic had plenty of breweries, and some of their names survive in labels brewed by other brewers, or merely in memory. You or your father may remember National Bohemian and Globe Brewing (briefly reopened as a microbrewery) of Baltimore; Diamond State of Wilmington; Washington's Christian Heurich, now resurrected as a contract brew by a descendant of the family who has vowed to build a new Heurich brewery; and Home Brewing of Richmond.

There were more than two thousand breweries in America at the turn of the century, mostly small, local breweries producing almost every style of beer, although lager was a clear favorite. The temperance movements, however, had not gone away.

The Great Killer of breweries in America was the little social experiment called Prohibition, which lasted from 1919 to 1933. By 1939, after this fanaticism had run its course and the industry had briefly boomed and settled down, only about five hundred breweries remained.

Everyone knows that people didn't stop drinking during Prohibition, but the quality of the beer they drank was dramatically affected. Some drank "needle beer," which was near beer injected with alcohol, or low-grade homebrew made with anything they could get their hands on. They used cake yeast and the malt syrup that brewers were making to survive. Other beer generally available during Prohibition was low-quality and relatively weak, made from cheap ingredients with large amounts of corn or rice for fermentation.

Illicit brewers used the high-gravity system: brew very strong beer, then water it down. This saved time and money, as did greatly shortened aging times. Federal enforcement agents knew that hops were a commodity really used only for brewing; brewers, therefore, lowered the amount of hops they used to avoid suspicion. For fourteen years, people drank literally anything that was called beer.

These changes brought about some long-term effects. The corn and rice and high-gravity brewing produced a distinctly lighter-bodied beer with an identifiable non-barley taste. Low hopping rates made for a sweeter beer. Over Prohibition's fourteen years, people got used to light lager beer. The process continued over the next three decades, as big brewers came to dominate the market.

The rise of big breweries and the decline of small ones can be tracked to several important developments. World War II brought a need to get lots of beer to troops abroad. Huge contracts went to the brewers who were big enough to fill them. Hops and malt for home-front brewing were considered largely nonessential.

Improvements in packaging made buying beer for home consumption easier. One of them took place in January 1935 in Richmond, where the first beer in a can, Krueger's Cream Ale, was produced (the can was a "flat top," not a cone top, as people often assume). Richmond remains a frequent test market for beer innovations, for reasons best known to marketers.

Refrigerated transportation enabled brewers to ship beer long distances to reach more customers. Refrigerated boxcars and trucks, as well as the new canning lines, required large capital investment possible only for successful, growing breweries.

Mass-market advertising during broadcast sporting events got the national breweries in front of everyone. The advertising further convinced Americans that light lagers were the only type of beer out there. Advertising was expensive but effective. The big breweries got bigger, and small ones went out of business.

Why did the rise of big national brewers necessarily mean that American beer would become all the same type of light lager? Simple reasons, really: Making it all the same is cheaper and easier. Success breeds imitation. Image is easier to market than flavor. A large national brand has to appeal to a broad audience of consumers.

This led to the situation in the 1970s in which one dominant style of beer was made by fewer than forty breweries. People who wanted anything else had to seek out the increasingly rare exceptions made by smaller brewers or buy pricey imports of unknown age and freshness. The varieties of beer styles were unknown to most Americans.

This is the real key to understanding the craft-brewing revolution. These beers are not better made than Budweiser; in fact, Budweiser is more consistent than many American craft-brewed beers. What craft-brewed beers offered was variety.

The American Brewing Revolution

How did microbreweries get started? Fritz Maytag bought the Anchor Brewery in San Francisco on a whim in the mid-1960s. He had heard they were going out of business and knew they brewed his favorite beer. Fritz was an heir to the Maytag appliance fortune and could afford to indulge his whims. But he got hooked on brewing, and Anchor led the return of beer variety in America. Fritz brewed Anchor's trademark "steam" beer, an ale and lager hybrid; he brewed the mightily hoppy Liberty Ale; and he brewed the strong, malty barley wine he called Old Foghorn. Things were off and . . . well, things were off and walking in the United States.

Next came the microbreweries. Ambitious homebrewers, maverick megabrewers, and military or businesspeople who had been to Europe and wanted to have the same kinds of beer they drank there saw a need for better beer. They started these small breweries, cobbling them together like Frankenstein's monster from whatever pieces of equipment they could find. The beer was anything but uniform—sometimes excellent, sometimes awful—but even so, it found a receptive market.

The revolution started in the West and grew very slowly. New Albion, the first new brewery in America since World War II, opened in Sonoma, California, in 1976. Craft brewing first came to the Mid-Atlantic in 1984, when the Chesapeake Bay Brewing Company opened in Virginia Beach. But it was, as was often the case, born too soon. Chesapeake Bay, or "Chesbay," as the beer was known, held on until 1992 before folding, but not before I got a chance to sample a couple of their beers. They deserved to survive. Chesbay made a brief resurgence recently, but it's down again, sadly.

Sisson's and Baltimore Brewing opened in Baltimore in the late 1980s, as did Old Dominion in Virginia, outside of Washington. Things started happening faster in the mid-1990s, when dozens of small breweries opened. Brewpubs popped up like mushrooms after the rain, microbreweries opened on a loan and a wish, and the do-it-yourself brew-on-premise stores looked like a popular wave. It was an optimistic time, and breweries like Frederick Brewing expanded exponentially and went public amid huge fanfare.

Then the long-anticipated shakeout hit the industry, and the press has gleefully reported several times since then that microbrewing is dead. Most of the larger micros had troubles, and some of the undercapitalized ones went under. The tragic events of September 11, 2001, hit the industry hard as people reevaluated their lifestyles. Some were hit harder than others. Old Dominion's Jerry Bailey told me that he didn't sell a bit of beer in the hotels around the Pentagon in the two weeks after September 11. "The bar managers said everyone was drinking hard liquor," Jerry said. Who could blame them?

Things looked bad for a few years. Has the hammer fallen? Will microbrewing last, or was it just a passing fad? In my opinion, the genie won't go back in the bottle. Brewpubs are established in their communities, and more are still opening. The area's smaller microbreweries are doing well; a number of them were returning to growth and planning expansions as I finished this manuscript.

People have discovered the many different ways beer can taste. No one thinks all wine comes in gallon jugs anymore, and everyone knows there are more types than red and white. Beer is on that same path.

How I Came to Love All Beer

My beer-drinking career has been reflective of America's beer revolution. I started with beers from big breweries, some that are no longer around. I had my first full beer as a freshman in college. When I was a kid, my father had often let me have sips of his beer with dinner. That was Duke Ale, from Duquesne Brewing of Pittsburgh, one of Pennsylvania's many defunct breweries. But I'd never had a beer of my own until my freshman year in college, when I got hold of a Genny Cream in a 16-ounce, solidly brown and green returnable, dripping with condensation. I drank it, and it was good.

I drank a lot more of them over the next three years. Genny Cream, Stroh's, and Rolling Rock were my staples, though I drank more than my share of National Bohemian when the money was tight. "From the land o' pleasant living!" we would holler out as we clinked the bottles.

Then one night in my senior year at Franklin and Marshall College, I met my medieval history professor for drinks, a special treat for a few legal-age students. The bar was the Lauzus Hotel, in Lancaster, Pennsylvania. Run by old Wilhelm Lauzus, an ex-German Navy man, the bar carried more than 125 different beers in 1981, not too shabby at all in those days. I had no clue and grabbed my usual Stroh's. My professor laughed and slapped it out of my hand. He pulled a German beer, an Altenmünster, out of the cooler and popped the swingtop. "Try this," he said, and changed my life.

It was big, full in the mouth, and touched by a strange bitterness that I'd never tasted before. That bitterness made another sip the most natural thing in the world, like pepper on potatoes. I've been looking for beers outside the American mainstream ever since that night.

It's increasingly easy to find that kind of beer in the Mid-Atlantic, where breweries are turning out everything from whopping Imperial stouts to crisp, bitter pilsners to rippingly hoppy India pale ales to bubbly, spicy hefe-weizens. Dogfish Head, a Delaware brewery that I've followed pretty closely since its first days, is recognized as one of the most innovative breweries in the country; you'll see why when you read that entry.

Is that all I drink anymore, beers like that? Well, no. When I mow my lawn, or when I'm getting down and dirty with a bunch of friends and a bushel of steamed crabs, sometimes I want a cold glass of something dashingly refreshing and fizzy. Then I might reach for a growler of Capitol City Kölsch, or maybe even some ice-cold pony bottles of Little Kings. Cold is good!

It's been good to return to the lower Mid-Atlantic from my home in Pennsylvania. I've lived in Maryland, Virginia, and the District in the past; Delaware was always right across the border from where I grew up in southeastern Pennsylvania. I have enjoyed traveling to the region's breweries and sampling these beers at the source. I met a bunch of new people and made a lot of friends. Beer traveling is a great way to have fun, and I hope this book will serve as a ready guide for your travels. Hoist one for me!

How to Use This Book

This book is a compendium of information about Virginia, Maryland, and Delaware breweries. It also lists some of the interesting attractions and best bars in the area. It offers facts and opinions about brewing, brewing history in the United States and the lower Mid-Atlantic region, and beer-related subjects.

It does not present a comprehensive history of any brewery, nor is it one of the ubiquitous books that try to rate every single beer produced by every single brewery. It is not a conglomeration of beer jargon—Original Gravities, International Bittering Unit levels, Apparent Attenua-

Delaware

❶ Iron Hill Brewery and Restaurant, Wilmington
John Harvard's Brew House, Wilmington
❷ Stewart's Brewing Company, Bear
❸ Iron Hill Brewery and Restaurant, Newark
❹ Southern Beverages, Inc./Fordham Brewing
Company, Dover
❺ Dogfish Head Craft Brewery, Milton
❻ Dogfish Head Brewing and Eats, Rehoboth Beach

tions, and so on. And it's not about homebrewing. Other people do a fine job on books like that, but it's not what I wanted to do.

It is a travel guide about breweries and the amazing region that is home to startling natural beauty and man-made wonders. Sharing information has been a central part of the success of the rise of microbreweries in the United States. I've been sharing what I know for more than twenty years, and this book and its companion volumes, *Pennsylvania Breweries* and *New York Breweries*, represent my latest efforts to spread the good word.

The book is organized in alternating parts. The meat of the book, the brewery information, is presented in seven sections. Each of these geographical sections—Delaware, Baltimore and the Bay, Western Maryland, D.C. Metro, the District, Richmond and Tidewater, and the Blue Ridge—is prefaced with a description of the area for those unfamiliar with it. The *A word about . . .* sections are intended as instructional interludes on topics you may be curious about. There should be something there for almost everyone, whether novice, dabbler, or fanatic.

The history and character of the brewpub or brewery, highlights, my observations, and other information are presented in a narrative section. A brewpub sells beer to be enjoyed on location, whereas a brewery sells its beer primarily off-premises. If any beers have won Great American Beer Festival (GABF) or Real Ale Festival (RAF) awards, those are noted, but not every brewery enters these competitions. The annual capacity in barrels, as listed for each brewery, is a function of the fermenting-tank capacity and the average time to

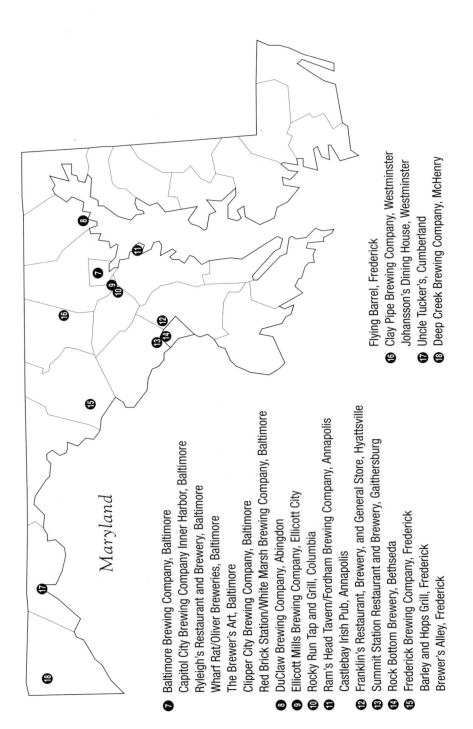

Maryland

7 Baltimore Brewing Company, Baltimore
Capitol City Brewing Company Inner Harbor, Baltimore
Ryleigh's Restaurant and Brewery, Baltimore
Wharf Rat/Oliver Breweries, Baltimore
The Brewer's Art, Baltimore
Clipper City Brewing Company, Baltimore
Red Brick Station/White Marsh Brewing Company, Baltimore

8 DuClaw Brewing Company, Abingdon

9 Ellicott Mills Brewing Company, Ellicott City

10 Rocky Run Tap and Grill, Columbia

11 Ram's Head Tavern/Fordham Brewing Company, Annapolis
Castlebay Irish Pub, Annapolis

12 Franklin's Restaurant, Brewery, and General Store, Hyattsville

13 Summit Station Restaurant and Brewery, Gaithersburg

14 Rock Bottom Brewery, Bethseda
Frederick Brewing Company, Frederick

15 Barley and Hops Grill, Frederick
Brewer's Alley, Frederick

Flying Barrel, Frederick

16 Clay Pipe Brewing Company, Westminster
Johansson's Dining House, Westminster

17 Uncle Tucker's, Cumberland

18 Deep Creek Brewing Company, McHenry

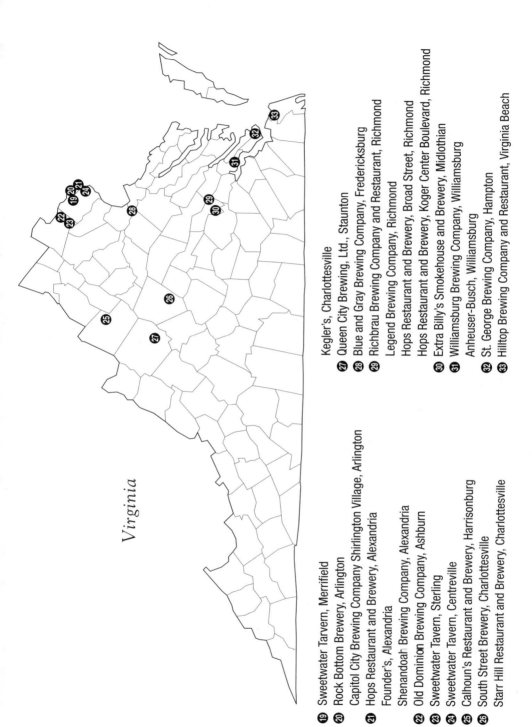

Virginia

19 Sweetwater Tarvern, Merrifield
20 Rock Bottom Brewery, Arlington
21 Capitol City Brewing Company Shirlington Village, Arlington
    Hops Restaurant and Brewery, Alexandria
    Founder's, Alexandria
22 Shenandoah Brewing Company, Alexandria
    Old Dominion Brewing Company, Ashburn
23 Sweetwater Tavern, Sterling
24 Sweetwater Tavern, Centreville
25 Calhoun's Restaurant and Brewery, Harrisonburg
    South Street Brewery, Charlottesville
26 Starr Hill Restaurant and Brewery, Charlottesville

    Kegler's, Charlottesville
27 Queen City Brewing, Ltd., Staunton
28 Blue and Gray Brewing Company, Fredericksburg
29 Richbrau Brewing Company and Restaurant, Richmond
    Legend Brewing Company, Richmond
    Hops Restaurant and Brewery, Broad Street, Richmond
    Hops Restaurant and Brewery, Koger Center Boulevard, Richmond
30 Extra Billy's Smokehouse and Brewery, Midlothian
31 Williamsburg Brewing Company, Williamsburg
    Anheuser-Busch, Williamsburg
32 St. George Brewing Company, Hampton
33 Hilltop Brewing Company and Restaurant, Virginia Beach

mature a beer. Lagers take longer, so on two identical systems with the same fermenter setup, an all-lager brewery would have significantly lower annual capacity than an all-ale brewery.

The other area beer sites I've listed for most breweries may include multitaps, historic bars, or restaurants with good beer selections. Whenever possible, I visited these bars and had at least one beer there. A few of these descriptions are based on recommendations from brewers or beer geeks I know personally.

Washington, D.C.

(See map on page 143)

Capitol City Brewing Company, Union Station
District ChopHouse and Brewery
Gordon-Biersch
John Harvard's Brew House, D.C.

Small Wonder, They Call It
Delaware

S ay "Delaware" to most people, and not much comes to mind. Maybe a weak "Dela where?" will escape their lips, but very few people get excited. I didn't realize how much I fell in that category until I started this book. Here's what I learned and why I think of all kinds of things when someone says "Delaware" to me now.

Delaware is a capital of business. Thanks to the state's liberal banking and corporation laws, more than 150,000 corporations call Delaware home—even if only through a mailbox. But the law firms and banks servicing those corporations are here, and some corporations have been smart enough to see the wisdom of basing themselves physically in Delaware: a well-educated workforce, proximity to Washington and New York, easy access to major airlines, and a much lower cost of doing business than in other big cities. And of course, the Du Ponts have always been here, a major force in American industry since their explosive beginnings.

Delaware is a tourism magnet. Whether it's for historic sites like the Du Ponts' former home at Wintherthur, the attractions of bird-watching in Delaware's wildlife refuges, the roaring thunder of NASCAR races at Dover Downs, or the beautiful beaches on the Delaware Bay, Delaware is the destination for many who do know of the Small Wonder. Weekend sailors cruise the Delaware Bay or sail right across the state on the Chesapeake and Delaware Canal.

Delaware is a breadbasket. Farms in southern Delaware, like their counterparts on the Eastern Shore of Maryland, raise hundreds of thousands of chickens for companies such as Perdue and Tyson, keeping you in chicken fingers. The large, irrigated farms of southern Delaware grow wheat and corn, and even some barley that Sam Calagione puts in Dogfish Head's Shelter Pale Ale every year. The bounty of the sea calls fishing boats every day from Delaware harbors.

1

Delaware was a key player in the beginnings of America. Caesar Rodney, the man on the horse on the back of Delaware's commemorative quarter, rode overnight through 80 miles of stormy darkness to cast the last-minute deciding vote for the ratification of the Declaration of Independence in July 1776, despite illness that had kept him confined to his home for months. When the independence thus declared had been won in truth, Delaware was the first state to ratify the new Constitution, a little head start on history that Delaware grabbed as grounds to style itself "The First State." As the second-smallest state in the Union—only Rhode Island is smaller—some compensatory puffery is to be expected.

It is small. This is the third brewery guide that I've done, and I'm used to cutting up states into easy-to-digest sections. But Delaware is a whole state, and you have to swallow it whole, without splitting the farms from the beaches, the capital of Dover from the financial weight of Wilmington, the liberal urban north from rural, conservative "slower lower Delaware."

Taken as a whole, then, Delaware is a state that puts me in mind of Belgium. It is small and lies between larger, very definitive cultures, Yankee and Southern. It has a culture of its own that is neither bold nor showy, but one that works for Delaware, a determined manner of doing things Delaware's way. It has taken its in-between position and made it valuable with liberal financial laws and no sales tax, leading many outlanders to do their shopping in Delaware. And there are a lot of breweries for a place its size.

Delaware has always had a lot going for it in its history, its geography, and its people. It is slowly waking up to just how well off it is, and other people are recognizing it as well. Dogfish Head's new brewery in Milton is in the middle of an ambitious project to create a wired, high-tech community. Iron Hill in Wilmington is on the city's new Riverwalk, a celebration of beauty the city had forgotten it had.

Things are happening in Delaware. It may not be a sleeping giant, but the little guy is waking up, and it looks like everyone's going to enjoy what happens when he does.

Note: Delaware state law prohibits smoking in bars, restaurants, and other public places.

Iron Hill Brewery and Restaurant, Wilmington

710 South Madison Street, Wilmington, DE 19807
302-658-8200
www.ironhillbrewing.com

After seven years of wanting to be here, Iron Hill has finally made a triumphant entrance to Wilmington. They're not just *in* Wilmington—they're one of the stars of the city's new Riverwalk attraction, a celebration of the Christina River. That's prestige, that's glory, that's due, that's—I'll tell you what that is, it's *convenient:* The brewpub is an easy five-minute walk from the Amtrak station in Wilmington. Sure beats running I-95 into town.

Oh, but it did my heart good to see Iron Hill's new brewpub standing two stories tall and hometown proud, with all the chain restaurants clustered around it. Wilmingtonians are rightly pleased to finally have an Iron Hill near enough to enjoy.

The partners are pretty pleased as well. "This is our state," says Mark Edelson, "and this is our home turf. Expectations are running high for this place, and we're up for it after a real smooth opening." They cheated a bit on the opening, bringing in experienced servers and kitchen staff from the other Iron Hills to make up about a third of the staff for the opening. That's the beauty of a successful large operation: cadre, and with it, the ability to replicate your successes and stamp out bad habits before they get rooted.

Mark and I were talking not long after the opening of the Wilmington Iron Hill. We were at the newest Iron Hill, in North Wales, Pennsylvania, on a chilly January morning watching the brewing staff manhandle the new brewhouse into the building. "You know," Mark confided to me, "I

Beers brewed: Year-round: Iron Hill Light Lager, Raspberry Wheat, Lodestone Lager (GABF Gold, 1997; Bronze, 2000), Anvil Ale, Ironbound Ale, Pig Iron Porter (GABF Bronze, 2002; RAF Silver, 2002 and 2003). Seasonals: Altbier, Barleywine, Belgian White, Bohemian Pils, Dry Stout, ESB, Hefeweizen, Imperial IPA, India Pale Ale, Lambic de Hill (GABF Gold, 2003), Maibock (GABF Gold, 1999; Bronze, 2000), Munich Dunkel (GABF Bronze, 2003), Nut Brown Ale, Oatmeal Stout, Oktoberfest, Old Alc, Russian Imperial Stout (GABF Gold, 2003), Saison (GABF Bronze, 2003), Tripel (GABF Bronze, 2002), Vienna (GABF Bronze, 1999), Wee Heavy (GABF Bronze, 1998 and 2001).

have to think to remember everyone's names now. We're working with a payroll of almost five hundred people these days." But I looked at that team of brewers, every one of whom had honestly volunteered to come out and shove a couple tons of steel around, and saw people who were happy with their work. Size has its pitfalls, but Edelson and Kevin Finn and Kevin Davies are neatly skirting them so far.

Size has its advantages as well, one of them being enough money to be able to do things right when you want to, instead of getting by and edging toward it. Wilmington is a mature Iron Hill, where the brewers are doing things the way they want to. Their locale has a great view of the Riverwalk, so they used it, with tall glass walls and extensive outdoor serving space (with heaters already installed for those cool fall days).

The brewhouse got the treatment as well, pushing through both floors and all encased in glass—plainly visible from the minute you walk in, just as it is in every other Iron Hill. "They thought they were working in a fishbowl before," said Mark, laughing as he indicated the vitreous expanse from floor to two-story ceiling. The brewhouse is ready for action, too, with a 10-barrel Specific Mechanical system that's about 15 percent larger than the systems in the other pubs, and tanks sufficient to serve everyone. For a while, anyway.

Iron Hill took a big step here when it opened, beer-wise. Wilmington was the official launch site of Iron Hill Light Lager. "We're competing with a lot of bars, right here," Mark explains, "and we weren't going to put national brands on tap. This is light, it's got a crisp apple finish, and the brewers are fully on board with it. We're picking up people who would be drinking basic spirits instead: rum and coke, screwdrivers. But now they're drinking beer." Light beer may creep out some beer geeks, but not this one. If it keeps people at Iron Hill drinking fresh housemade beer, it can't be bad.

They have plenty of room to drink it, too. Upstairs is all bar area. "We saw a real opportunity for the bar," says Mark. "We've always had this problem with bar overflow [into the dining area], but here it's all bar." The room has a long bar, tables, and high tables, plenty of space for the happy-hour crowd. The outdoor space opens off the second floor as well.

The Pick: I've come to like it only in the past year, but Anvil Ale has been getting more and more of my attention. It's a pale ale that's firmly hopped with East Kent Goldings, very spicy hops without the citrus cut that many American brewers treasure, and I am very impressed with their freshness. I'm also impressed with the solid malt body of this beer. No expense is spared on ingredients. "On the brewpub level, the incremental costs don't justify not using the best materials," Mark Edelson says. Amen.

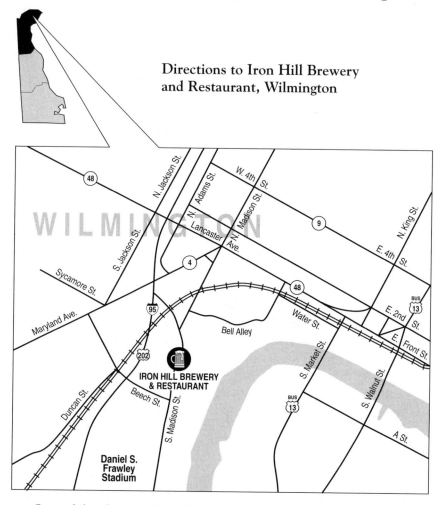

Directions to Iron Hill Brewery and Restaurant, Wilmington

One of the things I like a lot about the folks at Iron Hill is the way they're really committed to the industry. Mark Edelson has been contributing his time and considerable energies as a GABF judge for a number of years. More visibly, Iron Hill invites other brewers to their brewpubs on a regular basis for their Brewer's Reserve Nights, when each Iron Hill trots out something special and they all converge on one of the pubs, along with a guest brewer who brings something from his brewery. It's a great time, a real meet-the-brewer fest.

That's the latest from Iron Hill. Don't be surprised if you check my website after buying the book and find that yet another has opened. I hear the partners are taking a serious look at the long-neglected territory across the Delaware in southern New Jersey. When they're ready, they'll go, and they'll make it work.

Opened: September 2003.

Owners: Mark Edelson, Kevin Finn, Kevin Davies.

Brewer: Brian Finn, head brewer.

System: 10-barrel Specific Mechanical brewhouse, 1,400 barrels annual capacity.

Production: 275 barrels in September to December 2003.

Hours: 11:30 A.M. to 1 A.M., seven days a week.

Tours: Upon request.

Take-out beer: Growlers available.

Food: See entry for Newark Iron Hill (page 18).

Extras: Pool tables, live music (call for schedule), projection TV, large outdoor deck overlooking Wilmington Riverfront.

Special considerations: Cigars not allowed. Kids welcome. Vegetarian meals available. Handicapped-accessible.

Parking: Plentiful free on-site parking.

Lodging in the area: The Hotel DuPont, Eleventh Street and Market Street, 302-594-3100, is a four-star hotel. I went to a wedding reception here, and it was like being in a frothy novel, every whim catered to. Best Western Brandywine Valley, 1807 Concord Pike, 302-656-9436; Boulevard B&B, 1901 Baynard Boulevard, 302-656-9700.

Area attractions: The Du Ponts, in philanthropic tradition, left their extravagances to the public to keep up. **Winterthur** is the former home of Evelina Gabrielle Du Pont, located on DE Route 52, 6 miles north of I-95 (302-888-4600). It is a gorgeous place in its own right, but it is most known for its large collection of American furniture and decorative arts, including silver done by Paul Revere. The surrounding gardens, a consistent Du Pont interest, are part of a guided tour. To see how the Du Ponts made all that money, tour the **Hagley Museum** (6 Old Barley Mill Road, 302-658-2400), where restored mills line one of the few real water drops in the entire state: The Brandywine River falls 160 feet here. The old gunpowder mill is an education, as you note the thick stone walls on three sides, with wooden ones on the river side, where accidental explosions would blow out and do less damage. There are also exhibits on the modern chemicals produced by DuPont, such as Teflon and Nomex. The **Delaware Toy and Miniature Museum** (302-427-8697) is right by the entrance to the Hagley Museum and houses toys, miniature vases, and more than one hundred furnished dollhouses.

There is more to Delaware than the Du Ponts, of course. The collection of the **Delaware Art Museum** (2301 Kentmere Parkway,

302-571-9590) is strong in popular American artists and illustrators, such as Wilmington resident Howard Pyle and his students Maxfield Parrish and N. C. Wyeth. It also has a strong Pre-Raphaelite collection. If you'd like something a bit more lively, call the **Grand Opera House** for its schedule (818 North Market Street, 302-658-7897); besides actual operas, shows include symphonies and popular music; I saw David Bromberg there not long ago. Catch local baseball at **Daniel S. Frawley Stadium** (801 South Madison Street, 302-888-BLUE), home of the **Wilmington Blue Rocks** class A baseball team. Enjoy the game with local beer; Iron Hill is offered at the stadium.

Other area beer sites: Iron Hill is closely surrounded by whoop-'em-up nightclubs; do yourself a favor and go elsewhere. The **Washington Street Ale House** (1206 Washington Street, 302-658-2537) is a small place, but it has a reasonably good selection of taps. **Stoney's British Pub** (3007 Concord Pike, 302-477-9740) is north of town and does a good job with fish and chips and standard British taps. I'd also suggest that you head up U.S. Route 202 and duck across the Pennsylvania border just a few miles to **McKenzie Brew House** (451 Wilmington–West Chester Pike/Route 202, 610-361-9800), where brewer Scott Morrison brews some award-winning and truly outstanding beers; ask about his special beers in bottles.

John Harvard's Brew House, Wilmington

303 Rocky Run Road, Wilmington, DE 19803
302-477-6965
www.johnharvards.com

"'John Harvard's Brew House is a chain!'

"You'll sometimes hear that from the more exercised of the geekerie, with the strong implication that if it's a chain, it can't be good. Balderdash. I am not a big fan of chain restaurants; I'm convinced they are a sign that the Apocalypse is near. It is the increasing blandification of America that has fired me on a quixotic crusade against chains."

That's the standard text I've used for writing about four John Harvard's in my other books, *New York Breweries* and *Pennsylvania Breweries*. I do go on to note that although John Harvard's may be a chain, I'm still pleased with them and visit them when I can. A foolish consistency is the hobgoblin of little minds, as Emerson said (and a tip of the hat to Sam Calagione for making Emerson popular with beer geeks), and I like to think mine is broad enough to contain some apparent contradictions. I make exceptions for John Harvard's in my chain disdain by noting the relative amount of freedom their brewers enjoy in crafting their beers.

But faced with a region that encompasses a large number of brewpub chains, with very different policies on brewer freedom, suddenly I'm not so sure how I feel. Let's give you the John Harvard's story first while I think about it.

Beers brewed: Always at least seven beers on. Year-round: Light, Pale Ale. Seasonals: Scottish Ale, Munich Dunkel, Nut Brown, Schwarz-bier, Inebriator, Hefeweizen, Kölsch, IPA, Wit, Grand Cru, Barleywine, Presidential Ale (RAF Bronze, 2000), Pumpkin Ale, Winter Beer, and more.

The Pick: Inebriator says it all for me. Brian has crafted a doppelbock that is a true classic. It's malty-sweet, heavy and satisfying, and has that weird, fruity malt overdrive thing going that I love in the best German d-bocks. An excellent beer, a great doppelbock. Just wait till cold weather comes!

Grenville Byford and Gary Gut started the first Brew House on Harvard Square in Cambridge, Massachusetts, in 1992. Although there have been some failures, the chain is still strong, and the idea embodied in the company slogan, "Honest food, real beer," has proven attractive to the lunch and after-work crowds at the local pharmaceutical campuses.

The corporate history tells the tale of the young John Harvard watching William Shakespeare brew beer in Southwark, England. We are told that Shakespeare wrote, in addition to his plays and sonnets, a book of brewing recipes that John Harvard brought with him to America in 1637. The story is that the book was found in 1992 and is claimed as inspiration for the brewpub's beers. You can decide for yourself how "honest and real" the story is.

Don't doubt the sincerity of the slogan, though. The menu is innovative and eclectic, with a number of regional influences. The desserts are excessive, just the way you want them. A few local specialties may show up, but the food varies little from pub to pub. That, I'm not crazy about, but we are talking about chain brewpubs, not chain restaurants, so let's have a look at the beer.

The pubs have very similar brewing equipment, with which they brew the same core beers. Each location has a handpump for serving

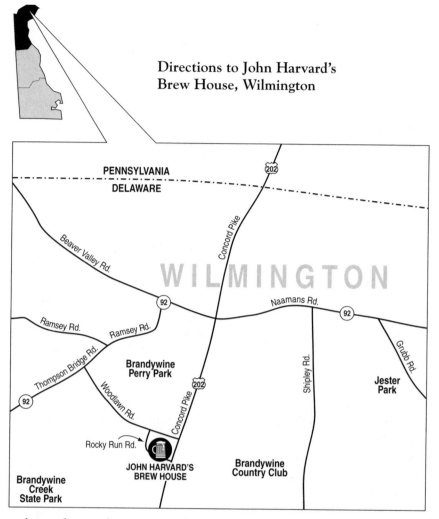

**Directions to John Harvard's
Brew House, Wilmington**

PENNSYLVANIA
DELAWARE

202

Concord Pike

WILMINGTON

Beaver Valley Rd.

92

Naamans Rd.

92

Ramsey Rd.

Ramsey Rd.

Thompson Bridge Rd.

Grubb Rd.

Brandywine
Perry Park

Shipley Rd.

Jester
Park

92

Woodlawn Rd.

202

Concord Pike

Rocky Run Rd.

JOHN HARVARD'S
BREW HOUSE

Brandywine
Country Club

Brandywine
Creek
State Park

cask-conditioned versions of some of the beers. The Brew Houses exchange recipes and information, a practice the brewers find very helpful. If a brewer runs into a problem, chances are someone else has had the same problem and can offer a solution, or at least some ideas. Brewers also formulate some of their own beers, and they are encouraged to tweak the core beers toward local tastes.

Brewer Brian McConnell has done that and more. More? Well, for one thing, Brian is an interstate brewer. He's the head brewer both here and at the John Harvard's in Springfield, Pennsylvania, so he's taking local tastes into account at the different brewpubs and is doing a great job, so far as I can see. Things tend to be malty and smooth here, with one big, snappy, hopped-up pale ale to keep the bitter lovers happy. "The IPA is bigger in Springfield," said Brian, which is quite interesting; six years ago, the Springfield drinkers liked their beers sweet and smooth. Maybe the Wilmingtonians will change, too, though with beers like Brian's Inebriator Doppelbock, I've no idea why they'd want to.

Brian has also brought home some Real Ale Festival medals for John Harvard's. The man has a penchant for strong, bottle-conditioned beers that translates into a delicious sense for the estery yeast effects that characterize that kind of beer.

That still leaves me thinking about brewpub chains. John Harvard's has relatively gentle direction from the top, a request for something light, something dark, a pale ale, a brown beer, and then do whatever you want—within reason, and don't forget to check with the other brewers—to fill the rest of the taps. At the other end of the spectrum is a place like Hops, where Dave Richter sends out recipes and ingredients, and there are four regular beers and one seasonal. Period.

But in the middle you've got Gordon-Biersch, with control almost as strict as Hops, and Iron Hill, with control almost as loose as John Harvard's, and maybe even looser (brewers have to make the four house beers, but they can really do *anything*—barleywines, double IPAs, pseudo-lambics—on the other taps). Sweetwater is almost a case where Nick Funnell is an executive chef and Jonathan Reeves and Greg Gerovac act as his *sous-chefs*, making the beer that he doesn't have the time to make, but still doing it his way. And the Rock Bottoms and the Chophouse darn near do what they want, with very little direction from headquarters at all.

What's a chain-hatin', beer-lovin', book-writin' guy to do? The tough part of all this is that the beers work. All these people are making well-crafted beer, some of them exquisitely great beer. How can that be bad? I guess my mind's going to have to open just a bit wider to park this big contradiction in the garage: I hate chain restaurants, but chain brew-pubs are fine by me. Sheesh. It's a tough life, making all these decisions. Let's go get a beer; the first round of Inebriator's on me.

Opened: April 1997.
Owners: Boston Culinary Group.
Brewer: Brian McConnell.
System: 7-barrel Pub Brewing system, 1,000 barrels annual capacity.
Production: 660 barrels in 2003.
Hours: Monday through Saturday, 11 A.M. to 1 A.M.: Sunday, 11 A.M. to midnight.

Tours: On request.
Take-out beer: Not available.
Food: The John Harvard's menu features upscale pub fare, including Asian crispadillas, chicken pot pie, steaks, Aztec chicken salad, calamari, and a few local specials.
Special considerations: Kids welcome. Some vegetarian meals available. Handicapped-accessible.
Parking: Large off-street lot.

Stewart's Brewing Company

219 Governor's Square, Bear, DE 19701
302-836-2739

I've seen brewpubs in old train stations, brewpubs in old homes, brewpubs in old banks, brewpubs in old convenience stores. Some brewpubs are in new buildings, some are in airports, and some are in bowling alleys. I've even seen more than one brewpub that's in an old brewery building.

Stewart's is in a former pet store in a strip mall, the Governor's Square Shopping Center in Bear, Delaware. I'd jazz it up, but to be honest, that's about all there is to the setting. From the front, it's just another glassy storefront with glass and metal doors, and the same brick overhead and white sign as most of the other stores in the shopping center. Inside, if you take away the brewhouse, it's much like any mall restaurant: drop ceiling, chairs and tables, bar with TVs in the middle.

Thankfully, the beer isn't ordinary; in fact, it's downright exceptional. After owner Al Stewart brewed for a while, and a couple other brewers came through, Al found his brewer: Ric Hoffman. Ric's worked wonders with this 7-barrel Peter Austin system, pulling beers out of here that once

Beers brewed: Year-round: Wacky Wheat Ale (high-quality raspberry and apricot extracts can be added at the bar if you'd like a fruit beer), Irish Red Ale, Big Bear Amber, Highlander Stout. Seasonals: Stumbling Monk Tripel, McBride's Strong Ale, Barleywine (GABF Gold, 2003), Maibock, Smoked Porter (GABF Bronze, 2001), Bohemian Pils, Oktoberfest (GABF Bronze, 2003). Other seasonals make rare or unique appearances.

more prove to me the utility of these direct-fire, largely manual systems and the much-derided Ringwood yeast.

I remember the first time I visited Stewart's. I was traveling with Michael Jackson, the world's foremost beer writer, acting as his native guide for the day. It poured down rain in biblical quantities, and we were running a full two hours behind schedule because of traffic delays. Al and his brother Greg, who was still involved in the business in those days, anxiously watched as Michael tasted the beers. I thought they were okay, but not very exciting. Michael thought they were "rather same-ish."

The Pick: I cannot resist that barrel-aged McBride's Strong Ale. I'm a sucker for these kinds of beers, bourbon lover that I am, and this is a solid one, fuming of whiskey but firmly structured under it. Stewart's has discovered whiskey, and it looks like a beautiful friendship.

Apparently that didn't matter to the locals and regulars at Stewart's, who just kept coming in and drinking the house beers and the guest taps of macros, Guinness, and Yuengling Lager. Enough of them came in that when the pet shop next door barked its last, the brothers expanded into the space. "It doubled our seating to over 325 and gave us more beer aging space," Al told me. "It's worked out very well." The expansion space is largely restaurant seating, including an area for private parties of up to eighty people that is seemingly always in use.

Then Ric Hoffman arrived, and things changed. Stewart's started entering competitions and winning medals, the regulars started getting excited about the beers, and people started talking about them. Ric's modest about his talent, but this is a light you can't hide under a basket. Even his Wacky Wheat Ale, a brewpub standard that's supposed to be about light, pounding quaffability, is chewy, with a surprising tinge of walnut and a background earthiness, a surprisingly complex lighter beer with a noticeable hop finish.

Let him loose on some bigger beers, and Hoffman and Ringwood shine. The 6.4 percent IPA, a light orange-gold in color, floats with hop and ester aromas, underlaid with classic British earthiness and solid malt, but firmly shot through and through with hops. McBride's Strong Ale is a fortified version of the brewpub Amber, aged for ninety-nine days in a Jim Beam barrel. It was like walking into a Kentucky rickhouse full of aging bourbon, oaky, vanilla-laced, and obvious wafting alcohol. Then Ric trotted out his 2002 Barleywine. It had oxidized a bit, but as is often the case with these big beers, it hadn't done it any harm, developing sherry notes on the big malty background palate, accenting the fruit and candy character of this big-mouthed beer.

"I'm doing more one-time, fun stuff," said Ric, pouring me a sample of his Loco Rico's Jalapeño Ale, a Stewart's Cinco de Mayo tradition:

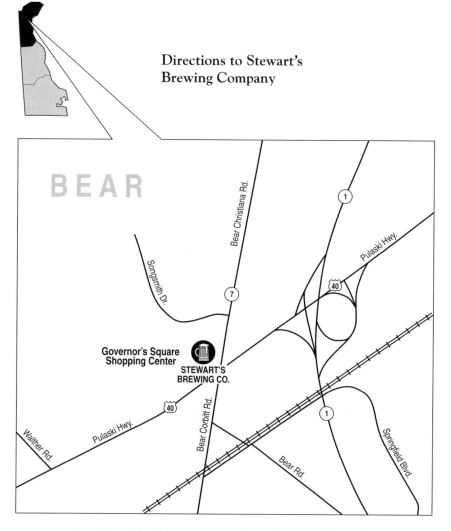

**Directions to Stewart's
Brewing Company**

one keg of Golden Ale, "dry-peppered" for the day. Oh yeah, fun, I had
to agree as I smelled the fresh pepper smell and tasted the tangy cap-
sicum in the ale, accompanied by just a hint of heat. For more traditional fun, stop by every other Friday for cask ale.

Who's drinking all the beer? "Well, it's traditionally a blue-collar
area," Ric explained. "But we get some transient high-income folks from
the banks and pharmaceutical companies. To be honest, after nine years,
we still don't have a good idea what our demographic is. People come in,
they drink, they watch TV. Things are good."

The eleven TVs have full sports satellite feed. The long central bar
is sports central on autumn weekends, when a customer can watch any

NFL game he wants. The food ranges from the lowliest pub grub—lowly, but I dare you to resist the onion rings when you see a plate of them go by your table—to steaks and seafood.

"We haven't done anything different," said Ric, always modest. "We're just getting better." Indeed, they are. If you think no good brewpub could be found in a mall, stop in and find out just how much better Stewart's has become. Like me, you may decide that the best way to get from Baltimore to Philadelphia is not necessarily a pedal-down rip up I-95. A nice detour along U.S. Route 40 where it cuts through Bear might just be a better way to do things.

Opened: July 1995.

Owner: Al Stewart.

Brewer: Ric Hoffman.

System: 7-barrel Peter Austin system, 1,000 barrels annual capacity.

Production: 603 barrels in 2003.

Hours: 11 A.M. to 1 A.M., seven days a week.

Tours: Upon request, subject to brewer availability.

Take-out beer: Growlers available.

Food: The onion rings are fantastic, and you should try the crab-stuffed potato skins. Stewart's does an entrée treatment of the famous Chicago beef on toast points. Crab cakes and steaks are also on the menu. The Black Forest sandwich goes particularly well with the beer, as does the rib-sticking meatloaf. And try the Scottish pork loin sandwich; it's different.

Extras: Lots and lots of TVs. Private banquet rooms available.

Special considerations: Delaware law prohibits smoking. Kids welcome. Some vegetarian meals available. Handicapped-accessible.

Parking: Large plaza lot.

Lodging in the area: Americinn Lodge and Suites, 875 Pulaski Highway, Bear, 302-326-2500; Howard Johnson Inn and Suites, 1119 South College Avenue, Newark, 302-368-8521; Red Roof Inn, 415 Stanton Christiana Road, Newark, 302-292-2870.

Area attractions: Bear is mostly about sleeping and shopping, but it's not far from Newark. Need an excuse to go to Newark? Why not show your prospective student the **University of Delaware,** where free tours are available (196 South College Avenue, 302-831-8123). The **Iron Hill Museum of Natural History** (1355 Old Baltimore Pike, 302-368-5703) is in a one-room schoolhouse built by the Du Pont family. This is actually a great exposition of why Iron Hill Brewery is called Iron Hill; there are old iron ore mining pits and industrial archeology exhibits, along with the usual stuffed animals and mineral displays.

Other area beer sites: Pretty slim pickins, folks. You can try the *East End Café* in Newark (270 East Main Street, 302-738-0880) for a decent bottle selection, or the *Deer Park Tavern* (108 West Main Street, 302-369-9414) for a couple of good drafts and some live music . . . and likely a bunch of UD students. Otherwise, you're looking at sports bars, college bars, or going to the brewpubs in Wilmington. One place you don't want to miss is *State Line Liquors,* just over the border in Elkton, Maryland (1610 Elkton Road, 800-446-9463), which has excellent selections of beer, wine, and spirits, as well as a fair selection of upscale food. The staff really knows the stock and will be happy to discuss it with you. I shop here fairly regularly from more than an hour away—it's that good!

Iron Hill Brewery and Restaurant, Newark

147 East Main Street, Newark, DE 19711
302-266-9000
www.ironhillbrewing.com

Iron Hill is one of the most successful small brewpub chains in the country. I have nothing to back up that statement: no numbers, no comparisons, no spreadsheets, nothing. I don't care, I'm sticking with it, because I know what I see. I see five busy brewpubs that all look terrific. They're all filled with bright, energetic staff that show more energy and customer-service savvy than you find most places these days. The food is excellent, fresh, and innovative without being outlandish. The brewers are proud, happy, technically proficient, and imbued with an honest camaraderie. And the beer, my heavens, the beer is just fantastic. That is success. You can't be doing that well, with so many happy people, and not be making it.

It all started here. Iron Hill was the product of a classic brewpub story: two homebrewers, Kevin Finn and Mark Edelson, met restaurateur Kevin Davies, and the three of them opened a brewpub. Many similar stories have taken place; few have turned out so well.

Some of the reason for their success was probably the planning that went into it. The partners planned for five years while looking for a suitable spot in Wilmington. "We just couldn't find a spot that suited us," Mark Edelson said. "We didn't want to be in Newark. We didn't want to be in a college town, where it's all about price competition for the college crowd. But friends convinced us to take a look, and we saw an opportunity to be something different."

As it turned out, Iron Hill had found part of the key to its success by opening in Newark: college students. Not low-price lager swillers, though; Iron Hill was looking for talent. "Our customers aren't the student crowd," Kevin Finn explained, "but our employees are. The labor market was tough at the time, but there are always energetic students looking for part-time work."

The location was another part of the story, and always has been with Iron Hill. The owners have always put a lot into finding just the right place to open a new brewpub, and it has worked phenomenally well. Their second brewpub, in West Chester, Pennsylvania, was jammed from day one and had to go to serving guest beers for a short period before more tanks could be brought in to keep up with the demand for the house beers. The latest one, in North Wales, Pennsylvania, planned for that but is still behind on seasonals because of demand for the regular beers.

The beer sold, but the partners followed the lead of Kevin Davies, the experienced restaurant man, and have never regretted it. "The key was concentrating on the restaurant end," said Mark. "That way, if the brewery didn't make it and shut down, we'd still have a successful restaurant."

If you've read much of what I've written, you'll know that I'm usually disdainful of the popular wisdom that "a brewpub is just a restaurant that happens to make beer." When I heard Mark say something

Beers brewed: Year-round: Iron Hill Light Lager, Raspberry Wheat, Lodestone Lager (GABF Gold, 1997; Bronze, 2000), Anvil Ale, Ironbound Ale, Pig Iron Porter (GABF Bronze, 2002; RAF Silver, 2002 and 2003), Radio Free Wheat. Seasonals: Altbier, Barleywine, Belgian White, Bohemian Pils, Dry Stout, ESB, Hefeweizen, Imperial IPA, India Pale Ale, Lambic de Hill (GABF Gold, 2003), Maibock (GABF Gold, 1999; Bronze, 2000), Munich Dunkel (GABF Bronze, 2003), Nut Brown Ale, Oatmeal Stout, Oktoberfest, Old Ale, Russian Imperial Stout (GABF Gold, 2003), Saison (GABF Bronze, 2003), Tripel (GABF Bronze, 2002), Vienna (GABF Bronze, 1999), Wee Heavy (GABF Bronze, 1998 and 2001).

The Pick: Get some Pig Iron in you. The beauty of this big, hefty porter is not so much that it's good, but that it's so darned good in every way. I've had cask Pig Iron that was mellow and wonderful; I've had the bourbon-aged Pig Iron, and it stood right up to the corn likker and met it, punch for powerful punch. This is the beer that convinced me that Iron Hill was a place to watch.

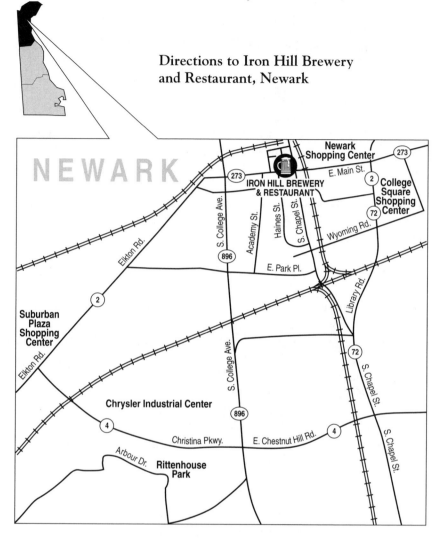

**Directions to Iron Hill Brewery
and Restaurant, Newark**

that sounded very close to that, I wrote Iron Hill off for a time. Then I came to realize that Mark was talking about worst-case scenarios, and that what he really was saying was that their brewpub was a great restaurant . . . that also made great beer. That was right about the time that they started doing just that.

The names of the beers—Lodestone Lager, Pig Iron Porter, Anvil Ale, Radio Free Wheat—all key around Iron Hill, a low local ridge near Newark that was mined for iron ore in the Revolutionary War (and is also blamed by University of Delaware students for the poor radio reception in the area). Pig Iron Porter was the beer that convinced me of Iron Hill's prowess. I went down to Newark and ran a sampler, and the beers were good; but the Pig Iron *rocked*. Eight years later, it's still my go-to beer when I'm at an Iron Hill. It's solid, rich, and balanced, with real hops and ester slicing right through.

It only got better. Iron Hill has gone from strength to strength in brewing, winning a number of prestigious medals for beers ranging from the excellently executed standard Lodestone Lager to 2003's medal for a lambiclike beer that was just astonishing. Helles, Imperial Stout, double IPA, ESB, a bourbon barrel-aged version of Pig Iron, Oktoberfest—the beers continue to astound. The brewpub enters local and regional festivals, acquainting more people with the beer. Under Edelson's sure direction, Iron Hill's brewers continue to improve, and the brewery's very loose hand on brewers' imagination is starting to attract the attention of hot brewers who very much want to work for the guys from Delaware.

Beer and food rule in tandem here, but Iron Hill, Newark, set a standard for architectural decor that has been kept in the other brewpubs. The distinctive lettering, the equally distinctive cast-iron decorative touches (including the hops-and-barley bird, designed by Kevin Finn's wife, Susan), the dark wood—all are repeated elsewhere. The open kitchen is popular with both the staff and the patrons; it adds some excitement and pulse to the atmosphere. And along the side wall stands the glassed-in brewery, plainly visible: *This is a brewpub.*

It all started here, and the crowds are still here, still mingling, still drinking every night. They're not the same people as eight years ago, but that's okay. Iron Hill isn't the same brewpub it was eight years ago. It's better. And the people who made it that way are working toward making it the best.

Opened: November 1996.

Owners: Mark Edelson, Kevin Finn, Kevin Davies.

Brewer: Justin Sproul, head brewer.

System: 10-hectoliter Specific Mechanical brewhouse, 1,000 barrels annual capacity.

Production: 675 barrels in 2003.

Hours: 11:30 A.M. to 1 A.M., seven days a week.

Tours: Upon request.

Take-out beer: 2 liter growlers available.

Food: Iron Hill has a way with food that I really like. The delicious salmon rolls with a wasabi dip, jerk pork tenderloin, and big hunks of beef to satisfy the guy in anyone—it's all good. I have to be honest, though: I'm going on other people's opinions when I say that, to a small extent, because I've never had room left for dessert. They look good on other people's tables, though.

Extras: Pool tables, live music (call for schedule).

Special considerations: Cigars not allowed. Kids welcome. Vegetarian meals available. Handicapped-accessible.

Parking: Lot in rear. Be careful parking on Main Street: the meters run till 1 A.M., and citations are swift.

Southern Beverages, Inc./Fordham Brewing Company

1284 MCD Drive, Dover, DE 19901
302-678-4810
www.fordhambrewing.com

It's quiet out here, considering you're in an industrial park. But it sprawls a bit, with plenty of trees and grass. The brewery sits on 20 acres of ground, including a small pond. It's very peaceful outside the brewery's back door. Peaceful, that is, until a huge C-5 on final approach to Dover Air Force base roars over and blots out half the sky.

It's a part of brewer Walter Trifari's workday that he doesn't even notice anymore. I understand; I used to live near a tank firing range, and my sleep was never disturbed by thunderstorms after that first month. Besides, Walter's got a much more interesting set of circumstances to occupy his attention. He's working big iron, a 50-barrel brewhouse, bottling line, and flash pasteurizer that are the likely future for this company.

Walter showed me around the place, happy to point out all the bells and whistles. Not all of them are working yet; that flash pasteurizer still needs some work. But it's all coming online, and he's brewing through it.

Mostly he's brewing Fordham beers, though the company is actually Southern Beverages. That's a long, complicated story, the kind you hear down here in the land of weird brewing laws. Let's just

Beers brewed: Year-round: C126 Light, Fordham Lager, Copperhead Ale, Oyster Stout, Tavern Ale, Atlantic Lager. Seasonals: Festbier, Black & Tan, Wizard's Winter Wheat.

skip over it by saying that brewing Fordham beers always comes first at Southern, and that the owners include Bill Muehlhauser, the owner of the Ram's Head Taverns. If we get any further into it, I'm gonna get a headache. Talk about tangled brewery DNA . . .

Jim Lutz is running things here. If you know anything about Mid-Atlantic microbrewery history, you know that Jim Lutz was the man at Wild Goose, the Eastern Shore microbrewery that gave craft brewing its first big start in the area. I remember vividly visiting Wild Goose in Cambridge, Maryland, for the first time back in 1991; it was a turning point in my life, when I first thought about getting involved in this business. Wild Goose brewed some astonishingly good beers, including the near-legendary Snow Goose. Then Lutz sold to Frederick Brewing and got out of the business.

The Pick: If you've never had an unfiltered beer, you may not understand why I'm picking the Tavern Ale. This is like beer just out of the tank: full of flavor, brimming with life, and quivering with hops. Fordham's fans and regulars asked, "Why don't you do any hoppy beers?" Tavern Ale was the brewery's surprise answer, not just hoppy, but alive.

"I got out," acknowledged Lutz. "I opened a couple of Dairy Queens. But then I looked at what Bill was doing with the Ram's Head. I've known him since 1990; I used to sell him a lot of Wild Goose. I still thought there was a niche for a competitively priced, nonquirky beers, and he needed his restaurants supplied. 'It'll work, Bill; trust me!'"

They tested the waters at leased brewery space in Alexandria, Virginia, the brewery behind the Birchmere nightclub where Native Brewing had had the run (Southern is also contract-brewing the Virginia Native beers.) Things went well, so they decided to open their own place. "We went out and found this 1998 JV NorthWest 50-barrel brewhouse that was at Butterfield Brewing in Fresno," said Jim. "We're at 15,000 [barrels] annual capacity to start, with room to grow. That's all we need right now.

"We're going to make beer," Jim continued, "and stay local. A lot of people lost sight of what a local brewery was supposed to be doing. I can knock the back wall out in a few years and add on. You can make a lot of beer with a 50-barrel brewhouse, but you can make a little, too." It helps when you get it for a great price, of course.

In case you were wondering why Maryland brewers moved from Virginia to Delaware to brew beer for Maryland markets, well, blame Maryland's laws again. "Because of our ownership structure," Jim explained, "we could not put a manufacturing facility in Maryland. The tax consequences of Virginia compared to Delaware were astronomical. Pennsylvania was just too far away. Delaware made sense, and we're centrally

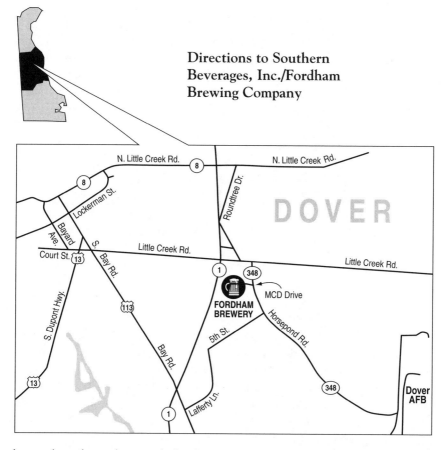

Directions to Southern Beverages, Inc./Fordham Brewing Company

located so that when and if it becomes time to ship beer further north and south, we're there."

Jim's willing to brew for people with a good idea and ready money. In addition to the Fordham brands, the brewery is currently brewing the Virginia Native brands, all the bottled Backfin Pale Ale for Clay Pipe, and Sir Walter Raleigh Lager, a brand for Apex Brewing of Apex, North Carolina. They also started brewing DeGroen's.

The brewery is banking its success on Fordham's stylistically proper beers. Jim Lutz wants to distance himself a bit from some of what's going on in craft brewing these days. "The whole 'microbrewery' term . . . I understand the definition, I've been in this a long time. We're not building a microbrewery, we're building a brewery. We brew beer people want to drink. We don't brew funky stuff, we brew with malt, hops, yeast, and water. We can take market share away from the big boys just by brewing good lager beer. We can't beat them with ads and marketing, but if we can get a piece of the local market share, we'll concentrate on that."

It might be a complicated story, but it's a simple aim: Brew good beer and sell it, supported by a number of pubs that are essentially tied houses. Get Jim Lutz back in the brewing business. Circumvent Maryland's screwy one-brewery law. And maybe, just maybe, drag central Delaware into the craft beer revolution. Not bad for a recycled Fresno brewhouse.

Opened: October 2003.
Owners: Jim Lutz, Bill Muehlhauser, and George Lawson.
Brewers: Walter Trifari, head brewer; Brian Pluto.
System: 50-barrel JV NorthWest, 15,000 barrels annual capacity.
Production: 6,500 barrels in 2003, with brewing at Alexandria facility.
Tours: Saturday, 11 A.M. to 2 P.M.; walk-ins welcome Monday through Friday.
Take-out beer: No retail sales. Free samples. Retail sales are available less than a mile away; ask for directions.
Special considerations: Handicapped-accessible.
Parking: Large free lot.
Lodging in the area: Comfort Inn, 222 South Dupont Highway, Dover, 302-674-3300; Little Creek Inn, 2623 North Little Creek Road, Dover, 302-730-1300; Dover Downs Slots and Hotel, 1131 North DuPont Highway, beside Dover Downs Raceway, 302-857-2190.
Area attractions: *Dover Downs* (south of Dover on U.S. Route 13, 800-711-5882) was known for harness racing for years before NASCAR came to town, and racing still goes on here from November through April; the slots go on year-round. The *Dover International Speedway,* NASCAR's "Monster Mile," thunders into full high-octane action two weekends every July and August; call for a schedule (302-678-0892). If you've really got the need for speed, call *Monster Racing Excitement* (800-GO-TO-WIN) about getting into the cockpit of a stock car and running the Mile yourself . . . or with a professional driver. The *Johnson Victrola Museum* (Bank Lane and New Street, 302-739-4266) is a tribute to this historic "talking machine." There are a variety of early recordings, played on antique and modern equipment, but it's worth going just to see the original painting of the dog Nipper, listening to "his master's voice," once the symbol of the Victrola company, now used by RCA. I love that painting. Dover is home to Dover Air Force Base, which is home to the *Air Mobility Command Museum* (the main entrance is on U.S. Route 113 south of Dover, 302-677-3376). There are exhibits both inside and outside of the museum; the indoor exhibits include one

on the WASPs, the women pilots who performed ferry service during World War II, who freed combat pilots by transporting aircraft to staging areas. Active-duty military are usually available outside to answer questions about the aircraft. It's free, but when the base is on alert, the museum is closed; call ahead.

Other area beer sites: There's really not much in Dover; check the Milton and Rehoboth listings at the Dogfish Head Craft Brewery and the Dogfish Head Brewings and Eats (page 28) or ask the guys at the brewery where to pick up a few six-packs.

Dogfish Head Craft Brewery

6 Cannery Village Center, Milton, DE 19968
302-644-4660
www.dogfish.com

Sometimes visiting Sam Calagione at Dogfish Head in Milton (and be sure you go to *Milton*, not *Milford*, just up the road, like I did one time) is like hopping on the Trolley with Mister Rogers to visit the Neighborhood of Make Believe. Put on your Dogfish Head "Off-center ales for off-center people" T-shirt and a pair of Chuck Taylors, and the Trolley takes you to the Brewery of Make Believe, where you meet people like Randall the Enamel Animal, Sir Hops A Lot, and—well, maybe we'd better not talk about what the brewers call World Wide Stout's alter ego. Your kid might pick up the book.

The beers in the Brewery of Make Believe are different, too. Look at Liquor de Malt; isn't he funny, boys and girls? What kind of beer comes in those big 40-ounce bottles with screwtops? Can you say "malt liquor"? Malt liquor is full of corn, and corn's not good for beer, is it? But Liquor de

Beers brewed: Year-round: Shelter Pale Ale, Raison D'Etre, Indian Brown Ale, Chicory Stout (RAF Gold, Best-of-Show Gold, 1998), 60 Minute IPA, 90 Minute IPA, Immort Ale (RAF Silver, Best-of-Show Bronze, 2001), Midas Touch Golden Elixir. Seasonals and one-shots: Pangaea, Festina Lente, Punkin' Ale, Au Courant, ApriHop, Weedwacker Wit, Snowblower Ale (the "Toolshed Series"), 120 Minute IPA, World Wide Stout, Olde School Barleywine, Prescription Pils, Liquor de Malt, plus a few more new ones every year.

Malt is made with very special corn: Aztec Red, Taos Blue, and Hickory Yellow. They're called heritage corn, and they give the beer a spicy note that adds to its bottle-conditioned character. Isn't that amazing?

And how about Miss World Wide Stout? The brewers have to feed her every day! You'd think she would get fat, wouldn't you? But she's always working, day and night, so she just gets stronger and stronger, and stronger and stronger and stronger, until she's the strongest dark beer in the world!

Enough, you get the idea, but the funny thing is, it's all true. I have never made a trip to Dogfish Head without Sam pulling out something truly different and asking, "What do you think?" This past Christmas, I was quite ill and couldn't make a big tasting party at the brewery, so Sam sent me a package with not one new beer, but three: Pangaea, a very nice, lightly spiced beer with an ingredient from each of the seven continents; Festina Lente, a peach-flavored lambiclike beer; and 120 Minute IPA, a ridiculously hoppy super-strength IPA that was over 20 percent ABV. "Tell me what you think," the letter said.

The Pick: Chicory Stout is almost forgotten by the geekerie these days, but that's a sad statement on the rush of the herd. It's a rich, coffee-tinged stout that warms and satisfies. I also have to mention the 90 Minute IPA, an absolutely sizzling IPA that in its bottle-conditioned form puts most "imperial" IPAs to shame with its bright hoppiness and shameless drinkability. One of my favorite Dogfish Head seasonals was 2003's Au Courant, a Belgian strong ale tweaked with a dose of red currants that I found delightfully understated, a great addition to the overdone winter beers out there.

There's always something new . . . except the equipment. When I made my visit, brewery operations head Andy Tveekrem was getting ready for the arrival of three big fermenters. "They'll be the first new brewing equipment Dogfish Head has ever purchased," Andy said, and having seen Dogfish Head's first production brewery, I could easily believe him. He smacked a seriously dented and dished tank that was being used as a hot liquor tank and grumbled, "Sam thinks that if something's dirty and beat up, it's got more character. We're getting him over that."

Sam doesn't mind his brewers ribbing him like that, because it's all about the beer. "I'm proud to be the least talented brewer in the company," he said with a big grin. "I am confident in our brewers. I can give them a concept, any concept, and they will execute it."

But Sam still does some things himself, like creating his gadgets. One of the first was for making 90 Minute IPA. Sam had this idea of continually adding hops to the brewkettle during the boil, to get away from what seemed to him to be an artificial division of kettle hops, bittering hops, and finishing hops. The first thing he tried was an old elec-

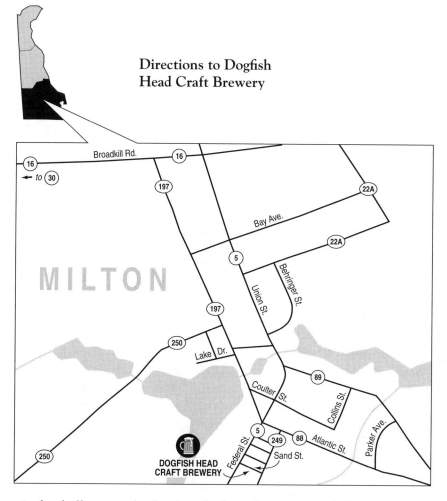

Directions to Dogfish Head Craft Brewery

tric football game, the kind with the vibrating metal field. Held suspended over the kettle, the game would slowly vibrate hops continually into the kettle. It worked, but it burned out in the hot, steamy air above the kettle, so they replaced it with Sir Hops A Lot, a pneumatically operated arm that dumps a measured amount of hops in the boil every fifteen seconds.

Randall the Enamel Animal was another invention. Brewers had added hops at every stage of brewing, from "mash-hopping" the boil in the kettle, dry-hopping in the conditioning tank, and slipping packets of hops into kegs. Sam wanted to go one step further. Inspired by a "hoppiest beer" competition, a West Coast Versus East Coast "Lupulin Slam" at the Brickskellar in early 2003, he came up with Randall the Enamel Animal. Randall is essentially a dispense system hopback or, as

Sam puts it, an organoleptic hops transducer mechanism. A cylinder is stuffed with whole-leaf hops, the cylinder is hooked into a draft line, the hops are saturated with beer, and then every drop of beer through Randall passes through the fresh hops, picking up incredible amounts of hop aroma. He's the "Enamel Animal," explained Sam, because beer that has been "Randallized" is hoppy enough to take the enamel off your teeth. It's brilliant, even if it has only limited applications.

Or maybe not that limited. Brewpubs and beer bars all over the country have purchased Randalls from Sam, who is selling them at cost. "Karmically, I don't want to make any money off this thing," he said. "I just want to sell them at cost. It's for hard-core beer bars and brewpubs. But I think any hard-core beer bar in American could use one to demystify hops. We don't want to make money; it's just good for the industry." And fun, too; he was talking about stuffing a Randall with whole-leaf spearmint and running his Weedwacker Wit through it.

It's not all nuts, of course. The brewery's tremendous growth is solidly built on beers like the 60 Minute and 90 Minute IPAs, the mild-mannered and locally popular Shelter Pale Ale, and steady markets for Chicory Stout and Immort Ale. Sam is proudest of the growth in revenue. "We grew 105 percent on revenues in 2003," he said, comparing it to a slightly smaller growth in volume. "Why does the brewing industry measure success by volume? Our revenues are climbing more steeply, because we're educating people that beer can be worth a higher price." Talk about good for the industry.

Sam does some stuff just for fun, like the Pain Relievaz project and the Woody Guthrie show. The Pain Relievaz was the first rap-brewing act, which spawned a CD called "Check Your Gravity" (released on the DFR/Dogfish Records label, of course). MC Lil' Guy and Funkmaster IBU (Bryan Selders and Sam Calagione) are pictured on the cover, working the brewhouse control board like a turntable. It's a pretty funny live show, especially when they do "(I Got Busy with a) A-B Sales Girl." The Woody Guthrie show is a one-man show Sam did, "channelling" the late folk-protest singer. It didn't get the reviews the Pain Relievaz did, but every artist has to suffer for his work.

Things are changing fast here at the brewery. Plans for a large on-site restaurant are proceeding swiftly toward a 2006 opening, as Dogfish Head moves into its role as the industrial cornerstone of a new planned high-tech community, Cannery Village, which is now being built and will double the population of Milton. Once the townhouses are all up, the brewery will be center stage, and Sam has plans that will make your day, including a large fountain with the dogfish logo in the basin and a merchandise yurt. "I've always wanted a yurt," says the least talented brewer at Dogfish Head.

I can't wait to see it, or to see what new beers Sam and his crew will dream up to celebrate its opening. I'll tell you what I think, Sam: I think it's the most exciting story in brewing right now, and it's about a lot more than weird beer and Randall. It's about steering your own course. Sail on.

Opened: July 2002.

Owners: Sam and Mariah Calagione.

Brewers: Andy Tveekrem, Bryan Selders.

System: 50-barrel Pub Brewing system, 25,000 barrels annual capacity.

Production: 14,000 barrels in 2003.

Hours: None yet; restaurant set to open in 2006.

Tours: Call ahead for current schedule; tour schedules will be changing when the restaurant opens.

Take-out beer: Individual bottles, six-packs, cases, and kegs available.

Food: By the time you read this, the restaurant may be open. Expect well-prepared food using local ingredients as much as possible.

Special considerations: Handicapped-accessible.

Parking: Free off-site lot.

Lodging in the area: Red Mill Inn, 150 Highway 1, Rehoboth Beach, 302-645-9736; Inn at Canal Square, 122 Market Street, Lewes, 302-644-3377; Sleep Inn, 1595 Highway 1, Lewes, 302-645-6464.

Area attractions: See Dogfish Head Brewings and Eats entry (page 28).

Other area beer sites: *The Rose and Crown* in Lewes (108 2nd Street, 302-645-2373) was recommended by Sam as having a decent selection of English ales and atmosphere. *Striper Bites Bistro* (107 Savannah Road, Lewes, 302-645-4657) has very good seafood and Dogfish Head beers in a bistro atmosphere.

Dogfish Head Brewings and Eats

320 Rehoboth Avenue, Rehoboth Beach, DE 19971
302-226-2739
www.dogfish.com

Dogfish Head is a point of land on Southport Island off Booth Bay Harbor, Maine.

That's to let you know: Don't expect the obvious from this brewery. Sam Calagione has been aiming at a different endpoint than most brewers from the very beginning, guiding his brewery and his life by lines from Ralph Waldo Emerson's essay on self-reliance:

> Whoso would be a man must be a nonconformist.
> He who would gather immortal palms
> Must not be hindered by the name of goodness
> But must explore if it be goodness for himself.
> Nothing is at last sacred
> But the integrity of our own mind.

Kind of puts reasons like "I started the brewery to brew beer like I had in England" in a different light, doesn't it?

Sam started the brewpub in Rehoboth back in 1995, and you could tell it was going to be different. No light golden ales and American wheats to cater to the beach crowd from this brewpub. Sam went right to work on a little half-barrel system, laying the groundwork for the strange, wild ride the years ahead would bring. He added fruits, spices, and wild sugars to his beers, and shortly after opening sent out hand-painted, hand-numbered bottles of something he called Immort Ale—originally known at the brewpub as Boothbay Barleywine—to members of the beer press. It was one of the most shockingly good beers I'd had in months, alive, complex,

Beers brewed: Year-round: Shelter Pale Ale, Raison D'Etre, Indian Brown Ale, Chicory Stout (RAF Gold, Best-of-Show Gold, 1998), 60 Minute IPA, 90 Minute IPA, Immort Ale (RAF Silver, Best-of-Show Bronze, 2001), Midas Touch Golden Elixir. Seasonals and one-shots: Punkin' Ale, Au Courant, ApriHop, Weedwacker Wit, Snowblower Ale (the "Toolshed Series"), 120 Minute IPA, World Wide Stout, Olde School Barleywine, Prescription Pils, Liquor de Malt, plus Lawnmower Light, a draft-only, pub-only summer beer.

smoothly melded, and rich. Who was this guy, and what was he doing?

Everything, it seemed. Wild ideas continued to flow at Dogfish Head, and the half-barrel system was supplanted by a 5-barrel system cobbled together from used and salvaged parts. (The old system's still around, and crops up in special projects at times.) Sam has a penchant for searching scrapyards for bits of steel that just ought to do *something,* and looking at them till he figures out what the something is. It soon became obvious that the something was getting bigger and bigger, and the brewpub took second billing to a production brewery up the road in Milton.

The brewpub steamed along, brewing pilot batches of some truly outlandish beers—mostly good, but there was a lavender-peppercorn hefeweizen that was simply bizarre, and I still rib Sam about it. Some of the beers got picked up at the production brewery: Aprihop, an IPA blended with pureed dried apricots that was surprisingly good and grew in popularity to the point that it was sold in 12-ounce bottles in 2004; Chicory Stout, a deliciously rich stout spiked with organic Mexican coffee and Saint-John's-wort.

Then Sam got a seriously new bee in his bonnet after a trip to the scrapyard, where he found a conical piece of stainless steel that looked like the tip of the Lunar Command Module. Welding and piping commenced, and the brewpub system began cooking up plain mashes with potato starch added, batches of molasses and water. Don't expect the obvious: Dogfish Head Brewery had added Dogfish Head Distillery.

"It's like a big homebrew system!" yelled Mike Gerhart over the roar of the propane burner under the brewkettle. "It's pretty basic, and it breaks down more often than a new system, but when it does it's more like fixing a bike, not like fixing a car. We get 10 barrels of wash [the distiller's term for the fermented beer] after fermentation, which goes to 30 gallons at 80 proof after the first distillation; when we run it through the still again, we get 15 gallons at 155 proof." Mike's a brewer with experience at Coors and Magic Hat, and a distiller with a degree from Scotland's prestigious Herriot-Watt University.

The Pick: I like the Aprihop a lot; it's one of my favorite fruit beers because of the way the apricot flavor sharpens the edge of the IPA-level hops. But I like the 60 Minute IPA even more. This deliciously hoppy ale proves that Dogfish Head isn't the "nuts and berries" brewery some jealous brewers accuse them of being. 60 Minute has a freshness that comes across beautifully in its bottle-conditioned form, one of the best bottle-conditioned American beers on the market; but it is phenomenal on draft, lively and aromatic, one of my favorite beers. (And if you're curious, yes, that's really my quote on the six-pack holders, and no, I don't get a dime for it.) If I'm going to pick a spirit, I guess it's the Brown Honey Rhum, a deep creamy rum with a pretty floral character. The Blue Hen Vodka's pretty good too.

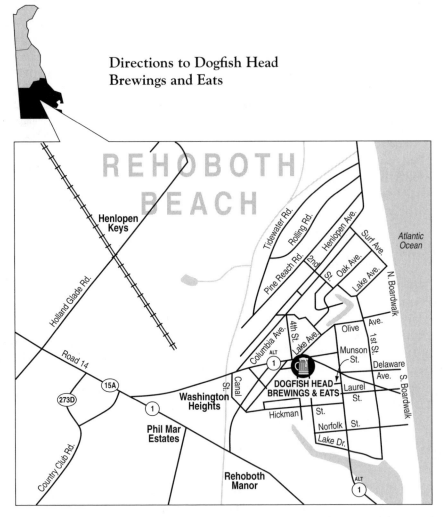

The spirits being produced are Blue Hen Vodka, Dogfish Head Brown Honey Rhum, Wit Rhum, and Jin. "The Jin's a work in progress," said Mike. "I'm still figuring out the botanicals; I want to try putting some hops in it." The vodka has been infused with a literal rainbow of flavors for sale at the bar: peach, chocolate, coconut, blueberry, and so on, and the bartenders are experimenting with them in true Dogfish Head fashion, mixing them with juices and sodas, using them in cocktails, mixing them with beer. "The pub gets first priority on the booze," said Mike, even though retail sales in Delaware and surrounding states are brisk. "We could go to two shifts and really pump it out, but it would lose a lot."

Why distill? "Our momentum as a brewery was headed that way," Sam said. "We were pushing the alcohol envelope on beer, and that led right to it. We just have our toe in it now, and there's not the same level of expectation as with the beer, but it's still all about excitement. That's what sells it. I've always felt that our products themselves are our marketing campaign."

The brewpub system is actually brewing beer again, too. "We keep one house beer on tap," said Mike, "kind of decided by what people want. It's important; people want to know it's made here. This is the source, where it started." Like the little sign says on the wall, the beer is "Imported—from the other room." You can get all of it for take-out as well: a growler, a bottle of Blue Hen Vodka, and a pizza. There's a wild night, all wrapped up in a paper bag.

With plans proceeding for a major restaurant at the big new Dogfish Head brewery up in Milton, it would seem likely that this brewpub is going to become a backwater again, just a beach brewpub that has a little distillery upstairs making gin, rum, and vodka. I'll say it one more time: Don't expect the obvious from this brewery. I don't know what Sam will think up next, but for as long as I've known him, the man has had a talent for coming up with an answer before anyone else has even thought about the question.

So figure on visiting this somewhat worn, comfortable brewpub, with its look of a family boathouse. The food is excellent, a menu that centers on the wood grill. Let me recommend the rockfish, one of the best simple pieces of fish I've ever had. The dining room is great for family dining, the bar is fun for adults. And . . . keep your eyes open. There's no telling what might be going on by the time you get there.

Opened: June 1995.

Owners: Sam and Mariah Calagione.

Brewer-distiller: Mike Gerhart.

System: 5-barrel "custom-built" system ("built out of old cannery cleaning equipment," Sam says), 600 barrels annual capacity.

Production: 200 barrels (counting wash for the still) in 2003.

Hours: Monday through Thursday, 4 P.M. to midnight; Friday through Sunday, noon to 1 A.M.

Tours: Upon request, subject to brewer availability.

Take-out beer: Growlers are available.

Food: It's all about the wood grill. The grilled fresh fish is outstanding and should be the first thing you try. Pizza's very good, and that's

saying something in a town with Grotto Pizza. And if you like burgers, just imagine them done on a real wood grill.

Extras: Live music Friday and Saturday nights, with nationally known
acts; call for schedule. Pool tables and TVs. Wide range of house-
distilled spirits, including a changing rainbow of infused vodkas.

Special considerations: Cigars not allowed. Kids welcome. Vegetarian
meals available. Second-floor dining room is not handicapped-
accessible.

Parking: Off-street lot, some on-street parking.

Lodging in the area: Crosswinds, next to brewpub, 312 Rehoboth
Avenue, 800-581-WIND; Delaware Inn B&B, 55 Delaware Avenue,
302-227-6031; Sea-Esta IV, 713 Rehoboth Avenue, 302-227-5882.

Area attractions: It's all about the boardwalk and the beach. Sixteen
blocks of boardwalk means sixteen blocks of games, rides, food,
and souvenirs, and that means happy kids—and an empty wallet.
Take 'em down to the beach! And if you really want a beach, why
not drive on past Dewey Beach to the *Delaware Seashore State
Park,* where the kids can splash and swim all day. If you want to
get out farther than the breakers, deep-sea sportfishing boats sail
out of *Anglers Marina* in Lewes; make your selections at www.
atbeach.com/fishing/lewes/. Or do you feel the need to shop in the
tax-free atmosphere of Delaware? Take a hike out to U.S. Route 1
to see the outlets lining the road for almost a mile. Nearly every
major outlet is here, and you're saving at least 6 percent already!
Finally, at a time of year when no one's thinking of the Delaware
beaches, a bunch of loonies from as far away as Illinois get together
in the fields outside of Harbeson on the first weekend after Hal-
loween for the *World Championship Punkin Chunkin Festival.*
Check out the website at www.punkinchunkin.com, and keep your
head down; competitors have been known to fling squash almost a
mile. Dogfish Head is heavily involved in the festival, so expect to
see plenty of Punkin' Ale there.

Other area beer sites: The Rehoboth *Ram's Head Tavern* (15 Wilmington Avenue, 302-227-0807; note that the Ram's Head Inn, also
in Rehoboth, is a gay B&B, so be precise when asking directions)
has been a blow-out success for the chain. Good place to get some
cut-above lagers. If that doesn't seem like much, remember: Ram's
Head, Dogfish Head, two Heads are better than none.

Micros, Brewpubs, and Craft Brewers

My son Thomas sometimes accompanies me on brewery tours. Much to my delight as a writer, he's fascinated by words and what they mean and how people use them. I've explained to him that much of what people say is said because they don't want to say something more blunt or honest. Code words, euphemisms, and evasions are part of our everyday speech. Here's a little secret of the beer world: "Microbrewery" is just another code word.

When the new brewing movement started in America in the 1970s, no one knew what to call these little breweries. "Brewery pub," "boutique brewery," and "microbrewery" were all used. By the early 1980s, two words had settled into general use: microbrewery and brewpub. (I didn't miss "boutique brewery" at all, either.) At the time, industry pundits defined a brewpub as a brewery that sold most of its beer in an in-house taproom. They defined a microbrewery as a brewery that produced less than 15,000 barrels a year. These terms gained legal recognition in some states, as deals were struck to allow the new businesses to start up and as tax rates were determined. The federal government acknowledged the special nature of small breweries in the early 1990s, granting a substantial tax break to those with an annual production under 50,000 barrels.

Eventually the industry itself came up with a whole set of labels. "Brewpub" continued to be used for breweries that sold the large majority of their beer on-premises by the glass. "Microbrewery" was for packaging breweries whose production was less than 50,000 barrels. "Regional" brewery applied to smaller breweries established before 1970 that did not distribute to all of America. Nationally distributing giants like Anheuser-Busch, Miller, Coors, and Stroh were dubbed "national brewers" or "megabrewers."

But the growth of some successful microbreweries has made even 50,000 barrels an uncomfortable fit. Boston Beer Company, the contract brewery responsible for the Samuel Adams line of beers, sells about a million barrels a year, and Sierra Nevada Brewing Company, an early microbrewery that produces all its own beer, is pushing 800,000 barrels. Clearly these are no longer microbreweries, yet their beer is exactly the same as it was. To be called a microbrewery has a cachet to it that most microbrewers don't want to surrender. What to call them?

Some propose the blanket term "craft brewery." This implies that the beer is somehow crafted, rather than produced in a factory. Craft breweries are different, the brewers explain, because the beer is made in single batches, not in several that are then combined in one huge tank or blended after fermentation to ensure consistency.

Putting a label on a brewery these days is not as easy as putting a label on a bottle. For example, what do you call DuClaw, forced by a stupid Maryland law to build a big production brewery to feed an expanding pub business . . . and forced by that same law to take the brewery out of their first pub? The Ram's Head Taverns have a similar, oddly synergistic relationship between the brewpub in their original Annapolis location and the production brewery in Delaware. Old Dominion has a big production brewery and a thriving brewpub in the same building. What about the three brew-on-premises in the area? These breweries aren't readily pigeonholed.

The fact is, "microbrewery" has always been a code word, and so has "craft brewery." They both mean the same thing. They describe a brewery that makes beer in an authentic manner—using ingredients and techniques appropriate to a given style of beer or brewing—and that brews beers other than mainstream American-style lager. What do I think such places should be called? How about *breweries?*

The distinctions are really all nonsense. Brewery size has nothing to do with the quality of a beer. Guinness Stout, the beer to which most microbrewers hopefully compare their own dry stouts, is brewed by a globe-girdling gargantuan of a brewer. Blending is likewise a nonissue. It goes on at microbreweries across the country.

In this book, I have bowed to convention and used the words *brewpub*, *microbrewery*, and *craft brewery*. Brewpub is the best of these terms. A brewery where beer is taken directly from the conditioning tanks to serving tanks and sold from a tap on-premises truly deserves a unique name. But if I had my way, the others would all be called simply breweries. To differentiate a brewery based on the kind of beer it makes seems to be missing the point. Categorizing them by size penalizes the ones that succeed and outgrow the class. Call them breweries, and then let the beer do the talking.

Baltimore
and the Bay

I understand that Baltimoreans are supposed to have an inferiority complex about their city not being Washington, or maybe about not being New York. Maybe it's because Baltimore, the biggest, most important city in the state by far, is not the state capital. Maybe it's because this is still a place where people work hard at physical jobs, a major and growing port city, a city that is more detached from its suburbs than other cities, a city that still defines itself as a city by its neighborhoods and stops at its borders, instead of undetectably blending into suburbs.

I've heard this from a lot of the people I talked to in Baltimore, I've read it as I learned about Baltimore, and I don't get it. I've enjoyed Baltimore since I was a kid and my dad would bring me down here to watch Orioles games at the old Memorial Stadium. Then I discovered crabs and I loved the place even more. Then Sisson's and Baltimore Brewing and The Brewer's Art opened . . . and I idly started to talk to my wife about moving to Baltimore.

This is a great town! So many cities walled off their waterfronts and ignored them. That's changing, but Baltimore's Inner Harbor was one of the first to embrace the waterfront and bring it back into the city. They've done so well that "Inner Harbor" seems to inevitably come after "Baltimore" when nonresidents talk about the town. It should. The Inner Harbor project was fantastically successful and brings thousands of tourists to Baltimore every year.

Baltimore is exciting, with nightlife popping all over the city. Canton is bustling, a scene most people outside the city haven't heard of. Fells Point is dotted with bars, some famous, some infamous, and it shows no sign of slowing down. Mount Vernon is picking up, with a big push from The Brewer's Art. The Inner Harbor is getting more night-lively every year as Capitol City gets more competition, and a core of activity has built up around the stadiums. Federal Hill has some bars that are get-ting serious attention from beerfolk inside and outside the city.

The Ravens have made Baltimore a city of champions again, but with a gorgeous ballpark like Camden Yards, who could hold some los-ing seasons against the O's? Orioles fans still flock to the park, drink the great food and beer available there (upper level, third base line, it's there, believe me), and still roar out the "OH!" in the national anthem to establish just whose ballpark this is. They know better days are com-ing, one of these days.

Baltimore has stature and pedigree; it has history. The excellent natural harbor made Baltimore a seaport in the 1700s, and it hosted the Continental Congress when Philadelphia was occupied by the British Army during the Revolutionary War. Baltimore's importance made it a target in the War of 1812, but Fort McHenry stood firm under the bom-bardment, saving the city and inspiring Francis Scott Key to write "The Star Spangled Banner" . . . and set it to an old drinking tune. When its prosperity was threatened by the rise of New York and Albany as ports after the opening of the Erie Canal, Baltimore responded with the country's first railroad, leapfrogging the whole canal idea. And any Bal-timorean, it seems, can tell you all this, and will, at the drop of a hat.

This is a cultured town. The Walters Gallery is an international treasure, an exquisite and vast collection of artwork tucked away in a Baltimore neighborhood. The Baltimore Symphony Orchestra is well regarded and well supported. The American Visionary Art Museum is a rare tribute to untrained, unknown, unorthodox artists that most cities would have swept under the rug. Baltimore has been home to a number of creative artists: Eubie Blake, Upton Sinclair, Gertrude Stein, and perhaps the most famous, Edgar Allan Poe.

And Baltimore was home to one of the foremost American essay-ists, at least in my estimation—H. L. Mencken, who undoubtedly would have hated this kind of listing. Mencken always believed Balti-more was one of the best cities on earth, citing much more simple rea-sons: a charming and comfortable homelife, local foods that were unparalleled, and young women of "incomparable pulchritude." Per-sonal loyalties leave me disinclined to comment on the last, but I don't believe anything major has happened to change Mencken's faith in the first two components. As the National Bohemian ads used to say, it is "the land of pleasant living."

I'd add beer to the list, of course. Mencken didn't because good local beer was a given in his day; it would be like mentioning Baltimore had air to breathe (although Mencken did usually mention local beer when he traveled and had very good things to say about the beer he had in St. Louis: Michelob). Baltimore is, in my estimation, one of the top beer towns in the country.

Why? Other cities may have more breweries, but Baltimore has DeGroen's making top-notch lagers, The Brewer's Art making all beautiful Belgian-styled beers, the Wharf Rat's gorgeously English ales, and Clipper City brewing American classics and thumping big beers like the new Heavy Seas line. Almost all bases covered, and what they don't have is brought to the table by a seriously underestimated set of beer bars. A small but growing number of bars are doing cask ale, and doing it right; the Baltimore chapter of the Society for Preservation of Beer from the Wood (www.spbw.com) makes sure of that.

Thank DeGroen's for a major aspect of Baltimore's beeriness; there's a DeGroen's tap in a lot of bars that otherwise have nothing but mainstream beers. Yuengling has cut into this over the past couple of years, but it's still common to walk into an otherwise mainstream-tap bar and find a flowing handle of DeGroen's Märzen. That's a good beer town.

When you come to Baltimore, then, come thirsty. Come hungry. Be prepared for "pleasant living." And if you overdo anything, just look to the Bromo Seltzer tower; you'll know what to do.

And drop me a line if you have an opinion on that "incomparable pulchritude" aspect. Professional curiosity, you understand.

I've also put Annapolis in this section and, by extension, the Chesapeake Bay. Annapolis is one of the prettiest state capitals in the country, old, historic, walkable, and with an admirable waterfront. Its definite attractions are described in the Ram's Head Tavern/Fordham Brewing Company listing on page 77.

The Bay is a phenomenon, nothing less, a huge estuary swarming with life. It fed the Mid-Atlantic region through much of its early history and continues to feed it today. The Bay is in trouble from farm runoff and pollution and overdevelopment, but it is finding new friends every day. Enjoy it, but think about what you do.

Rather than repeat the same lodging suggestions and attractions and bars over and over in the Baltimore entries, I've grouped them all here.

Lodging in the area: I stayed at the Wyndham Inner Harbor (101 West Fayette Street, 410-752-1100) on all my Baltimore research trips, and it's been great, but save some money and park in the underground lot across the street; it's well worth the short walk. Mount Vernon Hotel, 24 West Franklin Street, 410-727-2000; Scarborough Fair B&B, 1 East Montgomery Street, Federal Hill, 410-837-0010; Abercrombie and Badger B&B, 58 West Biddle Street, 410-244-7227; Clarion at Mount Vernon Square, 612 Cathedral Street, 410-727-7101. The Holiday Inn Express (1401 Bloomfield Avenue, 410-646-1700) is outside of downtown, but the savings can make it worthwhile, and you can always take the Light Rail in (call the MTA, 410-539-5000, to get route maps of the Light Rail, buses, and Metro subway system); there's a stop at Pratt Street right by the **Wharf Rat** brewpub.

Area attractions: First go to **Fort McHenry.** It's the inspiration for our national anthem, and it's inspiring. It's also a very pleasant park on a sunny day. (East Fort Avenue, just follow the signs, 410-962-4290). Then go to the **B&O Railroad** (901 West Pratt Street, 410-752-2490) to view the first railroad station in America; the country's first passenger trains ran from here to Ellicott City. The museum is built in the old roundhouse and houses many restored locomotives.

The main Inner Harbor attractions are the astonishing **National Aquarium** (501 East Pratt Street, 410-576-3800), with its shark tank and poison-dart frogs; the USS *Constellation*, the only Civil War naval vessel still afloat (410-539-1797); and the **National Historic Seaport of Baltimore,** which includes admittance to the **Top of the World** (an observation platform on the twenty-seventh floor of the World Trade Center, 401 East Pratt Street), the World War II–era submarine USS *Torsk*, the Coast Guard cutter *Taney*, the steam tug *Baltimore*, the fireboat base at Fort McHenry, and the **Baltimore Museum of Industry** (1415 Key Highway, 410-727-4808) for one low combined price. To get around to all that stuff, and to the bars in Fells Point, plonk down five bucks for a day's worth of riding on the **Water Taxi** (800-658-8947), which not only will get you around, but also could save you money on the stiff Inner Harbor parking, too. Fells Point parking is a lot cheaper!

Want to get some game? **Camden Yards** (333 West Camden Street, 410-685-9800) is the home of the Baltimore Orioles and is held to be one of the best baseball parks in the country. Baltimore is nuts about its football team as well; catch a game at **Ravens Stadium** (1101 Russell Street, 410-261-3267).

Baltimore's **Washington Monument** (609 Washington Plaza, 410-396-7837) is older than D.C.'s Washington Monument and was designed by the same architect, Robert Mills. The monument in the District of Columbia also was partly built with marble from quarries owned by Baltimore's Sisson family, as were many of the marble porch steps in South Baltimore. You can go up in the Baltimore monument, but there's no elevator.

Feeling like something uplifting? The **Walters Gallery** (600 North Charles Street, 410-547-9000) contains an absolutely stunning range of exquisite works of art, from antiquity through the modern era, including sculpture, paintings, tapestries, jewelry, arms and armor, and illuminated manuscripts. The gallery houses the collection of William and Henry Walters, who left the entire collection and the three buildings to the city of Baltimore. If you'd rather listen to your culture, contact the **Meyerhoff Symphony Hall** (1212 Cathedral Street, 410-783-8100) for the schedule of the Baltimore Symphony Orchestra, or the **Lyric Opera House** (128 West Mount Royal Avenue, 410-625-1600) for the performances of the Baltimore Opera Company.

Just to be a little different . . . The **Baltimore Streetcar Museum** (1901 Falls Road, 410-547-0264) is a rare, loving look at the original light rail systems that spurred huge urban growth one hundred years ago. On top of the movie, the exhibits, and the uniformed volunteers, there is a short trolley ride. The **American Visionary Art Museum** (800 Key Highway, 410-244-1900) looks kind of wacky, and you know what? It is. This is art by people who are not "artists," per se, but just have to create. Here's where they get their due, and some of it is exciting. Take a look. You might also want to check out the restaurant at the museum, the **Joy America Café** (410-244-6500); the food's innovative, the décor's amusing, and the beer's not bad.

Other area beer sites: Baltimore has a ton of great bars, and most of them have a decent beer selection. Let's get started!

Federal Hill

Right across the street—Cross Street—from Ryleigh's is the Cross Street Market, and the western end of it is **Nick's Seafood** (no phone). This is not fancy, it's just barely a bar, but it's so Baltimore: Nick's is about eating delicious seafood—fried, broiled, steamed, or raw—while muckling onto beers served in the biggest plastic cups I've ever seen, like a kid's beach bucket without the handle. There's not much selection, though you can get Clipper City's McHenry, but this is about crab and shrimp and tuna and rockfish, standing at the counter, and jostling and laughing. Just down Cross Street from Ryleigh's is the **Thirsty Dog Pub** (20 East Cross Street, 410-727-6077), a comfy joint with nice food and house beers done by Old Dominion (the house beers are a bargain, too). A little farther south is the **Ropewalk Tavern** (1209 South Charles Street, 410-727-1298), an extensive, friendly bar with a good selection of draft beer, though a bit light on locals, and more than twenty-five single malts. Cigar-friendly. Walk in the door at **Sean Bolan's Irish Pub** (1236 Light Street, 410-837-4440) and you'll know you're in the right place: You're looking at a handpump and a jacket-cooled firkin sitting on the bar, permanent fixtures at Sean Bolan's. Very impressive tap selections are the norm here, and it's three draft mugs for $4 through 7 P.M. (you can thank the Wharf Rat in Fells Point for starting that Baltimore craft brew tradition). **Little Havana** (1325 Key Highway, 410-837-9903) isn't in Federal Hill, it's down on the stretch of Key Highway between Federal Hill and Fort McHenry, but you should go over for a visit: It's like walking into another time, another place. I had some great empanadas here one day when I was caught without a brewery to visit (Globe Brewing, across the parking lot, had closed without warning), and I greatly enjoyed the slightly run-down Cuban nightclub look here. Great food, great view of the Inner Harbor, and some decent beer. One more: To my mind, the only place worth drinking in Inner Harbor is at **Capitol City,** but there was supposed to be a **Ram's Head Tavern** music venue going into the big **Power Station** complex; check the Ram's Head website, www.ramshead tavern.com for schedules.

Mount Vernon

Before you leave the **Wharf Rat** brewpub on Pratt Street and head up to Mount Vernon, take a look into **Max's at Camden Yards** (300 West Pratt Street, 410-234-8100), a cadet branch of the tap-massive, beer-mighty Max's on Broadway in Fells Point. There may not be quite as many taps here, but there's plenty to keep you happy before or after an O's game over at Camden Yards—where you'll find a happily decent selection of beer as well, by the way. Now, be on your way up Charles Street and slip into the **Belvedere Hotel** (1 East Chase Street, 410-347-0888, just around the corner from The Brewer's Art). The Belvedere's no longer a hotel, by the way, so don't figure to stay there. Keep to your left as you walk toward the back, and you'll be in the **Owl Bar,** a celebrated Baltimore bar in the grand old style. Note the stained-glass owls, intricate brickwork, and the pizza oven in the corner. Also note the pretty impressive tap selection, if you would, one of the better I found in Baltimore. When you're ready for something a bit more informal, stroll down Charles Street to **The Brewer's Art** because the best bar in its neighborhood is downstairs from the dining room in the brewpub's basement. You'll see all the house taps, plus an excellent bottle selection of German and Belgian imports and American craft brews. Best of all is the brickwork, which gives you that "drinking in the catacombs" feel.

Canton

Canton is hot and up-and-coming, and so is **Mahaffey's Pub** (2706 Dillon Street, 410-276-9899). Just look at that sign outside, one of those lit signs with big, black block letters: "CASK-CONDITIONED ALE EVERY DAY." You bet, baby! And look at the push taps: nothing even faintly macro here, or in the bottle selection proudly on display. Wayne Mahaffey's small, friendly corner bar has grasped good beer with both hands. Not far away is **Growlers Pub** (600 South Potomac Street, at the corner of Potomac and Fleet, 410-276-7553), another up-and-comer. Owned by John Bates, a fifteen-year veteran bartender at Racers Café, Growlers is dedicated to the good beer proposition and is way out in light beer land; "Baltimore's Fort Apache of beer," Baltimore beer demiurge Tom Cizauskas calls it. On down in the square, the heart of Canton, is **Looney's Pub** (2900 O'Donnell Street, 410-675-9235), which has a pretty good tap selection, well beyond the usual suspects for an Irish bar. Looney's is a sports bar, which normally leaves me cold, but I like this place, wall-to-wall TVs and all. The food's reasonably priced and the beer's good and the folks are friendly. Looney's is across Linwood Street from **Speakeasy Saloon** (2840 O'Donnell Street, 410-276-2977), another nice place with decent beer that is definitely worth your time.

Fells Point

It has to be faced: This is Baltimore's beer epicenter. Fells Point has always been stuffed with bars—it's a real maritime neighborhood, not a reconstruction—but thank the Wharf Rat for bringing good beer here. That's the **Wharf Rat at Fells Point** (801 South Ann Street, 410-276-9034), of course, not the brewpub. You'll find the Oliver's ales here, usually with cask ale as well, and a couple guest taps. The bar is rough-hewn, dog-friendly, and solid. And it's still three mugs of three different beers for three bucks until 7 P.M.; sample up! "Eat **Bertha's** Mussels," the bumper stickers say, and that's just what I did at this Fells Point institution (734 South Broadway, 410-327-5795), and had the chess pie, too. The food was delicious, the beer's largely local, and the bar's snug and cozy. While you're on Broadway, it's a good time to go to **Max's on Broadway** (737 South Broadway, 410-675-6297), a real temple of good beer that has more taps than you can sample in three nights of dedicated drinking. Not just a lot of taps, either. Max's has exceptional taps, surprising taps: Belgians, rare craft brew one-shots, and craft brews rarely seen in Maryland. Ask about Max's Beer Socials on Tuesday evenings upstairs; there are often interesting brews and giveaways. Just around the corner is a real sailor's bar, the **Whistling Oyster** (807

South Broadway, 410-342-7282), the kind of place where a sailor can pick up his mail when he's in port, a well-worn barrel-house bar that still manages to sport some good taps and friendly atmosphere. The **Cat's Eye Pub** (1730 Thames Street, 410-276-9085), I was told, is the place to go for real Irish traditional music in Baltimore; if that's your gig, that's your place.

There aren't any brewpubs in Fells Point, but **DuClaw** is opening one of their pubs there on the Bond Street Wharf, supplied with their excellent beers and the service they're known for (check www.duclaw. com for an updated address). A Fells Point classic that's usually quite busy is **John Steven Ltd.** (1800 Thames Street, 410-327-5561), where people go to talk (loudly and excitedly), eat the great food, and drink a very nice selection of draft beer at the grand old bar, a monumental backbar with pillars and mirrors. There's a very busy little bar in the back, too. I saved one of the best for last: **Duda's** (1600 Thames Street, 410-276-9719) is not about loud music or picking up girls; it's about great simple food, conversation, and a medium-size tap selection that manages to have some things you won't find elsewhere in Fells Point. They have the three different mugs for three bucks Fells Point thing going, so you can try a bunch of them. It's across Bond Street from the London Coffee House, where Baltimore's original charter was negotiated in the early 1600s. One more recommendation, but it's not a bar: I've recovered very nicely from two long bar sessions with a morning-after breakfast at the **Blue Moon Café** (1621 Aliceanna Street, 410-522-3940); the service and food are outstanding, and the coffee is exquisitely good. Be prepared to wait—it's worth it.

Northern Areas

The place to go for a beer up here is **Racers Café** (7732 Harford Road, 410-665-6000), a beer bar of long standing that was recommended to me by a number of Baltimore brewers, and they were right. Racers is the real thing, with excellent taps and free peanuts. They do winter beers in a big way, and every fall they have the Racers Real Ale Challenge, a real ale festival out in the backyard beer garden that they put on with Baltimore's Society for the Preservation of Beer from the Wood, a real ale enthusiast group. It's part beer fest, part harvest celebration, all fun.

If you want to get take-out beer, the best places in town are up here. Start at Racers; the package store next door is part of the same operation. The biggest selection in town is probably at **Wells Discount Liquors** (6310 York Road, 410-435-2700), which also has a great bourbon and rye section. Just south of there on York Road, in the Belvedere Square shopping plaza, is **Grand Cru** (527 East Belvedere Avenue, 410-464-1944), where you can have your beer and drink it, too. Grand Cru is a beer store *and* a draft beer and wine bar, and for a modest corkage fee, you can buy a big bottle of something Belgian (or German or British or craft-brewed American) and drink it there at the bar. Very upscale for a beer store. Finally, a little farther out is **The Old Vine** (6054 Falls Road, 410-377-9599), which not only has a small but very select offering of beers and whiskeys, but also sports a ton of wine and some delicious cheese, and it has staff who talk knowledgeably about all four, a rare and wonderful thing in itself.

Baltimore Brewing Company

104 Albemarle Street, Baltimore, MD 21202
410-837-5000
www.degroens.com

Theo DeGroen was a prince in European brewing. The DeGroens have owned the Grolsch brewery in Holland for several hundred years. Theo's father was the president. Theo himself was attending Weihenstephan, possibly the most prestigious brewing school in the world, working toward the five-year brewing engineer degree, when his father died tragically young. There was no question of Theo dropping out of school; his cousins were moved in to take over, and school continued.

Part of the Weihenstephan program is the *praktikum*, real-life experience working in a brewery. Theo worked at Park-Brauerei, where he was well liked. He was so well liked that the owners were grooming him to take over control of the brewery. And why not? He had the education, the brewing pedigree. But he felt he needed a better idea of how to run a business, so the prince came to America in the mid-1980s to earn an MBA from Duke.

The education must have taken, because while he was studying, he saw an opportunity. The Amer-

Beers brewed: Märzen, Dunkles, Pils (GABF Gold, 1996), Weizen (GABF Gold, 2002). Seasonals: Rauchbock (GABF Bronze, 1998; Gold, 1999, 2000; Silver, 2002), Altfest, Maibock, Helles, Weizenbock (GABF Silver, 1994), Doppelbock (GABF Silver, 1994; Gold, 1995).

ican small brewery movement was just gathering steam in the West, and Theo saw no reason why it shouldn't work in the East. As it happened, the water in Baltimore closely matches that in Munich, so in 1989, after he had raised $1.5 million in capital (part of it being his inheritance), he opened his German-style brewery in the city of H. L. Mencken. Henry Louis, always a Germanophile, and particularly with regard to beer, would have been proud.

The Pick: Under Theo's hand, the Märzen is tasting great—malty, and very drinkable. But you know who I love . . . the Rauchbock, the carnivore predator of the beer world, able to dominate much bigger beers by intimidation alone. Seriously, DeGroen's Rauchbock blows better-known smoked beers like Rogue Smoke and Alaskan Smoked Porter right out of the water with its densely packed juicy smokiness and rippling float of malt underneath, a full-rack-of-ribs beer, double-smoked-bacon beer, fork-tender-brisket beer. You cannot beat it for drinking with grilled beef, cheddar cheese, or barbecue.

"The focus here has always been the beer," I was told by Jamie Fineran, then the brewery's general manager. "Theo's no restaurateur, and he's never pretended to be one. The pub is a good source of cashflow and a showcase for the beer." Speaking as a beer guy, stuff like that is refreshing to hear, especially when you see it working.

The beer does work, and it's beautiful to see. The Märzen is the best-seller, the friendly, gently sweet, massive mug of the Oktoberfest, accounting for fully half of the brewery's sales, according to Jamie. "Every city's got its local amber beer," he said. "The Märzen is Baltimore's. It can be scary, though, having just one horse doing most of the work pulling the cart."

The Märzen is the big seller, but it is the Rauchbock that has won the most medals and probably has the most devoted following, a small but dedicated cult who worship its authoritative smoky maltiness, dripping with flavor and powerful enough to blow the shattered splinters of your teeth right out of your mouth, the beer that all others bow down to . . . Sorry. Yes, I belong to the cult, a member since the first sip. You will be, too, if you have a tall glass of Rauchbock with a juicy rare bacon cheeseburger.

There was a time not long ago when DeGroen's beers seemed to be on tap in every bar in Baltimore, an admirable ubiquity. That's slipped a bit in the past couple years, but they're still on in a lot of places. Why did Charm City take to their new beer so strongly? Jamie grinned. "That was me," he said. "I worked the streets for five years. We're into New York, Massachusetts, well into the Northeast, but the bulk of sales are still right here at home."

The hard truth, though, is that sales have slipped significantly. This may or may not be connected to the absence of Theo DeGroen. Park-Brauerei never forgot the prince, you see, and eventually made him an offer that led to his leaving America to head the brewery in Germany. Baltimore Brewing was left to soldier on. Problems started with the management of the pub, which actually closed for a short period before a new management company took over the lease. That seems to be working out, although when I visited, the pub was surrounded by construction. The African-American Museum was being finished next door, and across the street an instant neighborhood of middle-class townhouses was going up.

The beer sales slip came to a head in the spring of 2004, when head brewer Barrett Lauer abruptly left the brewery. Theo did what he had to do: He took a short leave of absence from Park-Brauerei, flew back to Baltimore, and started brewing like mad and filling up the tanks while searching for a new brewer. Jamie was working on the bottling line the morning I stopped by, and he was upbeat, as if things had taken a turn for the better. For the sake of the Rauchbock, I hope he's right.

"People discount how hard it is to make lager beer and get it in the package," Jamie said, when I asked him about what it's like running German styles in a market that's largely ales. "We've been successful, we've got them stabilized, but the customers are still looking for ales." Is that a long-term limitation on your market? I asked. "I think it's cyclical," he replied. "It's a matter of waiting it out."

Push the cycle, will you? Get tuned in to the lager wavelength; find out how good it is to drink cold-brewed mugs of malt goodness. Then maybe you'll be worthy to drink the Rauchbock.

Opened: December 1989.

Owner: Theo DeGroen.

Brewer: Theo DeGroen.

System: 17-barrel Kaspar Schultz system, 10,000 barrels annual capacity.

Production: 6,000 barrels in 2003.

Hours: Tuesday through Thursday, 3:30 P.M. to midnight; Friday through Sunday, 11:30 A.M. to midnight. Closed Mondays. Hours may change when area construction is complete; call ahead.

Tours: By appointment.

Take-out beer: 2-liter growlers available; call ahead for kegs.

Food: As you might expect, the pub menu has some delicious German selections, and I heartily recommend them to go with the beer. But the pork sandwich with a mug of Rauchbock is simply carnivore heaven.

Extras: Live bluegrass on Friday nights.

Special considerations: Kids welcome. Vegetarian meals available. Handicapped-accessible.

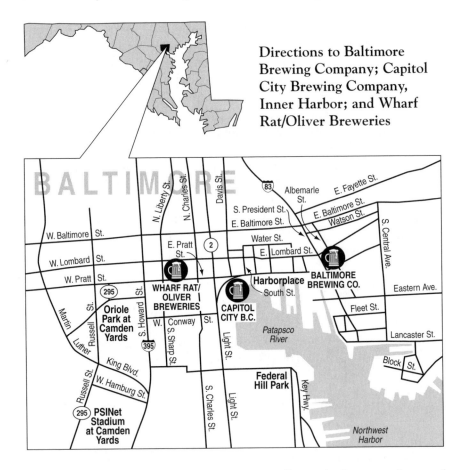

Directions to Baltimore Brewing Company; Capitol City Brewing Company, Inner Harbor; and Wharf Rat/Oliver Breweries

Parking: Metered parking is available on Albemarle Street and around the corner; a pay garage is one block south. Baltimore Brewing can be hard to find, but you've got a great landmark: Look for the **Shot Tower,** a tall, slim brick cylinder with a conical roof. You can see it from blocks away, and Baltimore Brewing is about a block and a half southwest. You'll never forget it.

Area attractions: The ***Star-Spangled Banner Flag House and 1812 Museum*** (844 East Pratt Street, 410-837-1793) is right beside the brewery and is the home of Mary Pickersgill, who sewed—with help—the famous flag that flew over Fort McHenry, a flag so big that they had to *spread it out in a neighborhood brewery.* You must go.

Capitol City Brewing Company, Inner Harbor

93 Light Street Pavilion, Harbor Place, Baltimore, MD 21202
410-539-PINT
www.capcitybrew.com

See the entry for Capitol City Brewing Company, Shirlington Village (pages 110–113), for the full Capitol City story.

The Capitol City pubs in D.C. are characterized by their buildings, big old government monumental–style beauties, hives of bureaucracy and mundane routine restored to a new life of leisure and indulgence. The Capitol City brewpub on Baltimore's Inner Harbor was purposely built for that life, a building that has but one aim: to provide a hospitable shelter for a deeply satisfying harbor view, a blue-water vista of the historic frigate USS *Constellation* and puttering water taxis, the skyward thrust of the National Aquarium, and the colorful swirl of waterside pedestrians.

Oh, it shelters one other thing as well. Capitol City, Inner Harbor, is the spiritual home of one of my purely favorite Capitol City beers, and one of my favorite big beers out of any brewery: the appropriately, honestly, bluntly named Fuel, one of the brewpub's winter seasonals. I made the mistake of declaring my love for this imperial stout when I was sampling this past December, and the bartender just smiled and poured me a full pint of the 9 percent beery berserker.

Well, what the heck, I figured, it's the last brewery I've got to sample today, and Dad's driving, so why not? I dove in. Ouch! Big, battering bitterness and the roar of malt are tempered with the beautiful punch of heavy-brewed Sumatra coffee added in the secondary, making for one serious pint of beer, a deadly good pint. Fuel is a popular tap here. I watched the bartender fill two growlers with it while I drank my pint, both for the same guy. What are you going to do with a whole gallon

Beers brewed: Year-round: Capitol Kölsch (GABF Silver, 2001; Gold, 2002), Pale Rider IPA, Amber Waves Ale (GABF Bronze, 2002), Prohibition Porter. Seasonals: Cherry Blonde Ale, Belgian-style Red Ale, Hefe-Weizen, Oktoberfest, Roggen Rye Ale, Pumpkinator Ale, Wee Heavy Ale (GABF Silver, 2001; Bronze, 2002; RAF Gold and Best-of-Show Silver, 2002; Gold, 2003), Slobberknocker Barleywine, plus Fuel.

of this jump-juice? I asked him. "Drink it!" he said with a big beer-geek grin.

Ah, December on the Inner Harbor. The wind, the cold, the cruel thin air. Thank you, Capitol City, for the shelter to keep me warm, and thank you for the Fuel to keep me going!

Opened: July 1997.

Owner: David von Storch.

Brewer: Mike Morris.

System: 15-barrel JV NorthWest system, 1,000 barrels annual capacity.

Production: 730 barrels in 2003.

Hours: 11 A.M. to 2 A.M., seven days a week.

Tours: Upon request, brewer's schedule permitting, Monday through Friday, from opening until 5 P.M.

Take-out beer: 2-liter growlers available; call ahead for half kegs (not all beers available in kegs).

Food: Largely as at Capitol City, Shirlington Village (page 110), with some small differences—mostly more crab.

Extras: The bar is well TV'd. Pool tables and video games available. The view is outstanding.

Special considerations: Kids welcome. Vegetarian meals available. Handicapped-accessible.

Parking: Pay garages available.

Ryleigh's Restaurant and Brewery

32–36 East Cross Street, Baltimore, MD 21230
410-539-2093
www.ryleighs.com

One of the best memories of my many visits to brewpubs is one of a dinner at Sisson's, Maryland's first brewpub, located in Baltimore's Federal Hill neighborhood across from the Cross Street Market. It was back in the early 1990s, and my wife and I drove down from Pennsylvania to meet my old friend Steve Van Albert and his wife for dinner. It was one of those perfect evenings.

Hugh Sisson's brewpub was alive with bustling waiters and bright with conversation, our food was zestily spiced (I still remember the superb fire in my mouth from the jambalaya and andouille) and brilliantly prepared, and the beer was perfect brew-pub-fresh stuff. I kept notes in a small beer diary in those days and can still read about how the "Marble Gold is clean and tasty, the perfect cold antidote to the heat of the jambalaya." It was a great time, and I wish I could go back there tonight.

Friends, I'm sorry to tell you that Sisson's closed. It was a great run, but sometimes even successful restaurateurs just get tired. But don't despair: There's still a brewpub at 32 East Cross Street, and oddly enough, you can still get Sisson's jambalaya there, and even Marble Gold, brewed by Hugh Sisson.

The brewpub is called Ryleigh's, and it is another example of the kind of brewery DNA that tangles through the Mid-Atlantic and refuses to die. Today Hugh Sisson happily brews Marble Gold over at Clipper City Brewing for the people who own his former brewpub, one of whom, Craig Stuart-Paul, used to own part of Oxford Class Brewing, which still survives in the form of one of Clipper City's beers, Oxford Raspberry. Ryleigh's usually has one of Clipper City's other beers on as a guest beer as well. The jambalaya? As the menu says, "Hugh left this one behind," and they were happy to use the recipe.

But it is *not* Sisson's. There's no bar to the left as you walk in the door. There's a double line of bricked archways running down the middle of the first floor. There's a raw bar every night. And the beers are all different, except for that Marble Gold. This is Ryleigh's now, and although there's still a hint of Sisson's left, it's a different place . . . as it should be.

"It's a sports brewpub," said partner-chef Tom Strawser. "There aren't that many of them." I'm not much on sports bars, because I'm not much on sports, but even I can see that they've put some thought into this one, and some money. The TVs are high-end flat-screens, with no distortion from any angle. You can see at least one screen from every seat in the pub, and that now includes the booths behind the main bar, which used to be deserted during big games because of their blind TV angle. "Every one of those booths has its own flat-screen now," Tom said, "and they are the hot seats. You've got to get in here early to get one. We had to do it, if we wanted to get people in every seat."

Beers brewed: Year-round: Dizzy Blonde, Marble Gold (brewed at Clipper City), Ryleigh's Best Amber, Raspberry Wheat. Seasonals: Ryleigh's Revenge IPA, Winter Warmer, others to come.

The Pick: The Best Amber is of a style that is more East Coast amber than West Coast amber. Out there, amber usually means sweet and touched with hop aroma. Here it's more like Ryleigh's Best Amber: malty, a caramel presence, and some surprising touches of roasted malt that keep the whole thing cleaned up and dry enough to tempt you to have another.

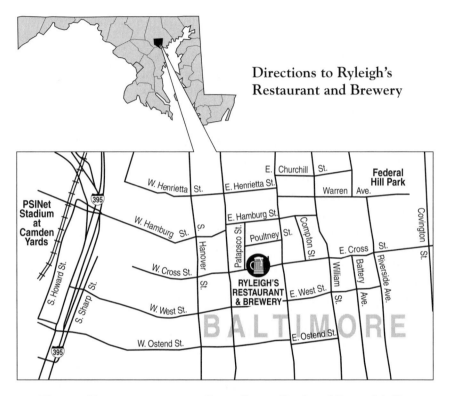

**Directions to Ryleigh's
Restaurant and Brewery**

Tom and his two partners—Craig Stuart-Paul and Brian McComas, whose daughter the pub is named for—are solid on "doing what you have to do." That's the first reason he gave when I asked him why they had kept the brewery. Space is at a premium in this building, after all, and the brewery easily could have been turned into more seating space for paying customers, an unfortunate trend that has crept up with brewpub turnover.

"No," Tom said firmly. "We had to keep it. This was Maryland's first brewpub. It's a big deal. Hugh Sisson got laws changed so this place could open. Besides, if you keep a close eye on your costs, you can get very aggressive on your draft prices, more than with kegs you're buying from the wholesaler. That's how we can do $5 pitchers of house beer on Tuesday nights." Nice to know it isn't *all* sentiment!

I'll always remember that night at Sisson's. Maybe I can't go back there, but I can still go to Ryleigh's, and I do.

Opened: November 2002 (as Ryleigh's).
Owners: Tom Strawser, Craig Stuart-Paul, Brian McComas.
Brewer: Brian Arnott.

System: 8-barrel Pub Brewing system, 800 barrel annual capacity.

Production: 750 barrels in 2003.

Hours: 11 A.M. to 2 P.M., seven days a week.

Tours: By appointment.

Take-out beer: Growlers available.

Food: It shouldn't come as any surprise that a brewpub right across from the Cross Street Market has a raw bar . . . and Ryleigh's is a good one. They also have steamed shrimp, clams, and mussels. Try the crab pretzels, lobster quesadilla, or one of the two different crab soups. When you're really hungry, tie into some of Sisson's Jambalaya, or pecan-crusted catfish, or some of the pub grub: wings, wraps, and burgers.

Extras: Extensive system of plasma-screen TVs for sports viewing, including individual screens in back booths on first floor. Tuesday is the night for $2 steamed crabs and $5 pitchers of house beer; Thursday sees $9.99 steaks. There's a brunch on Sundays.

Special considerations: Kids welcome. Vegetarian meals available. Handicapped-accessible.

Parking: On Cross Street, parking is limited and heavily enforced; metered parking on other area streets is not so bad, but be prepared to walk a couple blocks.

Wharf Rat/Oliver Breweries

206 West Pratt Street, Baltimore, MD 21201
410-244-8900

Look at all these beers! The Wharf Rat has always been known for a wide selection of taps. "I try to keep sixteen or seventeen on, counting the cask-conditioned versions as different beers," said brewer Steve Jones. "Because they are, you know. Why that many?" He smiled and shrugged. "Variety is the spice of life! They all sell well enough to stay fresh, and I can make enough different ones to keep it interesting."

Difference has been a part of the Wharf Rat since before it opened. To get to the root of the story, you have to grab the water taxi across to Fells Point and go to . . . the Wharf Rat. That's the bar Bill Oliver bought back in July 1987. "We had Coors and National Bohemian on draft when I bought the place," Bill said. "Most bars in Fells Point at the time were doing nickel drafts on two taps. I looked at that and thought, we have to do something different. So we went to twenty-eight taps, and we were the first in Fells Point to do an extensive draft selection."

Beers brewed: Year-round: SW1, Irish Red, Ironman Pale Ale, Old English Ale, Pagan Porter, Blackfriar Stout, Manchester Cream Ale, Best Bitter, ESB, Export Ale, Blonde Ale. Seasonals and one-shots: Summer Light, Biere de Garde, Vanilla Ice, Anniversary Ale, Winter Warmer, Scottish Ale, Cherry Blossom Wheat Ale, Golden Jubilee, Ginger Snap, Imperial Pale Ale, Harvest Ale, Hot Monkey Love Ale, Christmas Ale (or Merry Ole Ale) (GABF Silver, 1995).

Bar business in a popular area can be cutthroat, and quickly the competition started telling people that there was no way the Wharf Rat could be keeping all those beers fresh. "We knew we were," said Oliver, "but we started offering three different drafts for $2.50, just to keep it moving. Then people started putting in more taps, copying the success. We had to be different again, but how?"

Bill's father was originally from England and had emigrated to Canada, where Bill grew up, often hearing the sound of caps from his dad's homebrewed ales pinging off the ductwork in the basement. "I thought, that's it—we'll make Dad's ale," said Bill. "In May of 1992, Alan Pugsley started making Oliver's Ale for us at the old Wild Goose brewery in Cambridge, on the Eastern Shore."

But Bill wanted cask ale, and it just didn't make sense for Wild Goose to do it for them. "I used to pick up groceries at a wholesale warehouse right about where Camden Yards is now," Bill recalled. "I saw this building one day with a For Sale sign on it, and I bought it." He hired Pugsley, who was now doing business installing Peter Austin breweries up and down the East Coast, to put a system in the building, primed with the same authentic Ringwood yeast they used at Wild Goose.

"The first time we brewed was January of 1992, and I still remember that first pour," he said, a sentimental grin briefly lighting his face. "It was our first beer, SW1 Ale, and we were waiting to pour on this cold January day. We finally called the ATF and hounded someone down until they said, 'Yes, all right, here's your license number!' I hung up the phone and pointed to the bartender: 'Pour the beer!' And those first two beers went to a young couple in the bar, and the guy got right down on his knee and proposed to her." Then Bill laughed. "I have no idea if they're still married, but it sure is a great memory!"

Steve Jones doesn't go quite that far back; he's been brewing at the Wharf Rat since 1999. But he's a big part of it now, and the beers have his stamp on them. He's using all Thomas Fawcett malt, a York-shire malt to go with his Yorkshire yeast. You may see online reviews downchecking the Wharf Rat for the similarity of Steve's beers, but they're missing the point. Yes, the beers have a similarity; with the house yeast and common malt, it's inevitable. But the beauty of these beers is the differences Steve gets out of different blends of specialty malts and hops and different fermentation regimes. British beer is all about subtlety, the quench of a good pint, the liveliness of a cask in peak condition, and the Wharf Rat captures that quite well on most days.

Being situated across Pratt Street from the convention center and kitty-corner from Camden Yards, some days the Wharf Rat just gets hammered with crowds. Days like that, Steve just watches the tanks and hangs on. "We had some science conventions at the center," he recalled. "They get a lot of Europeans over for those, and those people really drink. Someone found out about our ales the first day, and I honestly thought they were going to drink us out of beer."

Part of the draw had to be the selection of cask ales. Steve tries to keep three casks pouring at all times, an amazing feat in a city where other regular cask taps are few. I know I've spent golden afternoons at the brewpub's outdoor tables drinking pints of the cask Best Bitter, and it's always been in grand condition.

You'll see guest taps of some fairly mainstream beers at the Wharf Rat, something that has led a few beer geeks to bad-mouth the place. Steve's blasé about the comments. "They were here when I got here," he said, "and I don't do lagers, so why not? We can compete, and the house beers outsell the guest beers." That's particularly true of the Ironman Pale Ale, the best-seller of the house beers, and one of the first cask IPAs I'd ever had back in 1996, when Bill Oliver brought it to a Philadelphia real ale event. It was so good that I still remember it: lightly carbonated, overflowing with earthy hops and the nutty notes of Ringwood.

Drop anchor at the Wharf Rat and try Steve's ales for yourself. Be sure to try the cask ales, be sure to try the draft versions, be sure to relax and enjoy your beers. Enjoy the difference, because that's what the Wharf Rat is—and always has been—all about.

The Pick: Ironman is my favorite if it's on cask; I can't resist the way the hops roar through the low carbonation. My everyday pick is the cask Best Bitter, mellow, estery, lightly hopped, with the understated malt complexity of a classic. This is an all-day beer, meant to be enjoyed in volume, and that's how I enjoy it the best. I do hope that Steve keeps on his "one-off" batch of Anniversary Ale, though—a wonderfully complex yet drinkable beer that rewards both the casual and the introspective drinker.

Opened: January 1992.

Owner: Bill Oliver.

Brewer: Steve Jones.

System: 7-barrel Peter Austin system, 1,500 barrels annual capacity.

Production: 1,000 barrels in 2003.

Hours: 11:30 A.M. to 2 A.M., seven days a week.

Tours: According to Bill, "Any time of day, as long as someone's here." Duck when you go in the brewhouse; it's low clearance down there.

Take-out beer: Growlers available, call ahead for kegs.

Food: English pub-style comfort food—fish and chips, bangers and mash, ploughman's lunch—plus American favorites as well, the old standbys: cheese fries, crab cakes, burgers, wings, and a long list of sandwiches. It ain't *haute cuisine,* but it pairs wonderfully with the 20-ounce pints of Steve Jones's English-type ales.

Extras: Live music; call for schedule. Large outdoor seating area.

Special considerations: Cigars not allowed. Kids welcome. Vegetarian meals available. Handicapped-accessible.

Parking: Numerous garages in the area.

The Brewer's Art

1106 North Charles Street, Baltimore, MD 21201
410-547-6925
www.thebrewersart.com

I like the bold statement The Brewer's Art makes as a brewpub name. Right away it lets you know that this place is out of the ordinary; no XYZ Brewing Company name, and no food-first, beer as an after-thought, "a brewpub is a restaurant that happens to brew beer" philosophy. The Brewer's Art has aimed beer-high from the beginning: It was the first brewpub in the country dedicated to Belgian-style brewing.

Why Belgian? "It's what we liked," partner Volker Stewart told me with a grin. "Seriously, the Wharf Rat was doing British ales, Baltimore Brewing and Fordham were doing lagers, and Sisson's had American micro-styles covered, so there was room for Belgian-style beers. There was an immediate positive reaction to them. Many people told us, 'I don't like beer, but I like this.'"

Stewart was a librarian at the University of Baltimore, when he met founding partners Tom Creegan and Johey Verfaille through homebrewing, and they decided to open The Brewer's Art. "It was almost a lemonade stand kind of idea," said Volker. The "lemonade stand" came together over the next year and a half.

"It's hard to find brewpub space in Baltimore," Stewart said, noting the expense of Inner Harbor locations and the reluctance of Fells Point residents to allow yet another liquor license in their neighborhood. But there are no residences on the block of Charles Street where the partners finally located, in the northern end of the city's Mount Vernon section, and the building, originally the "city house" for a wealthy banker, with a proud, column-framed entrance, turned out to be perfect for The Brewer's Art.

If you enter The Brewer's Art by stepping up between those columns and through the interior door to the right, you're presented with a small barroom, almost like a sitting room, with floor-to-ceiling windows overlooking the street (there's another entrance to the basement bar). The taps grab your attention: a dog's head, a cross, the business end of a full-size pitchfork. More about them shortly. Behind the bar, you'll find a deep selection of fine spirits, including exceptional single malts and bourbons. "They fit in with the artisan nature of our brewing," Stewart told me. The Brewer's Art also has a fine selection of guest beers in bottles, both imported and craft-brewed, often with the proper glassware.

To your left are the dining rooms, sophisticated and softly lit, decorated with hung artwork. The dining rooms draw a different crowd than the bar, diners from the nearby symphony and opera house. "We had to upgrade our wine selection for them," Stewart said. "But some of them have started drinking our beers and find that a big beer can match a big wine with food."

In the back is the brewhouse, a tight fit for the 10-hectoliter Criveller system. That's where brewer Chris Cashell has made the house beers since 1997, joined by Steve Frazier in 2002. The tanks are downstairs, where a major expansion took place in 2003. "We tripled our

Beers brewed: Year-round: Ozzy, Resurrection, House Pale Ale (brewed under contract at Old Dominion). Seasonal: St. Festivus, Wit Trash, Charm City Sour Cherry, Scarlet Fever, La Petroleuse. The following "rotating beers" may be available at any time through the year: Proletary Ale, Cerberus Tripel, Sluggo.

The Pick: I always reach for Charm City when I see it; the sour cherry flavor pairs up wonderfully with the tart Flemish-style brown ale for a glass that's beautifully refreshing. If you're up for it, Ozzie is ready to rock your world. This Belgian strong is as spicy, light, and dangerously drinkable as its inspiration, Duvel.

tank capacity," said Stewart. The tank room is clean and brightly lit, not the romantic image of a Belgian brewery, with cobwebs everywhere.

According to Volker, they are pretty much nonhoppers. "A lot of people who think they don't like beer really don't like hoppy beer." At The Brewer's Art, they are presented with beers like the popular seasonal, Charm City Sour Cherry Ale, a tart Belgian brown-style beer with sour cherries added. A recent addition is the Proletary Ale, "a beer for the people who wanted a porter," said Stewart. Proletary is hard to classify: opaque black, with a medium body, roasty character, and a surprising dash of smart hop flavor.

The "holy trinity" at The Brewer's Art are the three standard beers: Ozzie, Resurrection, and Cerberus, roughly a Belgian strong, dubbel, and tripel, respectively. The Ozzie is light gold, spicy, and dry, almost a vest-pocket Westmalle tripel. Resurrection is not your typical dubbel, being lighter brown and not overly sweet, though still a malt-balanced beer. Cerberus is the big (10 percent) beer, a roundish, sweeter tripel-style with a real heft to it.

Ozzie? Resurrection? Cerberus? It's quirky Belgian-style humor to go with the quirky Belgian-style beer. Ozzie is a Duvel tribute (catch the Satanic music connection?) and resides under that pitchfork. Resurrection is an Abbey-style beer, hence the wooden cross tap. Cerberus is the three-headed canine guard of the Greek underworld (tripel, get it?) and is tapped with a dog's head.

You should be able to find these beers in other places now, thanks to the expansion. But take that as a lure to try the beers on their home territory, because this is a place that will call you back once you've experienced it.

Opened: September 13, 1996 ("Friday the Thirteenth," Volker noted).

Owners: Volker Stewart, Tom Creegan, Steve Frazier.

Brewers: Chris Cashell and Steve Frazier.

System: 10-hectoliter Criveller system, 1,200 barrels annual capacity.

Production: 1,150 barrels in 2003.

Hours: Monday through Saturday, 4 P.M. to 2 A.M.; Sunday, 5 P.M. to 2 A.M. Dining room opens at 5:30 P.M.

Tours: By appointment only.

Take-out beer: Will fill other brewery's growlers; Brewer's Art growlers are "on the horizon." Call ahead for kegs.

Food: Combine Franco-Belgian brasserie fare with the wonderfully fresh seafood of Baltimore, and that's what you'll be sitting down to at The Brewer's Art. Simple, robust stuff that goes gloriously well with the house beers—and that's the whole idea.

Extras: "There are no TVs at the Brewer's Art!" Volker said proudly. And he's right, it's a plus.

Special considerations: Kids welcome. Vegetarian meals available. The Brewer's Art is located in a historical building and is not handicapped-accessible.

Parking: On-street parking can be tough; be prepared to walk. There is a garage at the Belvedere Hotel.

Clipper City Brewing Company

4615 Hollins Ferry Road, Baltimore, MD 21227
410-247-7822
www.clippercitybeer.com

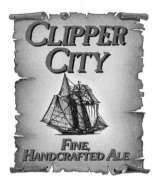

Hugh Sisson is here at Clipper City, and Ryleigh's is on Cross Street, because of an odd Maryland law. Maryland made brewpubs legal back in 1987 because Hugh Sisson and his family wanted to open the brew-pub on Cross Street. He got the law changed, and brewpubs became legal, but Maryland added a strange, unique caveat to the brewpub law: only one brewery. Not one license, though there's now a limit of two on those if you own a brewery, but only one brewery per company. So if Hugh had wanted to open, say, Sisson's II in Canton, he would have had to supply it with beer from the brewery on Cross Street.

The law still stands in all its quirky glory, and Hugh left the family business to start Clipper City, the production brewery he wanted. "I left for a variety of reasons," Hugh recalls. "The law in 1994 said I had to sell out of the brewpub to open the second brewery. Why did I want to leave? The brewpub wasn't growing anymore, and some of that was because of Mayor Schmoke's administration; nice guy, but not very effective. Not as many people were coming into the city, and competition had started. Maybe we could have opened more pubs, but there were problems.

"So I made the move, just as microbrewery brands exploded on the market," Hugh said with a sigh. "It was suddenly a different world. I wish we had an affiliated pub—it's a great market-ing tool—but Maryland law still denies it. This is a tough business, but I'm glad I'm not in a family business environment anymore. I'm here, this is what I do, this is what I will be doing."

How he came to run Sisson's is an interesting story. Hugh was a drama student at UVA, training that still shows in the cadences of his speech. "I figured I was going to head for New York and wait tables while I auditioned," Hugh said. "My dad

Beers brewed: Year-round: Clipper City Pale Ale, Clipper City Gold (GABF Bronze, 2000), McHenry, Oxford Rasp-berry Wheat Ale. Seasonals: The Heavy Seas line is all sea-sonals, including Storm Warn-ing Category 5 Ale, Small Craft Warning Über Pils, Red Sky at Night Saison, and more to come.

bought the bar on Cross Street, and I figured I might as well get some practical experience before leaving home." He chuckled darkly. "My first day on the job, my dad hands me the keys to the place, says 'Don't screw up,' and leaves."

"Well, I'd gotten the beer bug when I was in the UK as a student, so I started moving the bar in that direction. We started doing tastings, and I realized I didn't know anything about beer, so I started homebrewing. I wasn't a good homebrewer; I spent too much time working around the limitations of a home system. So I started thinking about putting a brewery in the bar, did some research, worked with a legislator, and got brewpubs legal in Maryland. We put in our system in 1989, and I still didn't know much about brewing!"

The Pick: My dad and I don't agree on much when it comes to beer; one of his favorites is Old Milwaukee NA. But it's an unspoken agreement that when one of us goes to Baltimore, we bring back McHenry. It's a good, clean, all-malt lager, a back-porch beer, a steamed-crab beer. I also like that Small Craft Warning: a big bock-strength lager, sure, and it's pretty clean, but what gets you is that big hop hammer that just doesn't stop whacking till the end of the glass. WHAM! WHAM! WHAM! Ahhhhh . . .

It was, as Hugh said, a more forgiving time. "I put together some credible beers pretty quickly and got good quickly. Suddenly I was really brewing, process manipulation and formulation, not spending all my time screwing with the equipment to make it do what I wanted."

Now he doesn't do any brewing. It's all about motivating the people who do the brewing. Hugh's job consists of quality assurance ("Perfection doesn't exist, you're never going to nail it; you need to be happy with continual baby steps"), branding ("Right or wrong, the game is about branding, and you're better off with multiple brands"), and . . . well, thinking. And Hugh is always thinking.

He thinks about his mix a lot. "Look, acknowledge that 95 percent of the market doesn't drink 'craft beer,'" he said. "So we created McHenry, a 'premium beer.' Now we want to get some support behind it, aiming it as 'the local suds.' Next we have the Clipper City beers, Gold and Pale Ale. They're good beers, but hard sells; there are a lot of pale and golden ales out there. We also have the Oxford Raspberry, with a new on-premise bottle." Hugh bought the struggling Oxford Class brewery in a noncash deal in 1998. "It seemed like a good idea at the time," he said.

That leaves Hugh's newest brand: Heavy Seas, an idea he's been kicking around for a few years, a "geek line" devoted to the hard-core beer geek. "Wine consumers read the second line of a label to see what a wine is, not just who makes it," Hugh said. "Beer drinkers usually don't. The whole point of Heavy Seas is a brand, a label, that the geeks *will* read. They're all big beers, all bottle-conditioned." They're doing well, too.

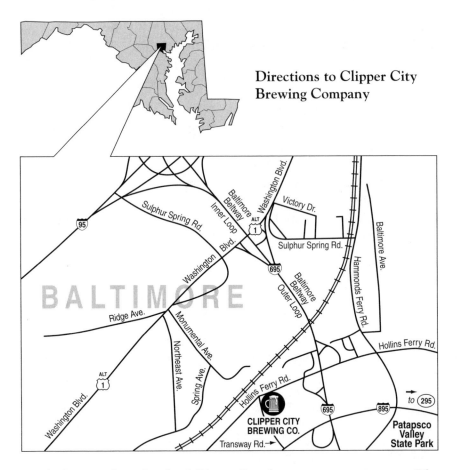

Directions to Clipper City Brewing Company

As I write this, the third Heavy Seas beer is just coming out. The first two, Winter Storm Category 5 Ale and Small Craft Warning Über Pils, were huge beers and big successes with the target market, and the Red Sky at Night Saison was eagerly awaited. "They're fun to make," Hugh told me. "At 6 to 7.5 percent ABV, they're not to cheap to make, but the market seems willing to pay for them. They have potential outside the area, too."

Hugh is gambling a bit, but he's gambled before. "It's a balance between being a brewer and a businessman," he said. "We have a unique approach; in the next three years, we should see some proof of whether it's working or not."

Like Hugh said, this is what he's doing now. But if he had it all to do over again? "I'd do a brewpub," he said. Would he want that strange little law changed? "No, rather the devil I know than a new one. At least someone big can't come in." You just have to wonder what things would have been like without that law.

Opened: December 1995.

Owners: Hugh Sisson, general partner; large group of limited partners.

Brewers: Scott Dietrich, head brewer; Matt Menke, Ernesto Igot, and Matt Saindon.

System: 50-barrel Pub Brewing system, 24,000 barrels annual capacity.

Production: 13,000 barrels in 2003.

Tours: Saturdays, usually the first and third of the month. Check website for dates.

Take-out beer: Maryland law limits sales to two six-packs each *after* a tour.

Special considerations: Handicapped-accessible.

Parking: Large free lot.

Red Brick Station/White Marsh Brewing Company

8149 Honeygo Boulevard, Baltimore, MD 21236
410-931-PUBS
www.redbrickstation.com

What if beers were to be delineated like wines are, split into types kept separate by parameters similar to the color and grape and tradition lines that divide wines? The lines that pop into people's heads immediately are those pigeonhole "styles" used by competitions and beer writers—and brewers, to be honest—to easily label beers. But what are those styles really based on, and what makes the real differences in beers that don't fit in those categories?

It all comes down to malts, hops, and yeasts. Most beer lovers know that more hops mean more bitterness, and some can identify the profile of hops generally classed as British, "noble," or American. Light and dark malts are quickly discernible, as are caramel and black malts. But beyond the very basic split of ale and lager yeasts, most beer drinkers do not have much of an idea about what different yeasts do to the flavor of beer.

Michael McDonald brews with an exception to that rule. Red Brick Station's brewer works on a Peter Austin system, using one of the best-known yeasts in microbrewing: Ringwood. Well-known does not equal well-liked, though. "Some homebrewers won't even talk to me because I brew with Ringwood," Michael told me. "They think they know Ringwood. Well, a little knowledge is a bad thing."

Michael got to know Ringwood at the Old Nutfield brewery in Derry, New Hampshire. "I really love the German lagers," he said, shaking his head and smiling ruefully, "but I keep getting sucked into brewing ales, especially with Ringwood." Then this must be hell for him, right?

"No!" he answered emphatically. "You can do a lot with Ringwood. It's so utilitarian, you can use it for everything. When the owners were planning this place, they stopped in brewpubs from Florida to Maine, and they loved Ringwood beers wherever they went. The Ringwood places had good ranges of beers."

So why do homebrewers not talk to Michael? Misunderstanding. Brewers who don't know what they're doing with Ringwood will screw up the fermentation regimen this 200-plus-year-old yeast needs for successful brewing. Treat it the wrong way, and Ringwood will produce heavy amounts of diacetyl, a compound that smells of butterscotch and theater popcorn butter. But it takes a simple step to eliminate that problem, a "diacetyl rest," and experienced Ringwood brewers like Michael know all about it.

"The temperature is key," he said. "Ringwood will generate heat very quickly, and there's no room for being lazy on a Peter Austin system; there are no electronic controls. There's not a lot of automation, but that's not all bad."

Neither is Ringwood, despite people who complain about its distinctive nutty flavor. "Some people call it that," said Michael. "I don't see it; it's more like toffee. It's fruity, estery, more distinctive than other ale yeasts out there. We get people who hate it, but people who like our beers enjoy that Ringwood character and seek those beers out."

They should look for the big ones, because that's where Ringwood really shines. Beers like Michael's Highlander Heavy, a classic Wee

Beers brewed: Year-round: Daily Crisis IPA, Something Red, Spooners Stout, Avenue Ale, Honeygo Light (any of these may be on cask). Seasonals: Big Gunpowder Pale Ale, Murf's Backdraught Porter, Highlander Heavy, Octopus' Pajamas, Old Crab Barley Wine, "They Made Me Do It" Blueberry Ale, Winter Solstice, Lord Baltimore Old Ale, EJ's Pumpkin Ale, Bishoff's Brown Ale, Bawlmer Best, Chesapeake Lager . . . "And the list will grow!" Mike promised. Red Brick also features a guest tap, with a rotating selection of local or nationally brewed craft beer.

The Pick: Something Red, the man calls it, flaunting his disregard for style categories. It's a smooth, rich, yet poundable ale with a great toasted malt flavor, almost a festbier of ales. My notes on this one read, "I'd like to shove this beauty down some hophead's throat." Always looking to broaden the beer geek's mind, that's me, and Something Red would succeed in that on a number of levels.

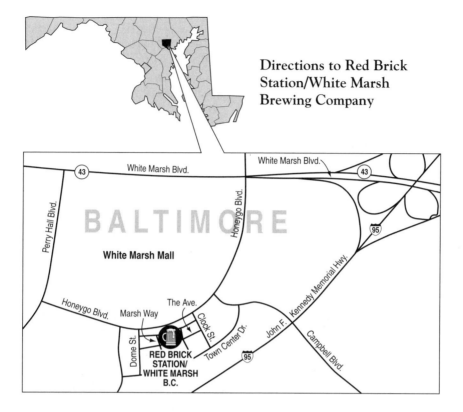

Directions to Red Brick Station/White Marsh Brewing Company

Heavy that comes on like a huge hunk of malt pudding with fruit salad heaped on top, chewy and dense, a ponderous but precise beer. "Thanks, Ringwood," Michael replied when I told him how great it tasted. "Not many yeasts could handle a beer like that."

But Ringwood can handle beers like the Daily Crisis IPA, a full-bodied IPA with a big hops profile that comes through just great, and even better on cask, the dispense system this yeast was bred for. Surprisingly, it can even handle Michael's Honeygo Light, a clean, grainy golden ale for the more timid drinker. "It's the best-seller," he told me. "If you're a brewpub and sell Lite, that's not right. If you're a brewpub and you refuse to *make* a light, that's just stupid."

Red Brick Station is all about beer, from light to dark, from the bar to the kitchen. Executive chef Keith Sappington likes the beers, and drinks the beers, and uses the beers in his special dishes. Some of his dishes you just need to have with beer, especially the well-named 3-Pint Curry: shrimp, chicken, and sausage in a cream curry sauce with fresh peas, a delicious dish that goes so well with Michael's Something Red, a malty amber that puts out the fire.

Putting out fire, by the way, is kind of a theme here. The brewpub is located on a plaza-strip called The Avenue. The Avenue is supposed to be Main Street, USA, and the brewpub got the site the developers wanted to be the firehouse. They're good sports, so there is a fair amount of firehall stuff in the pub: badges, equipment, helmets.

So if you're driving by on I-95, stop in. It's less than five minutes from the exit if you catch the light by the McDonald's. It's a good chance to get to know Ringwood. It's a friendly little yeast.

Opened: October 1997.

Owner: Bill Blocker.

Brewer: Michael McDonald.

System: 10-barrel Peter Austin system, 2,100 barrels annual capacity.

Production: 1,350 barrels in 2003.

Hours: 11 A.M. to 2 A.M., seven days a week.

Tours: Upon request.

Take-out beer: Growlers and half kegs.

Food: The crab soup is delicious, and you've read about the 3-Pint Curry. That's the kind of food you can get here: well-made, tasty, rib-sticking. "Comfort food," it's called these days, what would have been called "home cooking" fifty years ago. Sit down and enjoy it.

Extras: There are twelve TVs in the bar, and they're broadcasting sports and news all the time. Be warned: Ravens games are taken pretty seriously here.

Special considerations: Kids welcome. Vegetarian meals available. Handicapped-accessible.

Parking: Large lots all around the mall, but be prepared to walk a bit.

Lodging in the area: Hampton Inn White Marsh (8225 Town Center Drive, 410-931-2200) and the Hilton Garden Inn–White Marsh (5015 Campbell Boulevard, 410-427-0600) are both within easy walking distance.

Area attractions: *White Marsh Town Center Mall* is right where you are, with more than the ordinary run-of-the-mall shops, and the *Loews Theater* (410-933-9428) is right across the little square. But you can be fishing for bass or trout at *Gunpowder Falls State Park* in twenty minutes! A swimming beach and boat rentals are also available in the Hammerman area, but the best fishing is upstream. Check with the rangers: 410-592-2897.

Other area beer sites: *Della Rose's Avenue Tavern* is another bar on the Boulevard (8153-A Honeygo Boulevard, 410-933-8861), but if you're looking for serious beer, you'll be best served by heading up

U.S. Route 1 to Bel Air. The original **DuClaw** is out there (16A Bel Air South Parkway, 410-515-3222), and it's still a great place to drink and eat, even if they're not brewing there anymore. There's also a new branch of the great Federal Hill bar **Sean Bolan's** in Bel Air (12 North Main Street, 410-420-9858), and a visit to Sean Bolan's—wherever it is—is a can't-miss proposition. See the Baltimore bars also, particularly the Northern Area ones, but the Inner Harbor and Federal Hill are only twenty minutes away via I-95 and the Fort McHenry Tunnel.

DuClaw Brewing Company

1305-B Governor Court, Abingdon, MD 21009
410-515-3222
www.duclaw.com

DuClaw recently moved into a new phase in their history, and to tell the truth, as I write this, it hasn't actually happened yet, and I'm not sure what to call them anymore. Let me explain. Thanks to Maryland law, the company can have only one brewing facility. That was originally at the first DuClaw pub, in Bel Air. It was obvious that it was a brewpub; it was a bar and restaurant wrapped around a glass-enclosed brewhouse.

A few years later, DuClaw opened a second pub at the Arundel Mills Mall, a site that turned out to be more friendly to the DuClaw beers. "We do fairly well with house beer sales in Bel Air," brewer Jim Wagner said, "but we go through a lot of bottles of MGD and Coors Light. At the mall, we consistently sell twelve house pints for every bottle sold. The night we released Mad Bishop at the mall, I saw maybe five bottles of beer sold all night. I saw five bottles in the first ten minutes here [in Bel Air]."

Beers brewed: Year-round: Bare Ass Blonde Ale, Kangaroo Love, Ravenwood Kölsch, Misfit Red, Venom Pale Ale, Bad Moon Porter. Seasonals: 13 Degrees Hefeweizen, Alchemy Oatmeal Stout, Black Jack Imperial Stout, Devil's Milk Barleywine, Fantome English Brown Ale, Funk American Honey Wheat, Mad Bishop Oktoberfest, Naked Fish Chocolate Raspberry Stout, Old Flame Old Ale, Sawtooth Belgian White Ale, Twisted Kilt Scotch Ale, Serum Imperial IPA.

Jim and his boss, owner Dave Benfield, had good reason to remember that year's batch of Mad Bishop, Jim's Oktoberfest. Jim bet the servers that if they could sell 2,000 pints of Mad Bishop in two weeks, he'd die his hair green. Two weeks and 3,100 pints later, Jim was looking like Maryland's tallest leprechaun. He made out better than Benfield, though; Dave made a similar bet and wound up with a Mad Bishop tattoo on his calf.

The Pick: Day to day, I'll probably go for the Bad Moon Porter, with its black opacity, effortless power, and rich, creamy malt and chocolate flavor. Seasonal time makes it tougher, but I'd probably reach for the Twisted Kilt Scotch Ale. It's big, it's mean, it's raunchy with malt, it needs a shave, and I love it like a brother.

They take the beer pretty seriously at DuClaw, as a serious part of the business. I've never seen a brewpub that supports its house beers as strongly as DuClaw. The quality of the graphics and copy on the in-house marketing materials would lead you to believe these were national brands with major advertising houses behind them. Big banners with bold, edgy, well-executed graphics, table tents, and a sharp new tap trailer for beer festivals brazenly splashed with the despairing angel graphic of DuClaw's big barleywine, Devil's Milk. This is impressive, when you consider most brewpubs' idea of supporting the house beers runs to a chalkboard and some taphandles.

Jim Wagner knows how to have a good time—he and my dad had an energetic conversation about the joys of crabbing on the north Bay—but it seems that the best time he knows how to have is brewing, brewing the very best he can. He came to DuClaw in 1999 as an earnest homebrewer. "I was an avid competitor," Jim recalled. "I wanted a ribbon from every state competition. I have twenty-four." That's how he came to the brewpub: He won a chance to brew his homebrew at DuClaw, and by chance, they needed a new brewer. They liked his attitude and made him an offer. Once Jim realized it was an honest offer, he dropped his biomedical technician job and grabbed onto brewing with both hands.

The transition from homebrewer to pro brewer was one of the smoothest I've ever heard about. Jim was a very proficient homebrewer and a technical-minded guy, which helped. But it's his attitude about beer and brewing that helped the most, I believe. Jim's very concerned about the quality and consistency of his beers, not with the hoppiness, alcohol levels, or stylistic precision. Bravo!

Quality, consistency, and that strong marketing support have proved overwhelmingly successful. A third pub in Bowie is going gangbusters, and a fourth will have opened in Fells Point by the time you read this. It's been too successful for Jim to keep up, frankly. The 15-barrel system at Bel Air just couldn't brew enough beer, so there was a decision to make. The upshot was a plan to have the beers brewed at Clipper City

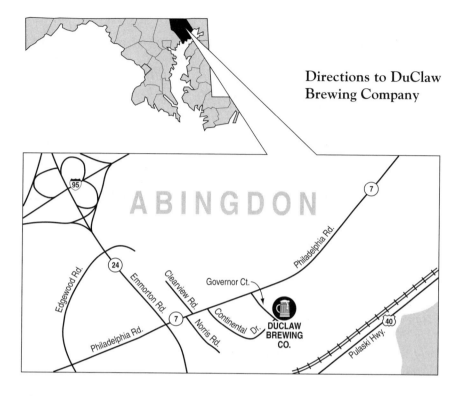

Directions to DuClaw Brewing Company

while Jim worked full-time on getting a much larger production brewery up and running.

That's the brewery I toured as the last research visit for this book. It's not far from the Bel Air pub, located in an industrial park in an old butter and margarine storage facility. There's a big new 40-barrel steam-fired DME brewhouse sitting in the corner, and five 40-barrel tanks fitted out with dry-hopping hatches in the top. There's a big cold box ("I know in a year we'll think it's too small," Jim told me with a grin) and a ton of new growlers. That's when you start to get a grip on just how successful DuClaw is: The pubs sold six hundred *new* growlers in *one month* in 2004. Not refills, new glass, about twenty each day.

Get another grip: The release parties DuClaw has for seasonal beers are promoted by an e-mailing to a list of more than ten thousand patrons, of whom 20 percent show up for any given release party, and over 40 percent show up to at least one out of three parties. That's a lot of people, and a lot of beer: They went through half the entire batch of 2004's Sawtooth White, supposedly a month's worth, in a week.

But what the heck do you call the place? It's not a brewpub, because they don't brew beer *in* the pub. In fact, because of another controversial

Maryland alcohol law, the pubs and the brewery have been split into two different companies; the law prohibits breweries from owning more than two retail outlets. But if they're a production brewery, they're a weird one, because they sell their beer only to another company, which for all intents and purposes is themselves. You could call them either, but which one is right?

Me, I call them DuClaw. And I drink Jim's excellent beer: the hoppy but extremely drinkable Venom and its somewhat scary big brother, Serum; the deep black and silky Bad Moon Porter; some of that creamy and spicy Sawtooth White; and Devil's Milk, a barleywine as smooth as finely tuned hydraulics, and as powerful. Who needs to label this place? Let's have a beer.

Opened: Bel Air brewpub opened 1996; brewery opened July 2004.
Owner: Dave Benfield.
Brewers: Jim Wagner, head brewer; Jared Mechling.
System: 40-barrel DME system, 5,000 barrels annual capacity.
Production: 2,100 barrels in 2003 (some produced under contract at Clipper City).
Hours: Varied; call individual pubs.
Tours: By appointment.
Take-out beer: Growlers available at pubs; call ahead for kegs.
Food: An eclectic, somewhat daring menu that has some comfort foods, too. Try a peppery slice of rare tuna au poivre, or Chicken Baltimore (did anyone guess that this involves crabmeat?), while your kids gobble mac and cheese. Something lighter? How about a Cuban sandwich, or a 'chicken salad salad'?
Locations: 16A Bel Air South Parkway, Bel Air, 410-515-3222; 7000 Arundel Mills Circle, Suite R4, Hanover, 410-799-1166; 4000 Towne Center Boulevard, Bowie, MD, 301-809-6943; 901 South Bond Street, Baltimore, 410-563-3400.
Special considerations: Handicapped-accessible.
Parking: Free on-site lot.
Lodging in the area: Super 8 Joppa, 1015 Pulaski Highway, Joppatowne, 410-676-2700; Quality Inn and Suites, 739 West Bel Air Avenue, Aberdeen, 410-272-6000; Holiday Inn Chesapeake House, 1007 Beards Hill Road, Aberdeen, 410-272-8100; Vandiver Inn, 301 South Union Avenue, Havre de Grace, 410-939-5200.
Area attractions: It's been a while since I visited the **Army Ordnance Museum** at the Aberdeen Proving Grounds (410-278-3602), but I remember it well. The museum itself houses a large collection

of weaponry, ranging from handguns to artillery (all inactive, of course), and around the museum are parked more than two hundred tanks and other armored fighting vehicles. There is nothing else like it in the world. If it looks like a duck and floats like a duck, chances are you'll find it at the **Havre de Grace Decoy Museum** (215 Giles Street, Havre de Grace, 410-939-3739), the finest collection of duck and waterfowl decoys anywhere, a celebration of a practical bit of folk art. The museum also has a decoy carving shop exhibit and duck-hunting equipage. The visitors center at the **Conowingo Dam** is open on weekdays; dam tours are given the first Saturday of each month (410-457-5011). You can drive straight across the dam and the Susquehanna River on U.S. Route 1 . . . and if you're north-bound from DuClaw's Bel Air pub, just turn right on MD Route 222 and go south through Port Deposit for a scenic detour around the recently raised $5 northbound toll on I-95 at Perryville. If you're in the mood, you can stop at **Hopkins' Crab House** (410-378-5250) and get a bunch of steamed crabs; watch for the sign on the river side of the road, about two miles south of the dam.

Other area beer sites: *Sean Bolan's,* the Federal Hill beer bar, has a branch out here (12 North Main Street, Bel Air, 410-420-9858). I haven't made it in yet, but I have no reason to believe it's any less great than the original. You're also close to the north Baltimore bars and liquor stores and Red Brick Station.

Ellicott Mills Brewing Company

8308 Main Street, Ellicott City, MD 21043
410-313-8141
www.ellicottmillsbrewing.com

I've been to Ellicott Mills a number of times over the years. It's fairly close to the interstates as I run down to D.C. and back home to Philly, I love good lagers, and Ellicott City pleases my quirky little heart with its quirky little ways. But the last time I was here was the first time I've ever been here in the rain and seen the real reason it's called Ellicott *Mills*, and why this little town is even here. It's the drop.

It's kind of hard to believe now, with Ellicott City looking so quaint and restored and touristy, and full of bars and restaurants and shops, but this place used to be a hive of industry, all powered by the Patapsco River and the Tiber Creek. Three Quaker brothers named Ellicott, from my home area of Bucks County, Pennsylvania, came here in 1772 and built a water wheel–powered sawmill, gristmills, and iron forges, harnessing the steep drop of the Tiber Creek to do their work.

The buildings weren't all originally the strong, granite structures you see today. A big fire in Ellicott City in 1903 took a lot of the buildings. Then in 1904, there was a bricklayer's strike, but the masons kept working, cutting out the granite you still see cropping out of the hills in town.

If you walk down the hill from the brewpub, you'll see the first railroad station in America, the Ellicott City terminus of the Baltimore and Ohio's 13-mile Old Main Line from Baltimore. That's also the site of the famous race between the Tom Thumb steam engine and a horse-drawn car—the horse won.

Beers brewed: Year-round: Kölsch, Boomerang, Märzen, Dunkel. Seasonals: OZ Wit, Ilchester Pale Ale, X.O. Special Reserve, Belgian Tripel (RAF Bronze, 2003), Scotch Ale. Ellicott Mills does a calendar of bock beers through the year: Jack Frost (RAF Silver, 2002), Big Red, Maibock, Firecracker, Bock of the Bat, and Doppelbock (RAF Bronze, 2002; Gold, 2003). Expect more ales as Darryl Nutter settles in.

The Pick: This one's easy. It's the beer I go to almost by reflex every time I come here: the Dunkel. It's smooth, lager-polished stuff, lightly malty and scarcely sweet, with just a hint of roastiness and a dry malt finish. Fill up the big glass and say, "Ahhhh!"

This is a town with some history, you understand. So is the brewpub: the building, the brewhouse, the brewer, and the beers. The building dates from the 1880s, originally built as a warehouse, then used as the headquarters of the Talbot Lumberyard. Partner Tim Kendzierski told me that Talbot's was "the edge" back in the late 1800s. "It was all boondocks past here," he said. "This was the place you bought the wood to build your house before heading out there." Talbot's had a hand-cranked elevator installed that still works, one of two left in America.

The brewhouse, a 20-hectoliter Czech-built ZVU system, is right there in the front bar, all copper vessels. But the serious old iron is over in the next building, where there are big 1950s-era German plate-frame filters and a cold lagering cellar with twelve horizontal tanks out of a scrapped German brewery. The original brewer, Martin Virga, brought all this stuff over from Germany. It's all lager heritage, a lager pedigree, that shows in the classic lagers brewed here at Ellicott Mills.

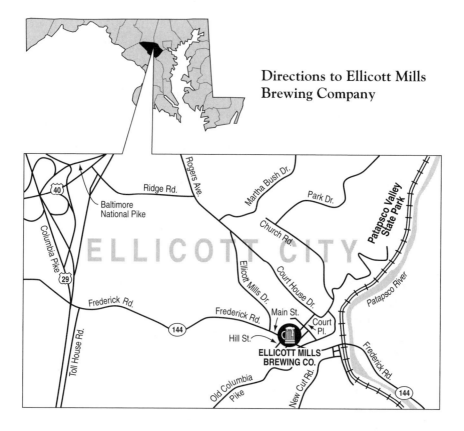

Directions to Ellicott Mills Brewing Company

The brewer has a history, too, but it's not with lagers. Darryl Nutter is an ale man from way back, a Wild Goose man, though he was an Eastern Shore man first, born and raised in Nanticoke. "I was a kitchen manager in Cambridge," he recalled, "and I met Jim Lutz when he came around selling Wild Goose. Well, then the restaurant closed and I needed a job. I was practically on the street. I went over to the brewery and asked Jim for a job."

Darryl started at Wild Goose in 1993, learning brewing partly from a Siebel course, "but mostly on-job training," he said. "We knew what we were doing wrong, but we were still making good beer: six tight-knit guys on a proven system . . . although, you know, those Pugsley systems were all built for a left-handed, 6-foot, 5-inch Englishman." Darryl laughed and I did too, picturing long, tall Alan Pugsley next to Darryl, a short fireplug of a man.

Darryl moved up to Frederick Brewing when they bought the Wild Goose brand. He started at Ellicott Mills in September 2003. "Going from Frederick to here," Darryl said with a laugh, "going from British ales to German lagers, from that huge place to this little system, was one thing. But open fermenters for lagers?" He shook his head, then struck a pose, declaratory finger in the air: "Adapt and overcome!"

How's the ale man adapting to lagers? "I always loved ales best," he said, "but the Märzen and Dunkel changed my mind. The four German standards will stay, and we'll continue doing the seven bocks year-round. Then I'll have at least one ale on, a strong beer, and just whatever else I feel like!" He's adapting, but it sounds like he's overcoming too.

History's one thing; what about the future? "We have a solid reputation and a solid group of regulars," Tim told me. "The beers are local favorites, and the people running things are experienced restaurateurs; that makes a difference." It certainly does; they're people with a history. Sounds like a match made in lager heaven.

Opened: May 1997.

Owners: Tim Kendzierski, William Pastino, Richard Winter, John Stefano.

Brewers: Darryl Nutter, Pat Groll.

System: 20-hectoliter ZVU system, 1,100 barrels annual capacity.

Production: 800 barrels in 2003.

Hours: Sunday and Monday, 11:30 A.M. to midnight; Tuesday through Saturday, 11:30 A.M. to 1:30 A.M.

Tours: By appointment only.

Take-out beer: Growlers available; call ahead for kegs (what's on tap is available).

Food: You bet there are German specials, but you'll also find all the brewpub favorites here. Watch out for the french fries; my dad is antifat and antisalt, but he couldn't stop eating them. There are always some good specials available, too.

Extras: Live music; call for schedule. The Batskellar is a convivial place, a classic German beer-drinking cellar . . . twisted a bit into modern times.

Special considerations: Kids are welcome. Some vegetarian meals are available. Handicapped-accessible in the rear (see the bar manager); the front entrance to this historic building is not handicapped-accessible.

Parking: Large metered lot in back; metered street parking.

Lodging in the area: Wayside Inn, 4344 Columbia Road, Ellicott City, 410-461-4636; Residence Inn by Marriott Columbia, 4950 Beaver Run, 410-997-7200; Paternal Gift Farm B&B, 13555 Route 108, Highland, 301-854-3353. There are also campgrounds at Patapsco

Valley State Park, along Marriotsville Road; call 410-461-5005 for park information, 888-432-CAMP for reservations.

Area attractions: Just walking around Ellicott City is a good way to spend some time; the homes are attractive and the stores offer interesting shopping. Down the hill is the **B&O Railroad Station Museum** (Main Street and Maryland Avenue, 410-461-1944), the other end of America's first passenger rail line, which starts at the B&O Museum in Baltimore, and the halfway point of the famous 1830 race between a horse and the Tom Thumb steam engine. The horse won. Call for the schedule at one of Maryland's best large live music venues, the outdoor stage at **Merriweather Post Pavilion** (10475 Little Patuxent Parkway, Columbia, 410-715-5560). Try the non–chain store shopping at **Historic Savage Mill** (8600 Foundry Street, Savage), a nineteenth-century textile mill turned into a shopping gallery with all single-proprietor shops. If you've ever driven past the National Security Agency sign on the Baltimore Washington Parkway and wondered just what goes on there, you can find out—or at least, you can find out what *did* go on there. The **Cryptological Museum** (Fort Meade exit off the Parkway, follow the signs to the museum and nowhere else; no phone) is the agency's exposition of what it does so very well: cracking and creating codes and ciphers.

Other area beer sites: Starting in Ellicott City, you can walk to three good bars. Just keep in mind that it's all uphill coming back. The **Tiber River Tavern** (3733 Old Columbia Pike, 410-750-2002) is a cool place to drink, built in a classily rebuilt old stable with a beautiful backbar and exposed beams. Not a big beer selection, but very nice whiskeys, and good service, too. Tucked up Tiber Alley, the shortest street in town and one of the oldest, is **Side Streets** (8069 Tiber Alley, 410-461-5577). There's just a tiny beer selection, but the spirits are excellent, as is the wine selection, and you can feel the age of the place, dating back to 1750. The small bar is downstairs; there is serious dining going on upstairs. The **Phoenix Emporium,** down by the railroad station museum (8049 Main Street, 410-465-5665), is well named; all the junk on the walls is priced and ready to be reborn as conversation pieces. The beer selection is ninety-nine different bottles, and it's a weird mix of very high-end stuff, rare eastern European beers, and complete crap. Don't underestimate it. You can still get ribs at **Bare Bones** (9510 Baltimore National Pike, 410-461-0770), but you can't get the house beers anymore; first the brewery was moved to Cockeysville, then the place did away with it entirely. There are still good taps.

Leaving Ellicott City, you can get introduced to the **Hard Times Café** chili chain in Columbia (8865 Stanford Boulevard, 410-312-0700). You'll see more of these mentioned in this book, and whenever you do, you can be sure of great chili (really, it's award-winning stuff), great music (the cafés pride themselves on their jukebox selection of classic western swing tunes), and . . . well, usually it's pretty good beer. The kid in the washtub logo is from a family picture, by the way. There's a **DuClaw** pub down in the mighty Arundel Mills Mall (MD Route 100 and Baltimore-Washington Parkway, 410-799-1166) and a **Ram's Head Tavern** (301-604-3454) at Historic Savage Mill. We like! Finally, for a great German experience, pack your dirndl and lederhosen for a weekend at **Blob's Park** (8024 Blob's Park Road, Jessup, 410-799-0155), a real old-style German beer garden that's been going almost every weekend since 1913, with a little time off after a fire . . . and a few weekends during Prohibition. Live polka music, a 2,000-square-foot wooden dance floor, and taps and bottles of great European beers will make you say *Gemütlichkeit!*

See also the Baltimore beer site listings (pages 39–43).

Rocky Run Tap and Grill

6480 Dobbin Center Way, Columbia, MD 21045
410-730-6581
410-551-4400
www.rockyrun.com

"This was a spot where restaurants came to die," Matt Hahn told me as we sat sampling beers at Rocky Run. As he reeled off the eatery failures that had occupied the same space, I was impressed at Rocky Run's success, but at the same time, I wasn't really surprised that all the other places had failed. Rocky Run is tucked into the back curlicue of Dobbin Center, a shopping center that occupies both sides of Dobbin Road, and I had just spent ten minutes looking for it on the wrong side of the road!

Good thing people who are smarter than I am live in Columbia, because not only did Rocky Run survive where all those other places had gone under, but it thrived to the point of spinning off two more Rocky Runs supplied by the same brewery (of course they are—it's Maryland!). It's an odd concept, dreamed up by some Canadian partners and named for something one of them saw on a sign somewhere and decided to use for a restaurant sometime.

The concept seems to revolve around illustration. The whole place swims with it, from the comical molded taphandles (with names like Barwench Brew and Big Gut Pale Ale, what could you expect?) to the big cartoony illustrations about the dining room (I like the shark, myself) to the butcher paper and crayons provided at your table so you can join the fun. Rocky Run is about having fun and laughing. Some of it is broad enough for a child to get; some is more eccentric, like the Spanish lessons playing over the sound system in the men's room.

Beers brewed: Year-round: Barwench Brew, Maple Leaf Lemon Wheat, Big Gut Pale Ale, Mountie Red, Brew House Barrel Stout. Occasionally added: The Witty Brit, Dunkel, Pumpkin Ale.

The Pick: Barwench Brew golden ale was a big surprise to me: it reminded me strongly of a beer I used to drink, back when I first started drinking beer, that was a bit different from Rolling Rock and Miller High Life: Molson Export. "The Ex" was beefier in those days, with more body and hops than it has today, and that old flavor was what I found in the Barwench. What a welcome memory it was.

Step into the long bar and you'll see commercial illustration on display: breweriana. There's a nice collection of these old brewery advertisements and promotional items: posters, metal signs, trays, barlights, and neons for breweries that exist only in the fading memories of senior citizens: Standard, Iroquois, National Bohemian—hey, wait a minute, I remember National Bohemian! Anyway, the bar's selection of breweriana is matched by the offerings of hot sauces and mustards, a spicy cornucopia of condiments guaranteed to raise your temperature a few degrees.

The beer's there to cool you off. Matt brews five regular beers and one seasonal at a time on a 3-barrel HDP system (appropriately Canadian) that's somewhere between a full commercial system and a BOP system. (I was quite surprised to see an actual six-kettle BOP-style brewhouse there, but Matt just uses the kettles as hot water and sanitizer reservoirs.) Matt brews the house beers on the 3-barrel system, then runs them off to plastic barrel fermenters. After fermentation and maturation, the beers are kegged and sent to the bar and the other two restaurants.

It is only a 3-barrel system, and it is supplying three restaurants, so obviously the guest taps are carrying most of the volume load. But consumption has increased to the point where Matt can no longer allow the

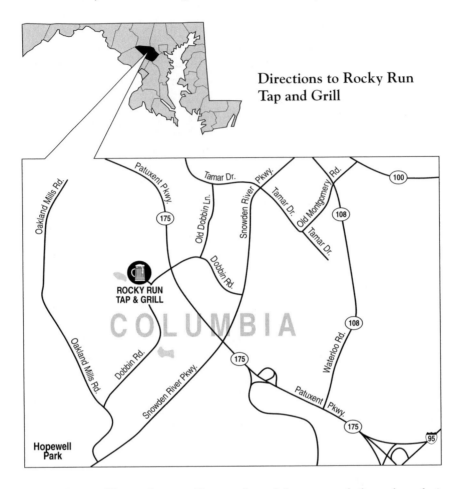

**Directions to Rocky Run
Tap and Grill**

bartenders to fill growlers, and his workweek has expanded to where he's brewing all the time.

He's up to it. Matt started homebrewing fifteen years ago, then started brewing on weekends at Ipswich Brewing in Massachusetts. "Brewing on their system kind of spoiled me for anything less," Matt admitted. From there he moved on to brewing at Oxford Class outside of Baltimore, then to Cleveland. "I answered an ad on the Pro Brewer online forum to get this job," he said, "and I've been here ever since."

The way Rocky Run is going, Matt's probably got a job as long as he wants it, although he may have to clean out those BOP kettles and press them into service. Still . . . they're Canadian, so that's only right.

Opened: August 1997.
Owners: Bert and Mike Donnelly.
Brewer: Matt Hahn.

System: 3-barrel HDP system, 600 barrels annual capacity.

Production: 400 barrels in 2003.

Hours: Monday through Thursday, 11 A.M. to 1 A.M.; Friday and Saturday, 11 A.M. to 2 A.M.; Sunday, 11 A.M. to midnight.

Tours: By appointment, or upon request, as available.

Take-out beer: None available.

Food: Rocky Run's menu doesn't miss much. Besides a full array of appetizers, soups, and salads, there are lots of sandwiches, fajitas, some real good ribs, pasta, and a variety of seafood dishes. If you like things on the spicy side, check out the assorted available hot sauces.

Extras: Lots of TVs dot the bar, and the NTN network trivia game is available.

Special considerations: Cigars not allowed. Kids welcome. Vegetarian meals available. Handicapped-accessible.

Parking: Large free lot.

Other area beer sites: Other Rocky Run locations are at 3105 St. Paul Street in Baltimore (410-235-2501) and 7900 Ritchie Highway in Glen Burnie (410-760-8850). Also see other local listings under Ellicott Mills Brewing Company (page 69).

Ram's Head Tavern/Fordham Brewing Company

33 West Street, Annapolis, MD 21401
410-268-4545
www.ramsheadtavern.com

Fordham Brewing was established in 1703 by Benjamin Fordham, an Englishman. The first time around, anyway. The one you'll find on West Street in Annapolis today was started in 1995 by William Muehlhauser. But the Ram's Head Tavern and Ram's Head On-Stage, which surround the brewery like the accretions of nacre on a pearl, started growing in 1984, when Muehlhauser bought the basement bar and named it the Ram's Head.

"It wasn't very big," brewer Jim Sobczak told me. "It was so small . . . well, you saw the bathrooms up the stairs, around the corner? They were outside then." Small beginnings, but Muehlhauser had big ideas, and they revolved around beer. He got in as many different beers as he could and started a beer club: drink one hundred different ones and you got your name on the wall. "They sold sandwiches by the pound, too," Jim said. "They weighed them right there, on the bar." Ah, the good old days.

The Ram's Head slowly grew, adding the upstairs bar, the kitchen, a big wraparound patio shaded by a massive and ancient wisteria vine, the covered stairs to the bathrooms, and then in 1995, the brewery. It's a beautiful German-make Beraplan brewhouse, a real showpiece, and that influence shows in the brew schedule, with Kölsch, helles, and a variety of seasonal bocks and altbiers showing up regularly.

Influence, yes, but not limitation; Jim regularly brews the unfiltered Tavern Ale and stout, as well as the German styles. The stout's kind of a funny deal. Jim brews only one stout, but there are usually two on the list: Oyster Stout and Genius Stout. What's up? The Oyster Stout, very popular in this bayside town, is carbonated; the Genius Stout is poured on a nitro tap, producing the "cascade" familiar to Guinness drinkers. (If those two names look similar, blame former Fordham brewer Allen Young, who had a thing for names like that; he also brewed a Young-Allen Lager when he was brewing up at the Kutztown Tavern, deep in Yuengling Lager territory.)

Jim's been brewing the beer for spin-off Ram's Heads in Rehoboth, Delaware, Savage and Crownsville in Maryland, and the newest one in Baltimore, or at least he was until the big new brewery opened in Dover. Well, no, that's not quite right, either, because Fordham was brewing over in Alexandria in the former Virginia Native brewery at the Birchmere nightclub. Muehlhauser purchased the Virginia Native brands and was leasing the brewery, but that arrangement ended in 2003. There's evidently still some confusion in the public's mind, because I still hear people refer to the Birchmere as a brewpub. With Fordham now having brewed in three different states, I know I was confused for a while.

It's all straightened out now, though. The big brewery in Dover brews the year-round regulars for all the bars, and Jim brews the regulars for Annapolis and the seasonals for all the venues. For now, anyway. The seasonals are well received. Hefeweizen is on all summer, there's a sticke-

Beers brewed: Year-round: C126 Light, Fordham Lager, Copperhead Ale, Genius Stout, Oyster Stout. Seasonals: Kölsch, Altbock, Weizenbock, Maibock, Wisteria Wheat, Edelpils, Festbier, Olde Ale.

The Pick: I'll take the biggest glass of Lager you've got, Jim. This beer's a well-tuned balancing act, with the malt in the front, solid and a bit juicy, supported by a bare framework of hops in the background. Each sip is deliciously German, and it's good in really big swallows, too.

altbock (an overstrength altbier that Jim runs through a hopback stuffed with whole-leaf Spalter hops), Weizenbock, witbier, Kölsch, Maibock, and the Edelpils, a hoppy Czech pilsner that Jim brews for his birthday.

The seasonal release parties keep getting bigger, and the seasonals sell like mad. With free glasses holding dollar drafts and a free buffet, it's no wonder! The big blowout is in September for the anniversary party. It starts at 7 A.M. with an "eggs and kegs" breakfast with dollar drafts of Old Ale, and moves on into the Festbier and popularly huge Calvinator Doublebock. It's a long, long day. "I was kind of hoping it wouldn't catch on," Jim wryly joked. Having been to a number of eggs and kegs, I know what he means.

If you're planning a visit to Fordham—and you should—don't forget to check the website or call to find out who's playing at On-Stage. In the ever-expanding saga of the Ram's Head, Muehlhauser bought the house next door when it went up for sale and found himself with a large room. What to do with it? "The music venue was a brilliant idea," said Jim. "It always sells out, it brings in people who have never had our beer before, and the only beer you can buy in there is our beer." The hall's table seating makes enjoying fine music and fine beer a treat. And after the show's over, you can get a free pint at the bar with your ticket stub. Deal!

"It's a different atmosphere up here on the hill," Jim noted. "There aren't as many tourists, and the mix of people is more diverse. It's a good mix, and it's stayed that way even though the place grew from 20 seats to 450." You do get more of the feeling of Annapolis as a small capital city up here, rather than the touristy sailing town with the Naval Academy across the water and bars every third door that you see down the hill. As Jim said, it's different. So's the Ram's Head, and with the upstairs and downstairs bars, dining rooms, shady patio, and exciting music venue, it's even different within itself. Just move around till you find the brewpub you like, and settle in.

Opened: September 1995.
Owner: William Muehlhauser.
Brewer: Jim Sobczak.
System: 15-hectoliter Beraplan system, 1,850 barrels annual capacity.
Production: 1,500 barrels in 2003.
Hours: Monday through Saturday, 11 A.M. to 2 A.M.; Sunday, 10 A.M. to 2 A.M.
Tours: Call for appointment (main number above, or 410-216-9730).
Take-out beer: Growlers available.

Food: Like crab cakes? How about a 10-ounce one? This menu has big cuts of meat and that honking big crab cake. Just feel like a sandwich? How about the Cobby Twister, a Cobb salad in a wrap? You can also get mussels, salads, or fresh-made soups.

Extras: Ram's Head On-Stage is an exceptional small music venue that books major acts. Check the website or call for schedule.

Special considerations: Kids welcome. Vegetarian meals available. Handicapped-accessible.

Parking: Some street parking (meters are heavily enforced); pay garage across the street.

Lodging in the area: Loews Hotel, 126 West Street, 410-263-7777; Super 8, 74 Old Mill Bottom Road North, 410-757-2222; William Page Inn, 8 Martin Street, 410-626-1506; Historic Inns of Annapolis, 58 State Circle, 410-263-2641. The *Private Pleasure* is a boat-and-breakfast that has two staterooms in a 1947 motor yacht. You get an evening sail, accommodations, and a continental breakfast. Not cheap, but what a story!

Area attractions: Before you do anything else, spend some time in Annapolis just walking, shopping (lots of navy souvenirs in town), and sitting by the City Dock at Spa Creek. This is one of the most beautiful and walkable state capitals and should be enjoyed. Find the **Kunta Kinte Plaque:** this is where Alex Haley's ancestor, whose story is told in *Roots,* first set foot in America and was auctioned as a slave, in 1767. Then walk up the hill and take the tour at the **Maryland State House** (State Circle, 410-974-3400), the oldest state capitol building in the country. Congress met here in 1784, while they were deciding where to settle; it's surprising that they ever left. You can catch a cruise of the bay with a number of services, but you can take a real sailing cruise on the schooner *Woodwind* (80 Compromise Street, 410-263-7837), and even help hoist the sails.

Now, have you noticed the energetic young men and women striding about town in crisp white uniforms? Follow one of them to the **United States Naval Academy** (Gate 1 is at King George Street and Randall Street, 410-263-6933), where you can tour the grounds with a guide, visit the USNA Museum in Preble Hall, and watch noon formation at Bancroft Hall. You'll feel like Tom Clancy when you're done.

Other area beer sites: If you're walking down Main Street toward the City Dock from St. Anne's Church, you'll hit the **Yin Yankee Café** (105 Main Street, 410-268-8703), an engaging sushi place with one

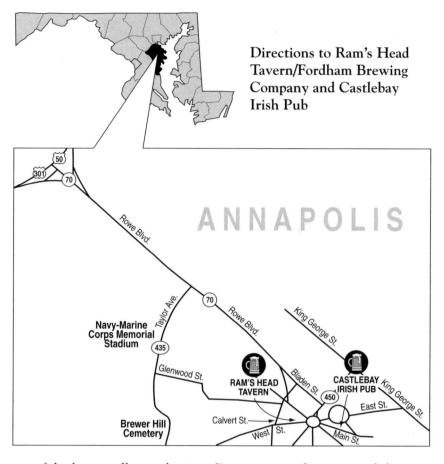

Directions to Ram's Head Tavern/Fordham Brewing Company and Castlebay Irish Pub

ANNAPOLIS

Navy-Marine Corps Memorial Stadium

RAM'S HEAD TAVERN

CASTLEBAY IRISH PUB

Brewer Hill Cemetery

of the best small tap selections I've ever seen: five taps, and the most common beer was Jever Pils—which went great with my salmon rolls. The decor is striking, the food is awesome, the music's happening. There are other sushi places in Annapolis, but this one has *beer*. The beer's not much down by the City Dock at **McGarvey's** (8 Market Space, 410-263-5700), though it does have the Aviator Red that Old Dominion brews just for this bar. But that's not the point! It's a beautifully classic Maryland bar with a massive backbar, the seafood's so fresh it's practically still flipping, and there's a roaring smell of Old Bay in the air. Tell your inner geek to shut up, and enjoy yourself. Right next door is **Middleton Tavern** (2 Market Space, 410-263-3323), where the beer selection is variable, but the old ambience is great, the crowd's lively, and the food's quite good. If you like the Fordham beers but you're looking for a different kind of bar to drink it in, run out to the **Ram's Head Roadhouse** in Crownsville (1773

Generals Highway, 410-849-8058), a Ram's Head that's been stripped down and rigged for speed, with an old-style roadhouse feel. Travel a bit farther south, to Edgewater, to visit **The Old Stein Inn** (1143 Central Avenue/Route 214, 410-798-6807), a German-American restaurant with a happily authentic *biergarten* and *bierstube*, where they have a great selection of German beers in glass and on tap.

Castlebay Irish Pub

193-A Main Street, Annapolis, MD 21401
410-626-0165
www.castlebayirishpub.com

"I never wanted this brewery."

This was the first thing Vince Quinlan told me when we started the interview. Trust an Irishman to have a good story!

All Vince wanted to do, it turns out, was to open a bar in Annapolis. The city wasn't wild about the idea, thinking that there were enough bars in the town already (in fairness, there are quite a few, but none of them seemed to be hurting from too much competition). So they made Vince a deal, a deal Vince thinks had them laughing up their sleeves as they proposed it. Open your bar, they said, but it has to be a brewpub.

"A brewpub in a place this size was just a slow way to go bankrupt," said Vince, "and that's what they figured. All right, I thought, I'll do it, but I'll put in a minimal system and make three drops of beer a week! My wife heard that, and said no, you'll do it right. So we got a 6-barrel brewhouse."

It wasn't quite that easy, of course. There was the ATF investigation to get through. "They checked everywhere I'd lived in the last twenty years, even did a felony search on me in Ireland through Interpol!" said Vince.

Then there was the problem of what to brew, and with Vince's experiences with brewpubs, it was

Beers brewed: Year-round: Three Nuns.

The Pick: Let's see . . . Sure, and it's Three Nuns. This is a beautiful nitrogenated Irish red ale, malty, sweet, with a slight edge of caramel and a delicious alefruit bouquet that is completely lacking from most beers of this style. Twist that with Three Nuns' dry finish and small but sure hop base, and you've got a beer worth traveling to taste.

a real problem. "I'd been to a bunch of brewpubs by then," he told me, "and 90 percent of what I'd tasted was horrible. I wanted one beer, done right." That beer was his Three Nuns: "None yesterday, none today, and none tomorrow," Vince laughingly explained. "It's an amber ale, with a nitro head, that's always consistent."

"Brewing," he explained, "is like cooking. The outcome depends on the skill of the brewer, the quality of the ingredients, and the desire, the passion of the makers. I didn't really plan the beer for men." That was a mystical moment, as Vince said that and paused for a puff on his cigarette, slowly rolling an eye at me. Who *did* he mean it for? The angels? "No!" he laughed. "It was for women! That's why I didn't overhop it like all those other beers I tasted at brewpubs."

Skill, passion, the taste of women—whatever the reason, Vince had the last laugh on the city. Not only is he still open, but he's doing well with his Three Nuns. "I make more money on that one tap than on any of the other eleven. It even outsells Guinness—in an Irish bar!" he said. "I'm brewing every ten days now, and it's all selling through that one tapline. I'm glad now that I started small. So many places went big, and half of them are out of business now."

Vince's business is good. His restaurant was rated one of the four best in Annapolis by the *Baltimore Sun*, serving up salmon Avoca, rack of lamb, and Irish standards like shepherd's pie, corned beef and cabbage, Irish stew, and bangers and mash. As he said, he has eleven taps of other beers running besides the Three Nuns, as well as a tap of Magner's Irish cider. There's also a very nice selection of Irish whiskeys behind the bar, and a fair number of single-malt Scotch whiskies.

"If you have your health and you're willing to work, life can be good," said Vince. He's certainly been working hard, and a little vindication never hurt anyone. He's getting ready for the next beer, though I happen to know he's been working on it for a couple years now. "I'm going to do an IPA," he said, "and it's going to be smashing. I'm going to call it Three Monks." He gave me one of his wry Irish grins. "Three Monks, to go with the Three Nuns. Have to keep religion alive somehow these days." If it turns out to be as good as Three Nuns, he'll have the last laugh indeed. Good luck to you, Vince!

Opened: October 1998; started brewing March 1999.
Owner: Vincent Quinlan.
Brewer: Bill Lawrence.
System: 6-barrel Pub Brewing system, 400 barrels annual capacity.
Production: 250 barrels in 2003.

Hours: Monday through Friday, 11 A.M. to midnight; Saturday and Sunday, 10 A.M. to midnight.

Tours: Upon request.

Take-out beer: Not available.

Food: Castlebay features a combination of the fresh seafood of Annapolis and the country food of Ireland, which has a seafood tradition of its own. So you'll find the traditional Irish pub dishes like shepherd's pie and corned beef and cabbage, crab cakes, "Galway Bay" style oysters on the half shell, and Irish oak-smoked salmon. Tuck in.

Extras: Vince Quinlan performed for years on the Boston to D.C. Irish music circuit, both on his own and as part of Celtic Folk, and now books Irish traditional groups at Castlebay. Call for schedule, and expect good things.

Special considerations: Kids welcome. Vegetarian meals available. Handicapped-accessible.

Parking: Metered street parking; small lots scattered around town. Best plan is to park once and walk; it's a pretty town for walking.

A word about . . .

Beer Traveling

First things first: "Beer traveling" is not about driving drunk from brewpub to brewpub. Beer outings are similar to the wine trips celebrated in glossy travel and food magazines; they're pleasant combinations of carefree travel and the semimystical enjoyment of a potion in its birthplace. To be sure, the vineyards of France may be more hypnotically beautiful than, say, the flatlands of the Eastern Shore, but you won't get any hot and steamy blue crabs with Old Bay seasoning in the Rhône Valley, either. Life's a series of trade-offs.

Beer traveling is sometimes the only way to taste limited-release brews or brewpub beers. Beer is usually fresher at bars and distributors near the source. And the beer you'll get at the brewery itself is sublimely fresh, beer like you'll never have it anywhere else—the supreme quaff. You'll also get a chance to see the brewing operations and maybe talk to the brewer.

One of the things a beer enthusiast has to deal with is the perception that beer drinkers are second-class citizens compared with wine and single-malt connoisseurs. Announcing plans for a vacation in the Napa Valley or a couple weeks on Scotland's Whisky Trail might arouse envious glances. A vacation built around brewery tours, on the other hand, might generate only mild confusion or pity. Microbreweries sell T-shirts and baseball caps, and beer geeks wear them. I've never seen a Beringer "Wine Rules!" T-shirt or a Chandon gimme cap. Beer-related souvenirs are plastic "beverage wrenches" and decorated pint glasses. Wine paraphernalia tends to be of a higher order: corkscrews, foil cutters, tasting glasses.

How do you as a beer enthusiast deal with this problem of perception? Simple: Revel in it. The first time my family went on a long camping trip with an experienced camper friend, we were concerned about wearing wrinkled clothes and sneakers all the time. Our guide had one reply to all our worries: "Hey, you're campers! Enjoy it!" It worked for us; it will work for you: "Hey, I'm traveling to breweries!" How bad can that be?

When you're planning a beer outing, you need to think about your approach. If you want to visit just one brewery, or perhaps tour the closely packed brewpubs in Washington and its suburbs, you can first

85

settle in at a nearby hotel. Get your Metro farecard or your walking shoes ready, and you're set to work your way through the brewery offerings. If you plan to visit several breweries in different towns, it is essential that you travel with a nondrinking driver. And when you're looking for that brewery in the mess of industrial buildings, here's a tip for you: Look for the grain silo. It's a dead giveaway.

You should know that the beer at brewpubs and microbreweries is often stronger than mainstream beer. Most brewers will tell you the alcohol content of their beers. Pay attention to it. Keep in mind that mainstream beers are usually between 4.5 and 5.0 percent ABV, and judge your limits accordingly. Of course, you might want to do your figuring before you start sampling.

About that sampling: You'll want to stay as clear-headed as possible, both during the day, so you can enjoy the beer, and the morning after, so you can enjoy life. The best thing to do is drink water. Every pro I know swears by it. If you drink a pint of water for every two pints of beer you drink (one to one's even better), you'll enjoy the beer more during the day. Drinking that much water slows down your beer consumption, which is a good thing. Drinking that much water also helps keep away the *katzenjammers*, as the Germans call the evil spirits that cause hangovers. There is, however, no substitute for the simple strategy of drinking moderate amounts of beer in the first place.

Beer traveling is about enjoying beer and discovering the places where it is at its best. You could make a simple whirlwind tour of breweries, but I'd suggest you do other things too. Beer is only part of life, after all. I've always enjoyed trips to breweries more when we mixed in other attractions.

D.C. Metro

No one travels between the Maryland and Virginia suburbs around
Washington. At least, that's what most people would tell you.
The Potomac is a barrier, they'll say, and people from Alexan-
dria wouldn't even think of going to Bethesda. Jerry Bailey at Old
Dominion told me that, and he lives in Bethesda and drives down to
Ashburn every day.

Maybe not absolute, then, but there is a very definite three-part
division in this area. Marylanders stick to Maryland, Virginians stick to
Virginia, and neither of them have much to do with people in the District—which suits the Washingtonians just fine; they don't feel the
need to leave the District very often.

There is a difference in the divisions because of the rivers. Where
the Potomac flows, the Virginia suburbs are separated from the District
and Maryland by bridges—and they are separated, not joined; the
bridges make the separation more real by bridging it, and by the nasty
traffic jams they can create. You can pass from Maryland to most places
in the northern edge of D.C. and back, and the only thing you'll notice
is a difference in the street signs. Down where the border is the Anacostia River, there is more separation.

So if these places are so divided, why did I lump the Maryland suburbs and "Northern Virginia" together as the D.C. Metro area? Practical
reasons, mainly—suburban Maryland doesn't have enough brewpubs to
make a large enough section by itself—but also because of the way the
federal government knits everything together here. The federal government is by far the largest civilian employer in the area, and along with
the military personnel, the intelligence agents, and law enforcement
officers, everyone has the same days off and gets paid at the same time.

That's been happening ever since the growth in the federal government begun by President Franklin Roosevelt. Before that, Washington

was a small, quiet town, and the suburbs were farm towns, if they existed at all. But the civilian mobilization to federal service begun in the Great Depression, and the massive growth in America's undersized military begun in 1940, expanded the government exponentially. As government responsibilities continued to grow, the population of federal employees grew right along in lockstep, until it reached today's immense level . . . and it is still increasing.

The city may house the huge bureaucracy (and it does, mostly, although more and more offices are being forced to the suburbs), but most of the bureaucrats live in the suburbs. That means there is quite a substantial middle class in this area. Federal wages generally are good wages, because the people who set them live here and are aware of the area's cost of living. Federal benefits are pretty good, including vacations and sick leave, because the federal employees' union is a strong one. Federal government is a growth industry, and when there is a recession, the government reacts by cutting taxes and increasing spending. The lobbyists and lawyers here, thousands of them, work on the same principle. These jobs are safe jobs, good jobs, and the D.C. Metro area thrives because of that.

I know. I lived here and worked as a librarian for the U.S. Army. Things were comfortable, except for the traffic and parking in the District, where I worked. There are good grocery stores and shops. The malls are tightly packed with high-end stores. The schools are very good. The worst problems anyone has to deal with in the whole area are sprawl and congestion, as well as the constantly rising cost of housing.

What does that mean for you? One thing it means is that you'll need a good map to get around out here, because the towns are as tightly packed as sardines in a can; one never really ends before the next one begins. You'll have to figure on traffic being heavy on the Beltway from 6 to 9:30 in the morning and from 3 to 7 in the afternoon, although the traffic never really becomes "light" anymore.

But you can also figure on a higher level of sophistication in these suburbs. The federal government puts a premium on education, and that shows. The *Washington Post* is one of the more intellectually playful newspapers in the country, and it is playing to its audience. The government attracts smart people, despite all the nonsense you've heard about government workers. You'll see that when you're here, along with a seemingly inevitable correspondingly high level of weary cynicism. Don't let that get you down; there are humans under that layer.

Enjoy what the suburbs have to offer. The restaurants and entertainment venues are excellent, the locals are sharp, and there is a surprising amount of beautiful scenery out here as well.

Franklin's Restaurant, Brewery, and General Store

5121 Baltimore Avenue, Hyattsville, MD 20781
301-927-2740
www.franklinsbrewery.com

This area has a lot of chain brewpubs: Capitol City, Gordon-Biersch, Hops, Iron Hill, John Harvard's, Rock Bottom, Sweetwater Tavern; if there were a Ram and a BJ's, it would be chain central. They're mostly good chains, as chains go, and between them they've brought a lot of awards home to the area. They're still recognizable as chains, though; the similarity of menus and signage gives it away.

If you want a completely different brewpub experience, one that I guarantee is unlike any other, get out to the good-beer desert they call Hyattsville. There, amongst the college-kid bars and gas stations, is a place called Franklin's Restaurant, Brewery, and General Store, where the flagship beer is very aptly called Anarchy Ale. Mike Franklin and his brewer, Charles Noll, have created something unique, and the wild business they've been doing since adding the brewpub to this deli, restaurant, and general store is a sign of how thirsty Hyattsville was for what they're selling. It was an instant success . . . after ten years.

Mike Franklin first opened his store back in 1992 in the one-hundred-year-old brick hardware store next door. "We converted the space to a general store with a forty-seat deli in the back," said Mike. "We've got cards, toys, wine, beer, food, hot sauces, all kinds of crapola, and we got a good lunch crowd."

They still have all kinds of crapola, and browsing it is an amusing way to while away the short time it takes for your meal to arrive. The bottled beer selection's worth a trip on its own, though how you'd be able to resist slipping into the bar for a draft while you did that is beyond me; the wine selection's almost as good, and there are lots of odd foods and candies and condiments. The range of toys goes from the silliest kiddie trash to some fun stuff for

Beers brewed: Year-round: Bombshell Blonde, Rubber Chicken Red, Twisted Turtle Pale Ale, Flagship ESB, Porter, and Anarchy Ale, an ever-changing hoppy ale. Seasonals: Private IPA, One Tonne Imperial IPA, Mr. Whipple's Tripple, and whatever else Charles decides to brew up; nothing is constant in the seasonals. Look for a nitro version of one of the regulars, and something on cask as well.

grown-ups—some of it real grown-up, so be prepared for the possibility of awkward questions if you go in with your kids—and there are some very nice foo-foo soaps and powders, too, if you're a beer writer looking for trinkets for your wife, for example.

Mike lives nearby and opened the place because there was nowhere to go in Hyattsville. "The deli went well enough to keep the doors open," he said. "But just enough. We decided that we either had to sell or expand, so we expanded." The brewpub and restaurant went into a new building, adjacent to the general store.

What's it like? Franklin's is very airy and open, with open stairways, high ceilings, and lots of glass. The colors are bright and lavishly applied, and there's plenty of brushed metal. The small bar area, up on the second floor, is a bit more restrained, but still much more open than you'll usually find. The servers move quickly, and bar service is good, though it does drag a bit on weekend evenings when people are standing five-deep around the bar!

How about that beer? Mike interviewed six brewers for the job before settling on Charles Noll. "They all brought their jugs," he said, "and Charles won. I'm not a beer geek, but I do have a sense of what good beer should taste like. He's also had experience on our kind of system, so that was a plus. I told him that as long as there are three or four anyone can drink, you can go crazy on the others." The three "anyone" regulars are Bombshell Blonde, Twisted Turtle PA (an English-hopped ale), and Flagship ESB.

And he does go a bit crazy on the others, something that shows in his signature beer, Anarchy Ale. One online reviewer said Charles "threw away his notebook after each batch"; that gave him a laugh. "No, we don't do that. I do save my notes!" he said. "For the most part, it's the most hoppy beer in the lineup, regardless of the color or the type of hops. The batch I've got on right now has got Cascade, Liberty, Tettnang, Fuggles, and Amarillo. I mess around with additions, too." I had a full pint of that batch of Anarchy; it was dark, medium-bodied, and bitter as a bad divorce. Anarchy is more than a name to Charles, by the way; he's an anarchist at heart, politically, and put anarchist history on the promotional T-shirt.

Some might say that nine to twelve beers on at any time is a little crazy, but not Charles. "We can do it, so I like to do it," he said. Not

The Pick: I'm picking two beers, given the huge and changing tap selection. First, the Anarchy Ale is a must, if only because of the gutsy concept: a big hoppy ale that's different every time Charles Noll brews it. Besides, if you order it, there's always a chance Charles might be there to tell you about America's forgotten anarchist history. I also want to note the rich, full Porter, full of malt and chocolate notes, chewy and satisfying. If people call Baltic porters imperial porters, this must be a foreign export porter.

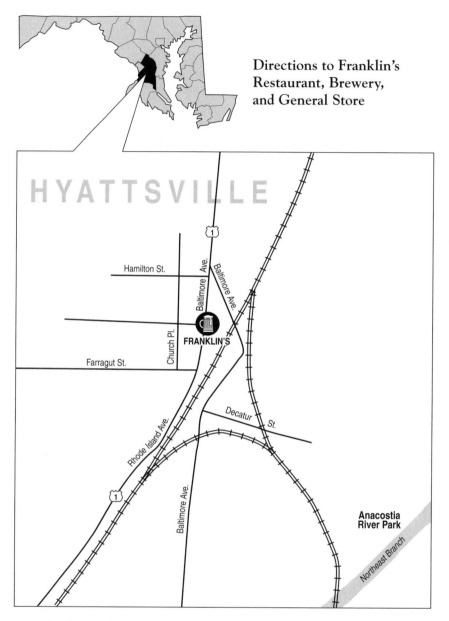

Directions to Franklin's
Restaurant, Brewery,
and General Store

enough choice for you? Try the nitro version of porter (who needs a stout with this big bad boy?) or the cask. Charles will throw even his big beers on cask into a small pin cask he got just for that purpose. I had his Mr. Whipple's Tripple that way last time in, the first time I'd ever seen a cask triple. "I was psyched to see when I came down to interview that there were already brewpubs like John Harvard's and the

Chop House doing cask ale," Charles told me. He's an enthusiast, and it's rubbing off on the customers.

Franklin's has a relatively small bar and a lot of tables, so plan accordingly. If you're traveling with kids, as I often do, it's a place they really enjoy: bright, busy, colorful, and right next to a whole bunch of weird and wonderful, inexpensive stuff for sale.

So pack up the minivan and head for Hyattsville. Where else can you get great beer, good food, a couple six-packs to go, a birthday present for your boss, and wind-up toys for the kids?

Opened: February 2002.

Owner: Mike Franklin.

Brewer: Charles Noll.

System: 10-barrel Bohemian system, 750 barrels annual capacity.

Production: 500 barrels in 2003.

Hours: 11 A.M. to midnight (or later), seven days a week.

Tours: On request.

Take-out beer: Growlers available; call ahead for kegs.

Food: The menu at Franklin's offers kind of twisted traditional foods: crab quesadilla, Thai pot stickers, skillet mussels. There's a lot of Asian influence, a good number of vegetarian items (like an eggplant parmesan sandwich), a variety of pizzas, and grilled sandwiches. It's a fun menu, and the beer matches up really well with it.

Extras: The general store is a great way to pass the time while you're waiting for your food; just be sure to leave your drinks in the dining room. You'll find all kinds of doo-dads, gadgets, toys for kids and adults, wine, beer, soaps, lotions, and *stuff*. A live music program is just getting started in the brewpubs; call for schedule.

Special considerations: Very kid-friendly. Good vegetarian items available. Handicapped-accessible.

Parking: There's a large city lot right beside the brewpub; there's a pay-by-the-slot system . . . but it's been broken for a long time.

Lodging in the area: Quality Inn, 7200 Baltimore Avenue, 301-864-5820; Best Western, 8601 Baltimore Avenue, 301-474-2800.

Area attractions: The **College Park Aviation Museum** (1985 Corporal Frank Scott Drive, 301-864-6029) is located at the world's oldest continually operating airfield, the College Park Airport, which has been open for business since 1909. Wilbur Wright taught two military men the intricacies of flight here that year. A very rare 1911 Wright Flyer B is in the museum, as is an animated Wilbur Wright. If you want more action, visit **Six Flags America** in Largo (13710

Central Avenue, 301-249-1500) and cut loose on the rides and in the water park.

Other area beer sites: There's not much out here that isn't college meat market, but that's why Mike Franklin opened his brewpub in the first place. There is a **Hard Times Café** (4738 Cherry Hill Road, College Park, 301-474-8880) for your chili fix and good beer to put out the fire. I used to see a girl out in Hyattsville, and I'd stop in at the **Colonel Brooks' Tavern** (901 Monroe Street NE, D.C., 202-529-4002) for a nightcap on the way back to my digs; the appeal of this tavern is in its barely acceptable tap selection (though it does come up with some surprises) coupled with a comforting patina of solid age. It's like comfortable old clothes. This is also a good place to mention the **DuClaw** pub out in Bowie (4000 Town Center Boulevard, 301-809-6943), which is flowing with their own good beer and good times.

Summit Station Restaurant and Brewery

227 East Diamond Avenue, Gaithersburg, MD 20877
301-519-9400
www.summit-station.com

"By God, I don't think you've missed a meal since I saw you last!" The familiar voice rang out behind me. I was sitting at the bar at Summit Station, swapping lies with a couple regulars while I waited for the waitress to find brewer Joe Kalish. I was starting to feel like a regular, in that relaxed, small-town welcome way, when Joe announced his presence with characteristic verve.

Joe's old school, a man with more than thirty years of brewing experience at places like Jones and Schlitz, but don't think he's a gray company man who didn't know how to handle the half-brewer, half-front-man world of the brewpub scene. He's a presence at the bar, simultaneously snarling and smiling, seemingly never slowing down, and staying on top of a quick-witted, profane, funny crowd of regulars with a quip, a grin, a barb, and a bark of laughter before running back to the brewhouse to check on the next batch of beer.

He took to the whole brewpub idea of beer, too. Don't expect to find Schlitz-like beer here in Gaithersburg; those big brewery years were evidently just holding Joe back. He was brewing a batch of his very popular Centennial Strong Ale when I stopped in. He brews this beer every one hundred batches. It's a powerfully hoppy beer that will finish out around 11 or 12 percent; the mash tun was stuffed to the brim with malts. His Irvington Pale Ale is a kicker as well, with plenty of hop flavor and sting, buoyed up by a steady pulse of malt.

His North Pole Porter shows off the malt side of the brewer's palette, a smooth, sweet, dark brown body tinged with garnet edges and brushed with hints of chocolate. The beer's named for a local aviator, Gus McLeod, who was so proud of his 1939 open-cockpit Boeing Stearman that he boasted he could fly it to the North Pole. His friends ribbed him unmercifully until he climbed in the airplane and did it in 2000, making him the first person to reach the North Pole in an open-cockpit aircraft. That's the kind of ornery behavior that would fit right in here.

Beers brewed: Year-round: Kölsch, Irvington PA, North Pole Porter, Nut Brown, Pale Ale, Diamond Stout. Seasonals: ESB, Alt, Amber Ale, Golden Ale, Scotch Ale, Belgian Ale, Cream Ale, Blueberry Wheat, Hefeweizen, Pumpkin Ale, Ebeneezer's Holiday Ale, Cupid's Cherry Wheat, Pooh's Honey Wheat, Granny's Apple Wheat, George's Independence Peach Wheat. Every one hundred batches, Joe brews his Centennial Strong Ale.

The Pick: Santa, stuff my stocking with growlers full of North Pole Porter! This is real porter, as it was meant to be made: a little sweet, easy to pour down the throat, smooth as glass, and refreshing to the point of ordering another.

Thirty years of big brewery experience did teach Joe plenty of good habits. The brewery is immaculate, everything's kept up to specs and hangs just so, growlers are clean and ready to fill, beers come out on time. I call around to every brewery in the Mid-Atlantic when I'm writing my regional news column for *Ale Street News*, and Joe is one of the few brewpub brewers who never hesitates. He always knows exactly what he's got on tap, what's coming on next, and what he'll have on in three months.

Summit Station used to be the Olde Town Tavern till Phil Bowers bought it in 1999 to go with his Frederick brewpub, Brewer's Alley. The Old Towne was a brewpub also, and Joe was the brewer, so not much has changed. Brewer's Alley brewer Tom Flores comes down occasionally, and the men exchange a few recipes, but mostly Summit Station just runs itself.

It runs fast, too. "My beer sales are up 8 percent for the year," Joe told me. "I'm keeping real busy brewing." The outdoor deck helps sales in the summer, as do events like the very nice occasional beer dinners. The

food's up to the beer's level; everything I've ever had at Summit Station was well made and pleasantly different from what you'd get elsewhere.

Gaithersburg, like any small town in the expanding surge of Washington's suburbs, is starting to sprawl and lose its definition a bit. There is a chain-based plaza at the edge of town; the I-270 expressway runs just west of the plaza, and that's where the traffic is, mostly. But the sidewalks outside Summit Station still have a fair amount of foot traffic, and the traffic light on the corner slows down friends and neighbors driving by. Joe waves to people he knows, they wave back, and small-town America survives another day longer at the local brewpub.

Opened: April Fool's Day 1993 (as Olde Town Tavern and Brewing Company); sold to Phil Bowers on April Fool's Day 1999 and renamed Summit Station.

Owner: Phil Bowers.

Brewer: Joe Kalish.

System: 7-barrel Pub Brewing system, 1,250 barrels annual capacity.

Production: 750 barrels in 2003.

Hours: 11:30 A.M. to 1 A.M., seven days a week.

Tours: Monday through Friday, 11 A.M. to 4 P.M., depending on brewer availability.

Take-out beer: Growlers available; call ahead for half kegs and sixtels.

Food: The food at Summit Station is top-notch, ranging from serious man-food pub grub, like burgers and chili, to the crisp, fresh, authentic Caesar salad with grilled chicken I enjoyed the last time I stopped in. Go hungry, and expect to be pleased.

Extras: Mug club and bimonthly beer dinners. Very nice selection of bourbons and single malts, and not the usual suspects. Live music; call for schedule.

Special considerations: Cigars allowed as of this writing, but Joe expects a smoking ban soon. Kids welcome. Vegetarian meals available. Handicapped-accessible.

Parking: Lot in the rear, plus large town lot behind brewpub lot.

Lodging in the area: Towneplace Suites, 212 Perry Parkway, 301-590-2300; Motel 6, 497 Quince Orchard Road, 301-977-3311; Best Western, 1251 West Montgomery Avenue, Rockville, 301-424-4940.

Other area beer sites: Mrs. O'Leary's (555 Quince Orchard Road, 301-947-1993) is Gaithersburg's Irish pub, with the Guinness, and the music, and the food; drop by and say hello. There's a **Hard Times Café** in Rockville (1117 Nelson Street, 301-294-9720), just waiting to serve you chili and beer. Once you're fueled up, take a trip over to Olney, where you'll find **Le Mannequin Pis** (18064 Georgia Avenue, 301-570-4800), a pleasingly Belgian place, with the food and the beer and the relaxed attitude that mark that country as so wonderfully civilized. If you haven't had the Belgian *cuisine de biere*, this is a must. Then relax at the **Olney Ale House** (2000 Olney-Sandy Spring Road, 301-774-6708), where I was shocked to find Randall the Enamel Animal (see page 25) when I last passed through. I was a pretty regular Ale House denizen for the year I lived in Maryland, but things had only gotten better: Randallized 60 Minute IPA, right there in Olney! Visit this neighborhood pub, which understands service, good food, and good beer.

Rock Bottom Brewery, Bethesda

7900 Norfolk Avenue, Bethesda, MD 20814
301-652-1311
www.rockbottom.com

GOOD FRIENDS. GREAT FOOD. GREAT BEER.

I just do not understand why people run down Rock Bottom brewpubs as being soulless places that serve competent but boring beer. When I think of Rock Bottom, I think of Van Hafig, who used to be at the Arlington Rock Bottom and is now wowing the beer-savvy people of Portland, Oregon, and Geoff Lively, who I hope is chained to a long-term contract at the Bethesda Rock Bottom. In my experience, Rock Bottom brewpubs are places with bright, technically skilled brewers who like to stretch things as much as they can.

That description fits Geoff Lively to a tee. He's been passionate about beer for most of his life and got an early start on homebrewing in college. Right out of college, he got a job with Mile High Brewing in Denver. "I got a thorough grounding in microbrewing and microbiology there," Geoff told me. "I was working on their quality assurance and quality control."

He grinned his usual broad, fierce grin at that point. "But now I've got my hands on everything!" he said. "I've got control of it, all of it." He sure does, even though it takes some walking to do that. The brewery had to adjust to the space here in this semibasement room, which originally housed offices for the Nuclear Regulatory Commission. So the brewhouse is over in one corner, the fermenters are over in another corner, and the serving tanks and cask storage are all the way down at the other end of the building and up on the second floor.

Not that you'll notice, because you'll either be eating white cheddar mashed potatoes and ribs at a table or quaffing Geoff's great beer over at the bar. You'd better be getting the cask, too, because this guy is good at it. Geoff's a big fan of cask beer and has carefully adjusted his cold room to ensure proper aging. "I put the casks at the end of the cold room

Beers brewed: Year-round: Lumpy Dog Light Lager, Rock Creek Pale Ale, Raccoon Red Ale, Brown Bear Brown, Stillwater Stout. Seasonals: Right on Rye (GABF Gold, 2003), American Dream Ale, Liquid Sun Hefeweizen, Extra Scary Beer, Oktoberfest, Velvet IPA, Anniversary Ale, Atom Smasher, Trouble (GABF Bronze, 2002; RAF Gold, 2003), Highland Courage (RAF Silver, 2003).

away from the fan," he explained, deadpan. "And they're right by the door, where I'm in and out. So they stay a little bit warmer, which is what you want." High-tech.

It's worth it, though; cask ale this good is worth a lot. It's worth a quick primer, too. Sit down and learn a little about this vibrant bit of beer heritage. Cask ale, real ale, or cask-conditioned ale is how all beers used to be consumed: right from the barrel, unfiltered and "alive." The brewer fills the cask with uncarbonated, unfiltered beer straight from the tanks, with the live yeast still in it. He may dose it with a small amount of sugar or fresh wort, and then he hammers home the bung to seal the cask. The beer will come to peak condition in the cask as it waits at the tavern . . . or in Geoff's not-quite-as-cold-at-this-end cold room.

The Pick: Well, my first pick would be anything on cask. Get a sample, say yes, and have a pint. If you can even entertain the thought of switching after that, think about the Raccoon Red, which Geoff describes as "a big whack of malt, a big whack of hops, just throw 'em in there together." It sure is, and the two whacks get along just fine. Final suggestion: If one of Geoff's special beers is available, a Belgian or a strong ale, save room for one. You'll be glad you did.

By the time the beer is tapped, it is lightly carbonated by a secondary fermentation done by the still-live yeast, fueled by the addition of sugar or wort. The cask has been sitting quietly, giving the yeast a chance to drop to the bottom of the cask; when the beer is ready, it is said to have "dropped bright." An ideal tapping will produce a clear glass of cellar-temperature (about 55 degrees F), lightly carbonated ale that has a fresh, estery aroma and flavor that cannot be matched by any other method of dispense.

Honestly, I've never had anything but an ideal tapping at the Bethesda Rock Bottom. Geoff usually has two casks on, and they're his babies, receiving a lot of his time and attention. The Pale Ale was on the first time I visited. It was during the sniper season in 2002, when the D.C. Metro area was gripped by the fear of two gunmen. I zigzagged down the sidewalk, ducked into Rock Bottom, had a seat at the bar, and saw cask ale.

Well, okay! I asked for a sample of the Pale Ale, something I encourage you to do whenever presented with cask ale—ask for a sample, because even when it's done properly, one man's perfect condition may be another woman's glass of weak alegar. My sample was delicious, so delicious that I immediately put the notebook and pen back in my pocket, forgot all about my usual running of the taps, and ordered a pint off the cask. Even a beer writer has to just relax and enjoy a beer sometimes!

Geoff likes to mess around with the casks. Take the Stillwater Stout, for instance. "I'll make a mocha or coffee stout by adding choco-

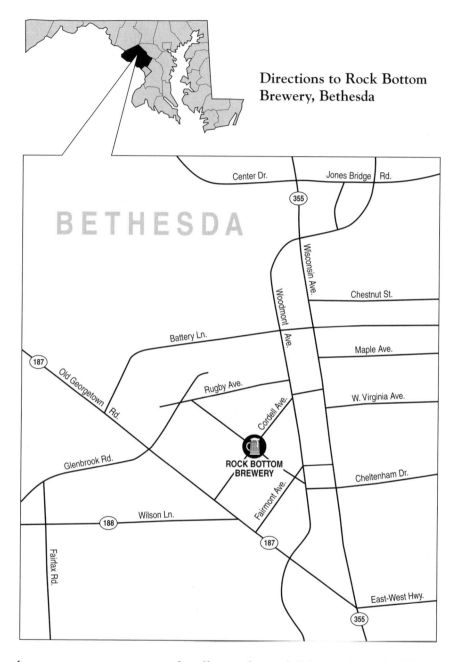

Directions to Rock Bottom Brewery, Bethesda

late syrup or coarse-ground coffee to the cask," he explained. "That's what happens with cask ales: You can play with spices, hops, little things like that, and you don't have to do a whole batch that way, just one cask." He'll play with the names, too, since the cask is technically a different beer. Take a look at all the cask markers behind the bar; they've all been used at one time or another and will be again.

There's a very serious side to this brewer as well—he's real serious about good beer. I got to see him do his Beer College training with a couple new servers. He teaches them about how all the different malts taste (chewing on samples), how the hops smell, what the yeast does, and how it all comes together. He's every bit as intense when he's doing lab work for Beer College, and the medals prove it.

Rock Bottom. Real beer. Believe it.

Opened: December 1996.

Owner: Rock Bottom Restaurants.

Brewer: Geoff Lively, brewer.

System: 7-barrel JV NorthWest system, 2,000 barrels annual capacity.

Production: 1,495 barrels in 2003.

Hours: Sunday through Thursday, 11 A.M. to 1 A.M.; Friday and Saturday, 11 A.M. to 2 A.M.

Tours: By appointment only.

Take-out beer: Growlers available. Geoff also occasionally bottles specialty beers; inquire about availability.

Food: Rock Bottom's menu really has a bit of everything, and everything I've ever had has been delicious. I particularly like the homestyle favorites, like chicken-fried chicken, alder-smoked salmon, jambalaya, and barbecue ribs. Don't miss the white cheddar potatoes, a Rock Bottom signature side.

Extras: The Rock Bottom Mug Club is free and has some cool benefits, including "club cash," good for discounts on your check. Ask at the bar. Patio seating available, weather permitting. Private rooms available for parties. Pool tables upstairs. Live music Saturday night. Call about tapping nights—first pint is free for the first hour!

Special considerations: Kids welcome. Vegetarian meals available. Handicapped-accessible.

Parking: Large town lot just south of the brewery.

Lodging in the area: Marriott Bethesda, 5151 Pooks Hill Road, 800-228-9290; Four Points Sheraton, 8400 Wisconsin Avenue, 301-654-1000; Holiday Inn Silver Spring, 8777 Georgia Avenue, 301-589-0800.

Area attractions: Bethesda is known for **Restaurant Row,** clustered all around Rock Bottom, where a number of odd and excellent eateries abound. Head up the Potomac, and you'll come to the **Clara Barton National Historic Site** in Glen Echo (5801 Oxford Road, 301-492-6245). This was the last home of the "angel of the battlefield," the strong woman who founded the American Red Cross. Farther upriver is the roar of the **Great Falls of the Potomac** in the **Chesapeake and Ohio Canal National Park** (301-299-3613). This is a hiking path, but the towpath is well graded; great for casual biking.

Other area beer sites: If you're looking for beers or bars in Bethesda other than Rock Bottom, you've got two choices: **Ri Ra Irish Pub and Restaurant** (4931 Elm Street, 301-657-1122), a chain, but not a bad one, or the by-now-familiar standby, the **Hard Times Café** (4920 Del Ray Avenue, 301-951-3300). But if you're willing to go a bit farther afield, there are a couple goodies out there. When I was an army librarian at the Walter Reed Army Institute of Research, I sometimes soothed the pains of the workday at the **Quarry House Tavern** (8401 Georgia Avenue, Silver Spring, 301-587-9406), a genuine old tavern, downstairs and dark, but always with something good on tap. I'm happy to report that not much has changed. **The Royal Mile** is the only Scottish pub in the area (2407 Price Avenue, Wheaton, 301-946-4511) and has a beautiful array of single malts to go with its solid tap selection.

Sweetwater Tavern, Merrifield

3066 Gatehouse Plaza, Merrifield, VA 22042
703-645-8100
www.greatamericanrestaurants.com, Sweetwater Tavern icon

Question: If you have a successful group of restaurants, and things are going well, why add brewpubs?

Answer: Quality and control.

That's why the Great American Restaurant group decided to open the three Sweetwater Taverns, and why Nick Funnell is masterminding their brewing operations. It was the first question I asked him. "So we could have what we wanted," he continued. "They started with a bakery for the restaurants. It made sense to build your own bakery for the same reasons: fresh bread, when you wanted it, the way you wanted it. The customers were happier, the managers were happier. I was happy, too; the bread at Sweetwater Tavern is excellent. And that led to . . . Why not beer? Why not a central brewery? There were legal problems, and there was the appeal of perceived freshness, the "right there" of it."

The Sweetwater Taverns are definitely different from the other restaurants in the Great American group, even aside from the obvious addition of the brewery. There's a southwestern, cowboys and Indians theme that's almost, but not quite, over the top. The beautiful thing about it is how un-self-conscious they are about it. The decor is like a five-year-old boy's dream—riding gear, pictures of Indians riding hard across the plains, buffalo, and cowboys—but the waiters don't wear cowboy boots and cap guns or call you "pardner." Thank goodness. There's themed and then there's stupid.

"It's one of those things every three-year-old boy wants to be, like a firefighter or a locomotive engineer," Nick said about the cowboy theme. He smiled. "And every twenty-one-year-old boy wants to be a brewer." Nick obviously did, and he got his wish. After brewing in the United Kingdom and at Dock Street in Philadelphia, Nick and his wife moved to Washington so Nick could brew at the short-lived Dock Street, D.C. (in the space now occupied by John Harvard's, D.C.). When Dock Street padlocked the doors and called it quits, Nick was lucky enough to land on his feet at Sweetwater.

Beers brewed: Year-round: Great American Restaurants Light, Great American Restaurants Pale Ale (GABF Bronze, 2002). Seasonals: Silverado Cream Ale, High Desert Imperial Stout (GABF Silver, 2001; RAF Gold, 2001, 2003; RAF Best-of-Show Bronze 2001, 2003), Pale Face Summer Wheat, Buffalo Tooth's Old Ale, Rusty Roadrunner Lager, Barking Frog Ale, Outlaw Ale, Jackalope Canyon Ale, Great American Restaurants Octoberfest, Crazy Jackass Ale, Painted Lady Lager, Hair of the Dog Lager, Yippee Ei O Springbock, Bishop's Pass Ale, St. Nick's Weizenbock, Sidewinder Holiday Bock, Chipotle Porter, Road Kill Barleywine Style Ale (RAF Silver, 2002), Boot Hill Brown Ale, Straight Shooter Stout, Iron Horse Lager, Red Tape Ale, Helles Out of Dodge, Wit's End Ale, Black Stallion Oatmeal Stout, Flying Armadillo Porter (GABF Silver, 1998), Ghost Town Pumpkin Ale, Happy Trails Christmas Ale, Kokopelli India Pale Ale, Last Chance Lager, Yellow Devil Pilzner.

"I've been here for eight years," Nick said, "having fun brewing great beer." As for the fun, well, he's always seemed cheerful enough when I've talked to him for my *Ale Street News* column. He has certainly been brewing great beers, a mess of them, and winning medals for them fairly regularly. His cask ale program is very popular with the local beer geeks, and why not, when he casks beers like his High Desert Imperial Stout, a beer that is more staunchly true to this austere style than any other American-brewed Imperial.

Nick's inspiration for that beer was the closest thing we have to an original these days, Courage Imperial Stout. He takes English inspiration—understandably—on other beers as well, often using English hops unfamiliar to most American drinkers until they meet them at Sweetwater Tavern. But I'd also venture to say that Nick tosses aside his English roots when he brews lagers, because his lagers, when he brews them, are better than any of the ones I've ever had from Great Britain.

The Pick: I've got three pubs to do three picks, so I'm taking full advantage of it. I've loved Nick's High Desert Imperial Stout from the first time I encountered its black, somewhat smoky, dryly rich character, tinged with the haughtily classic tarry notes you'd find in the archetype of the style, Courage Imperial. This isn't the sweet muck or black hopjuice you'll find sold as imperial stout in some brewpubs.

If you've seen the breweries at Sweetwater Tavern, you may have a hint to why the beers come out so well. Brewers as a class are tough on cleanliness; Nick's absolutely unyielding on it. "I am a stickler for that," he said. "But making quality beer comes first, always."

He doesn't stop at making it, either. If you want a growler at Sweetwater Tavern, don't expect your bartender to fill yours up; he won't. You'll get a Sweetwater Tavern growler, prefilled (if you already have one, you can exchange it for the filled one and just pay for the fill). Nick insists that growlers be cleaned at the brewery and filled on a special counterpressure filler that ensures proper pressurization and headspace in the growler, using CO_2 instead of air. A bit more work—a lot more, actually—but the beer comes first.

Just as he did at Dock Street, ten years ago, Nick brews a lot of beer styles, usually twenty-five in a year. What will you find when you stop in? "We always have five beers on," he told me. "The Great American Restaurant Light and Pale Ale are always on, and then I'll have something dark, something hoppy, something malty, something big, something like that. I try to keep a slightly different tap offering at each pub." Nick's also got a project going, barrel-aging some Imperial Stout. There's something I'd like to be in on when it happens.

One of the last questions I asked Nick was if the owners at Great American were happy with how the brewpubs had turned out. After all, it's been quite a while since the third one opened, and I'd expected more to come. "Yes, they're happy!" he said quickly. "They would build more if they could find good spots for them. But they're actually hard to find. The Potomac is also a big divide: Maryland is Maryland, Virginia is Virginia, and never the twain shall meet."

So maybe there are more Sweetwater Taverns in the area's future, and maybe not. I do know that if more pop up, the beer will always come first. You have Nick's word on it.

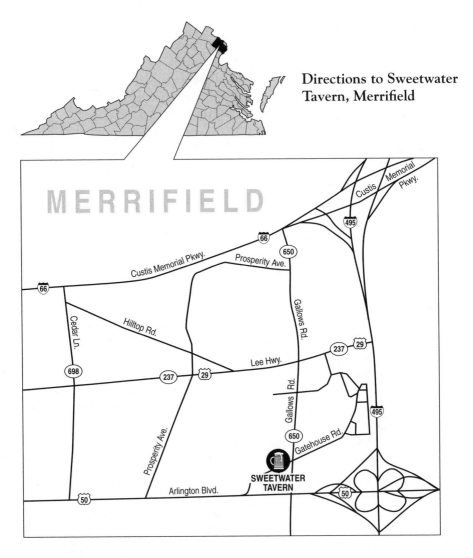

Directions to Sweetwater Tavern, Merrifield

Opened: August 1998.

Owner: Great American Restaurants, Inc.

Brewer: Nick Funnell, brewmaster.

System: 15-barrel JV NorthWest system, 1,700 barrels annual capacity.

Production: 984 barrels in 2003.

Hours: Sunday through Thursday, 11 A.M. to midnight; Friday and Saturday, 11 A.M. to 1 A.M.

Tours: On request, or by appointment, or just look through the glass.

Take-out beer: Growlers available; see narrative for details.

Food: First, I really, *really* like the way the first page of the menu is all about the beer—that says great things about priorities. I've eaten at the Sweetwater Tavern in Merrifield a number of times with my family and have yet to be disappointed. Food ranges from snacks to full-bore feasting: cheeseburgers, hickory-smoked salmon, roast chicken salad with dates and fresh corn, jambalaya, the inevitable and delicious crab cake, brilliantly cut and wood-grilled steaks and chops, and a flourless chocolate waffle with vanilla ice cream. Drool. Melt.

Special considerations: Kids welcome. A few vegetarian options are available. Handicapped-accessible.

Parking: Off-street lot.

Rock Bottom Brewery, Arlington

4238 Wilson Boulevard, Ballston Common,
Arlington, VA 22203
703-516-7688
www.rockbottom.com

Dollar draft night is insane. This Rock Bottom in the Ballston Commons Mall is pretty busy anyway, and it does some of the highest volumes of beer in the whole nationwide Rock Bottom operation. But on Wednesday nights, drafts go to a buck, and the bartenders' world explodes. "They pretty much just leave the Kölsch tap open and put empty glasses under it," Gary Winn told me. I didn't make it to a dollar draft night, and it wasn't an oversight; I'm too old for that kind of thing!

Rock Bottom needed it, though. Things were tough here when they were starting out. Arlington is a very competitive bar market, and there are probably fifteen bars within a five-minute walk of Rock Bottom. The brewpub needed something to get people's attention. It needed to get on the map. Dollar draft night did it. Even at brewpub margins, with most of the business going to a relatively inexpensive beer like the Kölsch, the bar just barely breaks even on the dollar drafts, but it's worth it for the food business, as well as the business the promotion has brought on the other nights from people who discovered they liked this brewpub.

This is a very busy, big brewpub. It has table seating for 420, plus the bar area. Thanks to the success of the big promotion, it's respectably filled most nights. The passing foot traffic from its location in the street-level floor of the Ballston Commons Mall is a continual stream, and a fair amount of it flows into Rock Bottom. And people drink a lot of beer once they get there.

That's why the corporate offices in Louisville, Colorado, sent Gary Winn to brew there. Gary's a hot young brewer, working in his third brewpub with the company. He was originally at the Rock Bottom in Westminster, California, then moved to the Walnut Brewery in Boulder, Colorado. Now he's come east to push the brews through here.

That's really all Gary's planning on doing. "I'm going to dial the Ballston Brown down a notch," he said. "It's a little big for a brown. I'm going to leave the others pretty much the way they are." I agreed with him on the Brown; good beer, but verging on porter territory. But the brewer who just left for another Rock Bottom location, Marty Brooks, definitely knew what he was doing, as the GABF Bronze medal he won in 2002 for his rye beer showed.

That's something that irks me a bit about beer geeks. Rock Bottom often gets very little credit from the geekerie, who usually say something like "It's a chain," or "The beers are all bland brewpub beers," or "They're full of yuppies." All I can figure is that these guys haven't actually spent much time in a Rock Bottom.

Take a closer look. I told you about Marty's medal. The guy who brewed here before he did, Van Havig, was a genius who cranked out some amazing beers, including a bottle-conditioned Saison that was simply phenomenal, and I wish I still had a couple bottles. Van went out to the Portland Rock Bottom, and he won a GABF Gold medal in 2002 for his Merry Prankster strong ale. And Geoff Lively, the brewer up at the Rock Bottom in Bethesda, has so many medals he's going to have to add an extra wall to the brewhouse to hold them all.

I've been to Rock Bottoms all across the country. If the idea of a chain is to provide the customer with a consistent product with no changes, well, Rock Bottom is a half failure, because while the menu's pretty much the same everywhere, the beer's different in every one. Do they all have a pale ale, a brown ale, a Kölsch, or some other light golden beer? Look

Beers brewed: Year-round: Mother Martha's Kölsch, Potomac Pale Ale, Ballston Brown Ale, Radio Towers Red (RAF Bronze, Best-of-Show Gold, 2001), Spout Run Porter. There is usually at least one cask ale on, sometimes two, and they are often tweaked: dry-hopping, a sack of coffee in the porter. Seasonals: Snake Chaser Stout, Catcher in the Rye (GABF Bronze, 2002), Hefeweizen, Double IPA, Oktoberfest, 1420 Shropshire Ale (RAF Gold, 2001), Oatmeal Stout, Imperial Stout, Bourbon-aged Imperial Stout, Dry Irish Stout, Pilsner, Wit, Scotch Ale, ESB, and probably more.

The Pick: I might give the geeks a hard time on occasion, but I like a nice hoppy pale ale as much as the next guy, and the Potomac Pale Ale has the hop thing going on, from the first bright, piney whiff to the light and frisky flavor, on through to fine hop finish. A very American pale ale that's light-bodied, well-hopped, and a lot of fun.

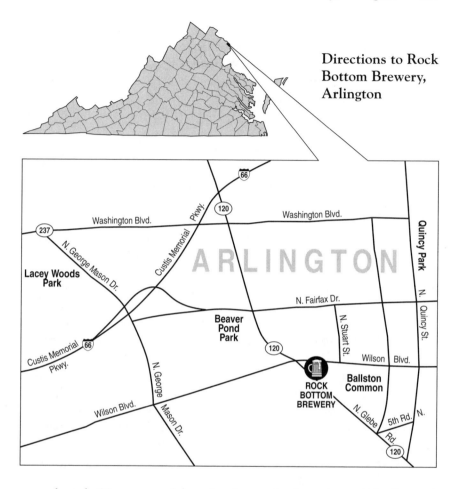

around: so do 80 percent of the other brewpubs. I was just at The Brewer's Art, one of the most different brewpubs around, and they had . . . a pale ale and a brown ale. They're standard beers; people *like* them.

Meanwhile, Rock Bottoms usually provide beers beyond the standards as well. Gary had just come to Ballston a few weeks before, and he already had two cask beers on: a cask version of the Radio Towers Red and a coffee porter that was electrifyingly java-soaked. "We usually have one cask coming on and one going," Gary said, "and sometimes they're both on at once."

Any place that has two cask beers on is okay by me, especially since they're good casks, in good condition. And if all the yuppies bug you, don't go on Wednesday. But do stop in for a visit. With the string these brewers have been running, you wouldn't want to miss the next medal winner.

Opened: August 1999.

Owner: Rock Bottom Restaurant Group.

Brewers: Gary Winn, brewer; Mark Braunwarth, assistant.

System: 8-barrel JV NorthWest system, 1,800 barrels annual capacity.

Production: 1,688 barrels in 2003.

Hours: Sunday through Thursday, 11 A.M. to 1 A.M.; Friday and Saturday, 11 A.M. to 2 A.M.

Tours: On request.

Take-out beer: Growlers available, call ahead for kegs. This Rock Bottom also has done occasional specialty bottlings; ask for availability.

Food: Rock Bottom's menu really has a bit of everything, and everything I've ever had has been delicious. I particularly like the home-style favorites, like chicken-fried chicken, alder-smoked salmon, jambalaya, and barbecue ribs. Don't miss the white cheddar potatoes, a Rock Bottom signature side.

Extras: The Rock Bottom Mug Club is free and has some cool benefits, including "club cash," good for discounts on your check. Ask at the bar. Patio seating available, weather permitting. Private rooms available for parties. Live music Wednesday, Thursday, and Saturday nights; call for schedule. And Wednesday is Dollar Pint Night, which is crazy. Be warned!

Special considerations: Kids welcome. Vegetarian meals available. Handicapped-accessible.

Parking: Metered street parking, but it's tough. There's a large parking garage in the same building with the Common.

Lodging in the area: Best Western Pentagon, 2480 South Glebe Road, 703-979-4400; Econo Lodge, 6800 Lee Highway, 703-979-4100; The Virginian, 1500 Arlington Boulevard, 703-522-9600; Arlington/Washington Travelodge Cherryblossom, 3030 Columbia Pike, 703-521-5570.

Area attractions: The *Ballston Common* is a big urban mall, of a type more often found in Europe. The *Newseum* (1101 Wilson Boulevard, 888-639-7386) is just what it sounds like: a museum of news. It's a museum of how news is—and has been—gathered, investigated, verified, and reported, with examples from the most gripping stories of history. A very exciting new museum.

Arlington National Cemetery (703-697-2131) is why most tourists come to Arlington. Here you'll find the Tomb of the Unknowns and the mast of the USS *Maine*, the eternal flame at the tomb of President Kennedy, the Tomb of the Unknown Dead of the Civil War and the Confederate Memorial, and the famous Marine Corps War Memorial. Our heroes lie quietly, at peace in a setting lovingly tended by a grateful nation. Even Robert E. Lee's home, subject to the cruel ignominy of having Union dead buried all around it so that he would never know a night's rest there, has now been restored, another symbol of a nation finally at peace with itself. It's easy to take the Metro to the cemetery; there's a stop right at the entrance. You can walk or take the quiet Tourmobiles (202-554-5100), which visit the major sites.

The **Netherlands Carrillon,** a gift from a grateful Holland for liberation during World War II, is outside the northern end of the cemetery. There are concerts through the summer; call 703-289-2530 for schedule.

Other area beer sites: You can easily walk to **CarPool** (4000 Fairfax Drive, 703-532-7665)—ha-ha, a little joke. CarPool is a huge place, cavernous, it's *automobilliards!* Lots of pool tables, plenty of bar space, some decent taps but nothing amazing, a big outdoor dining area, and pretty good barbecue; be sure to get the mac and cheese side—it's a vegetable, you know. If you're looking for hot entertainment, pony up the cover charge for **Iota** (2832 Wilson Boulevard, 703-522-8340), one of the top clubs for live music in the entire Metro area; the club's owners have a nose for up-and-coming bands. Beer's not bad, either. It's music of a different tenor at **Ireland's Four Courts** (2051 Wilson Boulevard, 703-525-3600), another of the profusion of Irish bars in the Metro area. Why so many? One friend thinks it might be because so many people come to this area from faraway homes, and Irish bars have common elements everywhere that make them feel at home. He may be right. Speaking of common elements: It's the home operation of **Hard Times Café** (3028 Wilson Boulevard, 703-528-2233), the one that started it all more than twenty years ago. Care for a bowl of red?

I've saved the best beer selections for last. It takes a careful eye to find **Galaxy Hut** (2711 Wilson Boulevard, 703-525-8646), an unassuming place that blends in with the rest of the block, no sign in sight. Step inside and it's small but mighty, "cool in a manly, artsy way," my notes say. There's art all over the place, but it's deliberately crude art; I like it. The Hut has a fairly small tap selection, but it's largely good stuff, and different from where the other area beer bars are usually headed. The other area beer bar is **Dr. Dremo's Taphouse** (2001 Clarendon Boulevard, 703-528-4660), which used to be the infamous Bardo Rodeo brewpub. While Dr. Dremo's is but a pale shadow of the inspired madness that was Bardo, that pale shadow is plenty nutty. The former car dealership is immense, with a ton of pool tables, and even more taps, great taps, a few surprises. One of my biggest surprises was the great view of the District from the main bar's east-facing windows.

Capitol City Brewing Company, Shirlington Village

2700 South Quincy Street, Arlington, VA 22206
703-578-3888
www.capcitybrew.com

This is where you're going to get the full Capitol City story, because this is where the big tanks that make Capitol City's best-selling Kölsch hang out, in the big brewery of the chain. It may not look like much, but this brewery does 2,500 barrels a year and is capable of cranking out 4,000 if things run flat out. Those are big numbers for a brewpub.

They have to be. Capitol City needs a big brewery just to keep up, now that it has to cover the demand at the original Downtown site (at Eleventh and H Streets, NW). The small system at the original site has been taken out. It just wasn't efficient to use a system that size to brew anymore. The system was sold to Thoroughbreds, a new brewpub in Leesburg, Virginia (see page 126). Shirlington also makes extra Kölsch for the Capitol City brewery at the Inner Harbor in Baltimore when summer drinking season hits, because that brewery just can't keep up with the demand. It keeps the guys at Shirlington stepping, brewing for two other places.

One of those steppers was John Bryce, fresh from closing his Blacksburg Brewing. You missed a good one there, but he has plans to head back to

Beers brewed: Year-round: Capitol Kölsch (GABF Silver, 2001; Gold, 2002), Pale Rider IPA, Amber Waves Ale (GABF Bronze, 2002), Prohibition Porter. Seasonals: Cherry Blonde Ale, Belgian-style Red Ale, Hefe-Weizen, Oktoberfest, Roggen Rye Ale, Pumpkinator Ale, Wee Heavy Ale (GABF Silver, 2001; Bronze, 2002; RAF Gold and Best-of-Show Silver, 2002; Gold, 2003), Slobberknocker Barleywine.

Blacksburg to open a brewpub after sharpening his skills and making some money at Capitol City; watch the book update page on my website for news. John led me down a tight set of spiral stairs from the brewhouse down to the lower level, where the bottom of the tanks and the cold room lurk.

He pointed out the three big 30-barrel tanks that are dedicated to brewing the Kölsch, Capitol City's best-seller and twice GABF medal winner. They soar right up through the floor to be visible from the sidewalk as you stroll along under the trees along the "village" street.

The Pick: We have to talk about the Kölsch; it dominates the conversation, speaking softly and carrying a big zwickel. Capitol City's version is clean, grainy, mellow, with just a hint of the alefruit that the cold conditioning is there to tame, and very refreshing and enjoyable. Nicely done, and not to be written off as "light beer." This is serious beer, just not an overwhelming style.

The Shirlington site was overbreweried from the outset, planned to pick up the slack in the system when the other sites came under pressure from seasonal swings. They pull a particularly heavy load in the summer, brewing for their own booming consumption, the Downtown site, and supplementing the Baltimore Inner Harbor site as well, where the summer demand on the Kölsch is fierce, as anyone who's ever been to Inner Harbor on a fine summer day can imagine. It's always full press time here at Shirlington. Capitol City used to brew lagers, but they just don't have the time anymore.

That's rough, considering that Capitol City was founded on German styles by the original brewer, Martin Virga, back in 1992 at the New York Avenue site. Virga formulated a German lineup, and the Kölsch quickly became the big hit. People just walk up to the bar and say "Kölsch." Kölsch traditionally "isn't kölsch" unless it's brewed within sight of the Cathedral Dome in Köln, Germany (one brewer I knew thumbtacked a postcard of the dome to the wall in his brewery), but Capitol City does what they can to make it as real as possible: the malts are German, the hops are German, the yeast is an authentic kölsch strain. The only thing non-German in it is the water.

The first brewpub was a big hit, which convinced the owners that they should open more. They opened the Capitol Hill pub in 1996 with the launch of MTV's Rock the Vote. The Capitol Hill site is located in a grand old post office building (the same building that houses the National Postal Museum) across the street from the beautifully refurbished Union Station. It took a while to catch on with the Capitol Hill crowd, but once people got used to the idea, things really went gangbusters there.

There was a Bethesda Capitol City that never did catch on and was subsequently closed. This Shirlington Village site was opened in March 1997, and the prime Inner Harbor location opened later that year, in

July. Things looked good, but it turns out now that Capitol City was growing right into the craft-brewing slump, the flat period in the late 1990s when a combination of financially shaky breweries, subpar beer from subpar breweries, and an apparent desire by journalists to write an end to craft brewing combined to undermine people's confidence in brewpubs and small breweries; not a good time to be expanding.

However, Capitol City hung in there through the shakeout, hung in through the severe blow to the local hospitality business brought on by the tragic event at the Pentagon in September 2001, and hung on through the bad economic times that followed. Now they are benefiting from their persistence as craft brewing's second wind lifts the industry. They are growing, and still looking to grow; whether that means on-site growth or a return to growth through opening new brewpubs remains to be seen.

What is Capitol City? What's the concept, what defines it? The chain is finding its way to a higher level of dining, while still delivering a good brewpub experience in a casual setting. The beer is happily wandering all over the map, anything within reason: rye beers, Scottish ales, barleywines, double IPAs.

The barleywine—Old Slobberknocker—and Double IPA are "stealth beers." Not in terms of sneaking up on you with unexpected strength, though they can do that, but in the way they're released. The brewers will just put them on tap, no fanfare, and sometimes just in one five-gallon keg at a time. It's fun for the regulars, and it makes these big beers last longer; like lagers, they take up tank time the brewers can ill afford.

But don't fret about Capitol City's capacities. Even with the burgeoning demand for Kölsch, this crew finds room in the schedule for regular seasonals and for experiments like the Saison and Roggen Rye I tried on this visit. Like the other small brewpub chains in the Mid-Atlantic, and some of the larger national ones as well, Capitol City lets its brewers express their own personalities. It's most appropriate in this constitutional home of the freedom of expression.

Opened: Company started August 1992; this location opened March 1997.
Owner: David von Storch.
Brewers: Sam Fernandez, John Bryce.
System: 15-barrel JV NorthWest system, 4,200 barrels annual capacity.
Production: 2,500 barrels in 2003.
Hours: 11 P.M. to 2 A.M., seven days a week.
Tours: Upon request, brewer's schedule permitting, Monday through Friday, from opening until 5 P.M.

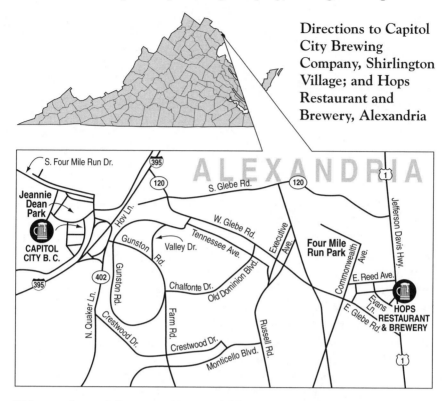

Directions to Capitol City Brewing Company, Shirlington Village; and Hops Restaurant and Brewery, Alexandria

Take-out beer: 2-liter growlers available; call ahead for sixtel or half kegs (Oktoberfest, Imperial IPA, and Wee Heavy not available in kegs).

Food: Tim Campion is the head of food at Capitol City, and he's got some good stuff ready for you. Let him take you on a menu ride, from the obligatory crab dip to the delicious pork rolls at the start, through a seafood-slanted main menu that also has a delicious vegan Pacific Rim pasta dish, all the way home to the Jameson Goes Bananas, a banana bread pudding version of bananas foster that will have you groaning. Don't forget your complimentary pretzels and mustard!

Extras: The bar is well TV'd. Pool tables and video games available. The brewery has an Oktoberfest celebration every fall and invites about twenty-five breweries from the region to bring an Oktoberfest beer (and others). It's a great fest, giving you a good chance to try a bunch of festbiers and meet some brewers; they like this one. Look for this year's date on the Capitol City website.

Special considerations: Kids welcome. Vegetarian meals available. Handicapped-accessible.

Parking: Street parking and free lots, but be prepared to look for a while; this is a popular area.

Founders'

607 King Street, Alexandria, VA 22314
703-684-5397
www.foundersbrew.com

Like its Old Town, Alexandria, setting, Founders' has a history. Founders' is where the Virginia Beverage Company was, with the same brewing equipment that Jason Oliver, now brewing at the D.C. Gordon-Biersch, used to man. Steve Winterling, the man who opened and owns Founders', was a chef at Capitol City's brewpubs for four years. His brewer and partner, Bill Madden, was the head brewer at Capitol City till he joined Steve in 2004. From this mix of D.C. Metro brewing influences has sprung a new brewpub that is neither a reincarnated Virginia Beverage Company nor a redone Capitol City, but something new, which is just what Winterling had planned.

"I wanted a place of my own," Steve said, echoing the thoughts of chefs worldwide—a place where things could be done the way he wanted, done the way he thought was right, a place that would succeed or fail on his merits. "I had just started looking when I saw an ad in the *Post:* 'Brewpub for sale.' Well, I knew brewpubs, and I had a brewer partner at the time, so I went and took a look. The owner, Milton McGuire, wanted to sell the place pretty quickly, I guess. I made him an offer, and he got back to me with an acceptance in two hours!"

The whole sale was finalized in less than two months, and in February 2002, Steve had himself a brewpub. He and his partner had split amicably, recognizing that their styles just would not work together. So after redoing the kitchen and bar and redecorating the dining room, he opened Founders' in March. The brewpub was named for the founders of Alexandria, who are further memorialized in the names of the individual beers. "But for us, 'Founders'' refers to the founders of the restaurant," said Steve, "my dad, Grayson Winterling, and myself."

Paperwork snafus would hold up brewing till July, by which time Steve had found Brian Hollinger, an experienced brewer. Hollinger agreed to brew for six months while training Steve. So back when I interviewed him for the book, Steve was managing,

Beers brewed: Year-round: Dick's Kölsch, Fitzgerald's Alt, Smoot's Stout, Harper's American Pale Ale. Seasonals: Wise's Weiss, Burke's Bock, Octoberfest.

brewing, and cooking. He was holding up well, but he was at the point where he was ready to hire a brewer. Then Bill Madden came to mind, and instead of hiring a chef, he got a new partner.

"I can brew," Steve said. "I'm a chef; I can follow a recipe. But I can't formulate new beers." It's plain from his experience that he recognized the need, which puts him ahead of a number of other brewpub owners. Madden will add the missing element of brewing creativity to the mix at Founders'.

So what has Steve wrought at Founders'? It is a stylish spot with a coppery pressed-metal ceiling and dark green color scheme, a well-decorated dining room that features not only the house beers, but also the surprisingly good products of Virginia's vineyards. A prominent map of Virginia pinpoints the thirteen vineyards represented in Founders' cellar.

The Pick: Go light, my friends: Dick's Kölsch is my advice to you. Stephen may have had more than a little help on this one, given the overall award-winning excellence of Capitol City's Kölsch, but I'd be the last to begrudge him any assistance, and now that Madden's on board, it can only get better. This is a delicious light golden ale; a bit of jammy fruit smeared across the lightly malty middle and a slightly bitter finish make for a great pint-after-pint beer.

It's no surprise that the trained chef lavished his attention on the menu. "I wanted to open a restaurant and brewing company," Steve told me. "And I was targeting a particular group when I decided to make the place nonsmoking. I didn't want a bar with a bunch of young kids drinking and smoking; I wanted an older crowd, a more stable crowd . . . well, a more moneyed crowd that would be willing to spend some money on good food."

They've got their chance. Founders' menu, according to Steve, features "a little bit of everything": a variety of steaks; veal chops; salmon; a delicious-sounding seared ahi appetizer with spinach, onion, and avocado; and some innovative sandwiches for the lunch crowd. It's a menu that comfortably straddles the pub and the restaurant, keeping almost everyone happy.

It made one person happy recently. "One of the members of BURP [a D.C.-area homebrew club] was in with his wife," Steve told me. "They had dinner and enjoyed themselves greatly. As they were leaving, the fellow's wife came over to me and said, 'You know, this food is really too good for a brewpub.' Well, I went home. The day just wasn't going to get any better than that!"

Stephen Winterling has started a new history for this building in Old Town. It's his own place . . . but you're more than welcome to visit.

Opened: March 2002; brewing started July 2002 (not connected to the brewpub that was in the building, Virginia Beverage Company).

Owners: Stephen Winterling, Bill Madden.

Brewer: Bill Madden.

System: 7-barrel DME, 750 barrels annual capacity.

Production: 250 barrels in 2003.

Hours: Monday through Thursday, 11:30 A.M. to 11 P.M.; Friday and Saturday, 11:30 A.M. to 1 A.M.; Sunday, 10 A.M. to 8 P.M.

Tours: On request or by appointment.

Take-out beer: Not available.

Food: Stephen has a menu to play with, and he uses it; there's a bit of everything here, from wings to a seared ahi tuna with spinach, onion, and avocado. There are steaks, veal chops, salmon, and a variety of high-end sandwiches. See if it really is "too good for a brewpub."

Extras: A Sunday brunch buffet is served from 10 A.M. to 2 P.M.

Special considerations: No smoking. Kids welcome. Vegetarian meals available. Handicapped-accessible.

Parking: Street parking is fierce competition at times; you could take the Blue/Yellow line on the Metro to King Street Station, though it's a bit of a walk.

Lodging in the area: The Holiday Inn Select (480 King Street, 800-368-5047) is expensive, but very nice and right in the heart of Old Town. Travelers Motel, 5916 Richmond Highway, 703-329-1310; Best Western Old Colony, 1101 North Washington Street, 703-739-2222.

Area attractions: *Mount Vernon* (at the southern terminus of the George Washington Memorial Parkway, 703-780-2000) is the major attraction here. You can tour the house, the outbuildings (don't miss the distillery, recently restored with the help of several Kentucky bourbon distillers I know who looked really funny in colonial garb), and the vineyard, where George and Martha Washington are buried together. Take a moment to walk to the hill's edge overlooking the Potomac River and try to imagine it two hundred years ago.

The Masons built their own *George Washington Masonic National Memorial* (101 Callahan Drive, 703-683-2007), a six-tiered tower modeled after the ancient Pharos of Alexandria. Washington was a "worshipful master" of the Masons, and this shrine honors his life. There are a number of Washingtonian artifacts: the family Bible, a clock stopped at the time of his death by the attending doctor, and others. The observation deck on the top floor will give you a grand view of the District's high points.

See old-time town life and politics—okay, see where they would have happened—at *Gadsby's Tavern Museum* (134 North Royal Street, 703-838-4242). Gadsby's, as was true with taverns in any

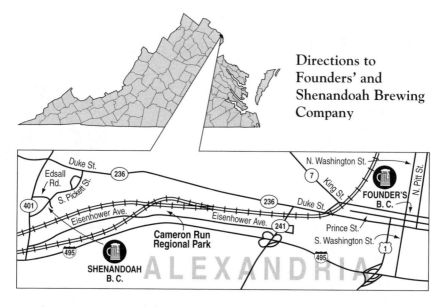

Directions to Founders' and Shenandoah Brewing Company

American town of the time, was the social center of Alexandria. It makes you wonder why there ever was such a seditious organization as the Anti-Saloon League.

If you've seen all that, take some time and walk around on the brick sidewalks of Old Town, looking at the small old homes, some of which are now selling for more than $600,000, and shopping in the boutiques.

Other area beer sites: *Union Street Public House* (121 Union Street, 703-548-1785) has a definite air of class to it, from the neatly attired bartenders working the big central bar to the old brick walls and tin ceiling, and everything trimmed with lots of wood. The tap selection, listed over the front door, is not bad at all. *Pat Troy's Ireland's Own* (111 North Pitt Street, 703-549-4535) has the usual draft suspects for an Irish place, live Irish music every night, and good food, recommended to me by someone who'd read *Pennsylvania Breweries* that I happened to meet at *Bilbo Baggins* (208 Queen Street, 703-683-0300). The taps at Bilbo Baggins were simply awesome, with a very low crap-to-tap ratio, and the bottle selection was almost as impressive. There's a big wine list, small but select groups of bourbon and malts, and excellent food; definitely recommended. *Murphy's Grand Irish Pub* (713 King Street, 703-548-1717) has a bigger tap selection than most of the area's Irish joints and is very busy and cheerful. A bit farther out, you'll find another *Hard Times Café* (1201 King Street, 703-683-5340), always a haven for thirsty, hungry travelers.

Hops Restaurant and Brewery, Alexandria

3625 Jefferson Davis Highway, Alexandria, VA 22305
703-837-9107
www.hopsonline.com

See the entry for Hops Restaurant and Brewery, Richmond (pages 226–229), for full details about the Hops chain.

Dave Richter, director of brewing operations for the Hops chain of brewpubs, told me about the brewer here at Alexandria, Derek Hudson. "Derek's been with us for quite a while," he said. "He trained here in Tampa, then opened a few stores for us. He made the move up to management, and he was running one of the Richmond operations. But he quickly learned that there are a lot more headaches in running a place than in brewing beer. He went back to brewing, and he's doing a great job; the Alexandria location is one of our busiest stores."

They had Hops' new Love Handles Low Carb seasonal on, cashing in on the Atkins craze. "My marketing people talked us into a low-carb beer," Dave said, "and it was a real challenge. We had to change the grain bill completely and add enzymes. But it's selling quite well for us. Put it up against Michelob Ultra, and it's a better beer." Well, maybe. But like Michelob Ultra, what Love Handles mostly reminded me of was mineral water. I'm just not a low-carb kind of guy. That's why I got nachos to go with it.

Beers brewed: Year-round: Clearwater Light, Lightning Bold Gold, Thoroughbred Red, Alligator Ale. Seasonals: Flying Squirrel Nut Brown Ale, Love Handles Low Carb, Powder Horn Pilsner, Big 'Skeeter Pale Ale, Lumberjack Oatmeal Stout, Beat the Heat Wheat, Single Hop Ale, Royal English Amber, Star Spangled Ale, Hoptoberfest.

The Pick: Alligator Ale is the biggest flavor in the four core beers, but my Pick is the Lightning Bold Gold. This beer caught me off guard. It's Coors Light light in color, but it has more body than the Silver Bullet and real malt flavor behind it. It's not going to wean you off something like Old Dominion's Millennium, but it is a stealth mainstreamer, one that could easily be a stepping-stone to better beer for your light beer–swilling buddies.

Opened: May 1999.
Owner: Avado Brands.
Brewer: Derek Hudson.
System: 7-barrel Pub Brewing system, 800 barrels annual capacity.

Production: 362 barrels in 2003.
Hours: 11 A.M. to 11 P.M., seven days a week.
Tours: On request or by appointment.
Take-out beer: Growlers available.
Food: I enjoyed everything I had at Hops. The food was freshly made, and the open kitchen here was a great idea. Pretty entertaining, too—those guys were having fun. The fresh, hot potato chips are great. Resist the temptation to top them; they're better plain. Steaks are good, pork chops are better, and all are done on the grill. Sandwiches are well made, desserts are ample. Dig in.
Special considerations: Kids welcome. Some vegetarian meals available. Handicapped-accessible.
Parking: Large plaza lot.

Shenandoah Brewing Company

652 South Pickett Street, Alexandria, VA 22304
703-823-9508
www.shenandoahbrewing.com

The first time I ever saw a brew-on-premise (BOP) shop in Canada, I couldn't stop laughing. The neat line of small copper brewkettles, each with their little oblong lid and piping, made me think of Andy Griffith in *No Time for Sergeants*, when he was on bathroom detail and proudly made all the toilet lids stand to attention for his commanding officer. The fellow who owned the place couldn't figure out why I was laughing, and it wasn't really something I cared to explain.

I'm over that now, and Shenandoah didn't fill me with anything but interest in how things worked. Owner Anning Smith took me through the whole thing. "The first thing we do when they come in the door is help them figure out what they want to do," he said. That can be fun, as it often involves trying some of the numerous beers on tap at the pub area to get an idea of what things are like.

"Once they select one," he continued, "we'll pull a recipe sheet and get the ingredients out. We do try to encourage people to set up an appointment; that way we can have the base wort boiling ahead of time." One advantage Shenandoah has over other BOPs is the big 5-barrel brewing system they use to make their commercial brews; while other places add malt extract syrup to water, Anning or brewer Shannon McKissick can brew up fresh batches of base wort.

What's next? The specialty malts and hops the "brewers" selected in the recipe process are put in the small kettle with the hot wort and allowed to steep for a certain amount of time. Then the grains are removed, the wort is brought to a boil, and the final hops additions are made, along with any additions of malt extract. The extract is added as needed to bring the wort up to the required concentration of sugars. As Anning says, this is really "scaled-down microbrewing, not scaled-up homebrewing."

Beers brewed: Year-round: White Water Wheat Beer, Big Meadow Pale Ale, Skyland Red Ale, Old Rag Mountain Ale, Stony Man Stout, Black and Tan (premixed Big Meadow and Stony Man). Shenandoah Root Beer is also year-round. Seasonals: Old Dusseldorf Ale, Dark Mexican Lager, Bavarian Weizen, Strawberry Chicha, Raspberry Cider, Ginger Beer, and a wild host of others. With this small system and plentiful small-keg taps, Anning and Shannon have the freedom (and the will!) to make any kind of beer they want, and generally, they do.

When the hot wort's ready, they pipe the 11-gallon batch from the kettle through the heat exchanger and into a special plastic barrel with a screw-in plastic closure. There's a bit of fun at this point. The wort needs to be aerated to give the yeast enough oxygen to get it going at the proper speed. This is achieved by the simple method of rolling the heavy barrel across the brewery floor, usually back and forth between two people. There's usually a lot of grinning and laughter during this process. After the aeration is done, it's time to add the standard ale or lager yeast. There are specialty brew days during each month, when Shenandoah runs up special batches of yeasts and ingredients—hefeweizen yeast and specialty malted wheat, for instance.

That part takes about three and a half hours, at the end of which Anning or his wife, Laura, or Shannon or her husband, Mike, rolls the barrel back to the fermentation room and cleans up the mess. The three and a half hours explained why they opened the pub area. "The people are sitting here for three hours anyway," Anning said. "We just wanted to offer them some kind of simple food." It's good, but it isn't fancy: The entire menu consists of four different chilis, beer queso dip with tortilla chips, meatball sandwiches, PB&Js, and chips and peanuts—Virginia's own Route 11 chips (www.rt11.com) and Virginia Diner peanuts (www.vadiner.com), if you please.

People sit at indoor picnic tables during the boil, mostly family members who come along for the beermaking. "A big part of the business," Anning explained, "is middle-aged guys, so we keep it family-friendly. They can even make a batch of root beer if they want to." There are toys, TVs, and books and magazines for the family members who might not be quite as interested in the brewing as the brewer. It's nice to see families in the brewery, talking among themselves, and the kids playing together.

The Pick: Easy call: Stony Man Stout is great. It's not overly dry, with a ton of flavor edging over into a character you want to call rich, but it's still quite drinkable in large quantities. A pounding stout, and that's a good thing to find in America, where all too often brewers err on the side of full, high-alcohol stouts.

Everyone goes home after pitching the yeast—and maybe a few cold ones at the bar; brewing raises a thirst. They come back in two to six weeks to bottle. "They get about five cases per batch," Anning said. Everything is prepped for them: The beer is racked to a new container and lightly filtered, bottles are washed and ready. Labels are another matter. People are given lots of help in designing their own, with the ability to add photos, drawings, and all kinds of personal touches, just as you would if you had your own brewery and your own beer . . . which you do have at Shenandoah, kind of.

Of course, it's Anning and Laura and Shannon and Mike's brewery, mostly, and they're making their own beers, too. Big Meadow Pale Ale and Stony Man Stout, their best-known beers, celebrate well-known spots in the Shenandoah Valley and are available in 12-ounce bottles out in stores. The big, very different Millennium Ale is available in 22-ounce bottles at the brewery only; it's an oak-aged barleywine inspired by Finnish *sahti*, a rye beer filtered through juniper branches. Millennium Ale is truly unlike anything you've ever had before.

"We did about 330 barrels of our own commercial beer in 2003," said Anning, "and about 300 barrels of customers' batches." Not bad for a little brewery that sells brewers' dreams. These days I still smile when I see a BOP, but it's because of those fulfilled dreams, the beer passions realized, not because of any thoughts of old movies.

Opened: May 1996.
Owners: Anning Smith, Shannon McKissick.
Brewers: Anning Smith, Shannon McKissick.
System: 5-barrel HDP system plus eight 11-gallon HDP BOP kettles, 1,100 barrels annual capacity.
Production: 630 barrels in 2003.

Hours: Thursday and Friday, 4 P.M. to 11 P.M.; Saturday, 10 A.M. to 11 P.M. Closed Sunday through Tuesday. Wednesday, brewing or bottling by appointment only.

Tours: *Tour* the brewery? You can walk right in and *use* it!

Take-out beer: Growlers available, and you can have other (clean!) growlers filled. Six-packs and cases of Shenandoah's commercial beers also available.

Food: Four types of chili, meatball sandwiches, and beer queso dip make up the menu, with PBJs for the kids. There are also excellent Route 11 chips (all flavors) and Virginia Diner peanuts available.

Special considerations: Kids welcome. One of the chilis is vegetarian. Handicapped-accessible.

Parking: Off-street lot.

Old Dominion Brewing Company

44633 Guilford Drive, Bay 112, Ashburn, VA 20147
703-724-9100
www.olddominion.com

Drive all the way out VA Route 267, the toll road to Dulles, and then keep going past the "gotcha" toll onto the Greenway, get off at the next exit, go past MCI's warren of buildings, past the light, and take the next left, then the second left after that, and go to the last brick building on the left . . . you're at Old Dominion's brewpub, and the first sign you'll ever see is the one at the door. I asked Old Dominion president Jerry Bailey how people ever found this place. "Grumbling and moaning all the way," he said with his usual grin, "but they do find us."

They're probably happy once they do, because they're sure to find something to please them. Old Dominion's pub typically pours more than twenty different beers on three sets of sixteen taps and two beer engines. It's the only brewpub that I've ever been to while writing the three brewery guidebooks where I had to decline sampling *everything*. I just hit the highlights, skipping the beers I'd already grown familiar with and a few that were just too scary for midday drinking—the over 10 percent ABV Millennium barleywine, for example.

Why is a brewpub in the back of a business park, anyway? And why is a Peace Corps veteran, who then had a career in the State Department's USAID program doing community-development and family-planning work overseas, running that brewpub? "I wanted to do good, and I gave it a good shot," Jerry said, "but I got frustrated. Then in 1989, a friend suggested opening a brewpub. We could be on the front edge of things."

Jerry's job was all about research, so he went to work on the brewpub idea. He didn't like it, but he did think running a small brewery could be fun. "I got a book, got an accountant, got a lawyer, and started writing a business plan," Jerry recalled. "It was just like writing a research paper, didn't seem that hard to me. I showed it to my neighbor to see what he thought of it, and he immediately offered to invest." Friends and neighbors would eventually come up with $800,000 in capital.

Old Dominion was up and running, with its distinctive stag logo. "It's a white-tailed deer," Jerry told me. "It's the state animal of Virginia." The beer sold well, despite the usual small-brewery problems with distribution, and the small brewery was growing fast. They did private-label beers for restaurants and contract brewing for people who had an idea for a beer but no brewery. One of the best known of these is Tupper's Hop Pocket Ale (and its sister beer, Hop Pocket Pils), brewed for Bob and Ellie Tupper, D.C.-area beer enthusiasts who donate half of the profits from sales of their Hop Pocket hop-rockets to charities benefiting the homeless. Old Dominion even started brewing a very popular and successful root beer.

"We were on and off again about the idea of a pub," Jerry said. "Yes, let's; no, what are we thinking;

Beers brewed: Dominion Lager (GABF Bronze, 1990; Gold, 1997), Golden Lager, Victory Amber Lager, Dominion Ale, Pale Ale, Belgian-Style Brown Ale, Black and Tan, Blonde, Stout, Oak Barrel Stout (there are two different versions; the actual aged-in-bourbon-barrels version is available only at the brewpub, and it's worth the trip). Seasonals: Millennium, Summer Wheat, Octoberfest (GABF Bronze, 1996), and the Spring Brew and Winter Brew, both of which are "brewer's choice" each year. Old Dominion bottles an excellent root beer, diet root beer, and ginger ale, all made with cane sugar.

Old Dominion also contract-brews a number of beers for a variety of restaurants, brew-pubs, and would-be brewers: Hard Times Select (GABF Bronze, 1992), Aviator Amber, Tupper's Hop Pocket Pils (GABF Gold, 2001), Tupper's Hop Pocket Ale (GABF Gold, 1997), Starr Hill (Mojo Lager, Amber, and Pale Ale), Great American Restaurants Pale Ale (the GAR Pale Ale served at Sweetwater Tavern is brewed there, and the Old Dominion–brewed version is served at the group's other restaurants), New River Pale Ale (GABF Bronze, 2000), Brewer's Art Pale Ale, J. Paul's 1889 Amber Ale, Old Dubliner Amber Ale, Siné Irish-style Red Ale.

maybe later. The main reasons to do it were to sell our draft beer in growlers and to get more visibility." In 1996, they took the step and built the pub. It was very successful, and growler sales were as profitable as projected. Jerry told me that one year they filled more than two hundred in ninety minutes on Christmas Eve. Things were booming, and the brewery kept hitting capacity limits and expanding.

Then in 1999, growth hit a plateau. "There was some saturation of the market," Jerry said, "and we got a bit lackadaisical about our promotions and our graphics." He got a pained expression. "They said our artwork was staid. You wouldn't believe what new artwork costs!" Things only got worse in 2001, when the telecom bubble burst and suddenly the people from MCI-Worldcom weren't coming in anymore, the people from AOL weren't coming in. When the airliner slammed into the Pentagon on September 11, the whole area tanked.

After three years of slowly declining sales, Old Dominion is on the comeback trail. Yes, there are new graphics, the sodas are "going bonkers," Jerry said, and the winter and spring seasonals for 2004, a Baltic porter and an "imperial" pilsner, were very successful. But the big bright spot is the unlikely hero of the brewery: Oak Barrel Stout, the brewery's stout aged in bourbon barrels.

The beer was a runaway success on draft at the pub; they couldn't keep up with it. "If I could find a way to bottle this," Jerry told me in 2003, "I'd be a rich man." He never did find a way to bottle it, but he did find the next best thing: a treatment of the stout involving toasted oak chips and fresh vanilla beans that made mass production of the beer in bottling-size runs feasible. Six-pack sales are climbing steeply, and overall sales for the first half of the year were up 6 percent. Staid would appear to be a thing of the past.

As Jerry and I sat in the pub, sampling his wares, I couldn't help thinking back to the frustrated USAID worker who wanted to help the world. Was it worth it? I asked Jerry; do you like it? "Yes!" he answered immediately. "It's the best job I've ever had." It shows in the beer.

The Pick: With more than twenty beers on tap at any one time, you can't expect me to stick to one for the Pick! First is the Victory Amber, served unfiltered at the pub, a smooth and wonderfully drinkable beer that makes you wonder why any lager is ever filtered. Then it's Tupper's Pils, clean, bright, brisk, and zesty with hops, a slap in the face to beer geeks who think lagers are boring . . . or staid. I have to pick the Oak Barrel Stout, and I prefer the draft: a hugely intense beer, stuffed with marshmallow, vanilla, and graham, and everything comes together so well in the mouth—a fantastic snowstorm beer. Finally, it's the big boy I just couldn't pass up: Millennium barleywine, brewed once a year, and massive, hoppy, showing colossal amounts of alefruit, and capable of years of aging to a mellow nuttiness. Oh, and the root beer is an excellent example of the beverage; don't miss it.

Opened: October 1989.

Owners: Private investors.

Brewer: Kenny Allen, brewmaster.

System: 25-barrel JV NorthWest system, 35,000 barrels annual capacity.

Production: 25,000 barrels in 2003.

Hours: Monday through Thursday, 11:30 A.M. to 9 P.M.; Friday and Saturday, 11:30 A.M. to 10 P.M.; Sunday, noon to 6 P.M.

Tours: Saturday, 2 P.M. and 4 P.M.; Sunday, 2 P.M.

Take-out beer: Six-packs, cases, growlers; call ahead for kegs.

Food: The food in the pub is solid brewpub fare: burgers, steaks, salads. It's well made, tastes great, and goes really well with the beer.

Special considerations: No smoking. Kids welcome. Vegetarian meals available. Handicapped-accessible.

Parking: Large lot; can accommodate anything up to a tour bus.

Lodging in the area: Days Hotel at Dulles, 2200 Centreville Road, 703-471-6700; The Norris House Inn, 108 Loudon Street SW, Leesburg, 703-777-1806; Bailiwick Inn B&B, 4023 Chain Bridge Road, Fairfax, 703-691-2266; Country Inn and Suites, 45620 Falke Pike, 703-435-2700.

Area attractions: There's not much out here except Dulles Airport; lucky for you, that's where you'll find the new ***Smithsonian National Air and Space Museum's Steven F. Udvar-Hazy Center*** (14390 Air and Space Museum Parkway, 202-357-2700). This new facility houses the great majority of the Smithsonian's aviation collection. About 20 percent is on display at the Mall museum or out on loan; the rest is here. The Enola Gay is here, and the Smithsonian's Concorde; the space shuttle Enterprise also has come to rest here. This is a gorgeous, exciting new museum for the aviation fans who just can't get enough of the Air and Space Museum. There is a shuttle service between the two.

Other area beer sites: The ***Buffalo Wing Factory and Pub*** (434761 Parkhurst Place #100, Ashburn, 703-729-4200) has started serving Old Dominion beers; soothe the winged heat with some. Another Irish pub? Sure, why not! Try the ***Old Brogue*** (760C Walker Road, Great Falls, Virginia, 703-759-3309) against the others. We've been talking Hard Times; it's the considered opinion of impartial judges that the ***Hard Times Café*** in Herndon (428 Elden Street, 703-318-8941) may have the best beer selection of any in the chain. Worth a look! A bit farther out but well worth the trip is the ***Tuscarora Mill*** in Leesburg (203 Harrison Street, 703-771-9300), a beer-

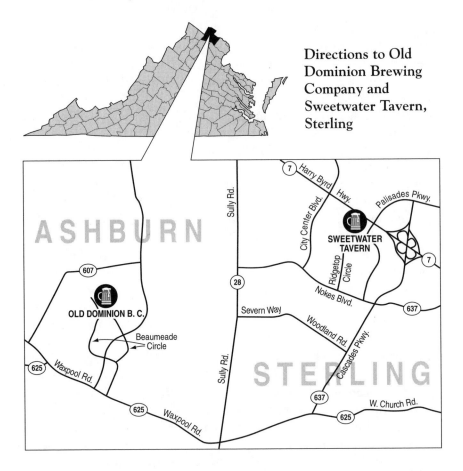

Directions to Old Dominion Brewing Company and Sweetwater Tavern, Sterling

oriented and beautiful old place that's been doing the good beer thing for a while. It's a converted nineteenth-century mill, with hardwood floors and a sense of solidity to it. There's also a new brewpub in Leesburg that was just a bit late for inclusion in the book: **Thoroughbreds Grill** (50 Catoctin Circle NE, 703-554-1207). The brewer, Dean Lake, is a seasoned Old Dominion veteran, and his first beers, a pale ale and a porter, are very traditional in style, and have been well-received by the local customers.

Sweetwater Tavern, Sterling

45980 Waterview Plaza, Sterling, VA 20166
571-434-6500
www.greatamericanrestaurants.com; Sweetwater Tavern icon

Beers brewed: Year-round: Great American Restaurants Light, Great American Restaurants Pale Ale (GABF Bronze, 2002). Seasonals: Silverado Cream Ale, High Desert Imperial Stout (GABF Silver, 2001; RAF Gold, 2001, 2003; RAF Best-of-Show Bronze 2001, 2003), Pale Face Summer Wheat, Buffalo Tooth's Old Ale, Rusty Roadrunner Lager, Barking Frog Ale, Outlaw Ale, Jackalope Canyon Ale, Great American Restaurants Octoberfest, Crazy Jackass Ale, Painted Lady Lager, Hair of the Dog Lager, Yippee Ei O Springbock, Bishop's Pass Ale, St. Nick's Weizenbock, Sidewinder Holiday Bock, Chipotle Porter, Road Kill Barleywine Style Ale (RAF Silver, 2002), Boot Hill Brown Ale, Straight Shooter Stout, Iron Horse Lager, Red Tape Ale, Helles Out of Dodge, Wit's End Ale, Black Stallion Oatmeal Stout, Flying Armadillo Porter (GABF Silver, 1998), Ghost Town Pumpkin Ale, Happy Trails Christmas Ale, Kokopelli India Pale Ale, Last Chance Lager, Yellow Devil Pilzner.

See the entry for Sweetwater Tavern, Merrifield (pages 101–105), for the main Sweetwater Tavern story.

Greg Gerovac mans the brewhouse here in Sterling, where the Sweetwater Tavern is located in a big office campus. The campus fire-insurance lake is attractively positioned right outside the back of the brewpub. Wisely, a patio has been added on the back to overlook the lake, with tables and a separate bar. I ate lunch out there with Nick Funnell (the pulled pork sandwich, and he's right: it goes very well with the pale ale) and enjoyed the scenery. There are heaters and glass doors for cool weather in the fall and spring, so you can enjoy it right through the waterfowl migrations.

As in the other brewpubs, the brewhouse is right out front as people enter the pub. Greg has added a personal touch to his domain: He will often write up a quick note on what he's doing and post it on the door so that people can have some idea of what's going on in the brewhouse. Very friendly.

The three brewpubs have similar menus—southwestern, but not unrelentingly so. You'll find things like Tex-Mex eggrolls, smoked salmon appetizers, that pulled pork sandwich . . . but not a lot of items. What sells best on the menu? I asked Nick. "Well, everything," he said. "I'm not being sales-oriented there. It's a relatively small menu, because if something doesn't sell, we take it off." After a brief tour of the kitchen, which included dropping in on a server training session and a look at the chilled meat-cutting room, I was convinced of the total commitment to quality food. I already knew that, though; we stop in here for a meal fairly frequently on trips to see family in Richmond.

Opened: November 2001.
Owner: Great American Restaurants, Inc.
Brewers: Nick Funnell, brewmaster; Greg Gerovac.
System: 15-barrel JV NorthWest system, 1,500 barrels annual capacity.
Production: 1,037 barrels in 2003.
Hours: Monday through Thursday, 11 A.M. to midnight; Friday and Saturday, 11 A.M. to 1 A.M.; Sunday, 11 A.M. to 11 P.M.
Tours: On request, or by appointment, or just look through the glass.
Take-out beer: Growlers available; see Sweetwater Tavern, Merrifield, listing (page 103) for details.
Food: Same as at Sweetwater Tavern, Merrifield (see page 105).
Special considerations: Kids welcome. A few vegetarian options are available. Handicapped-accessible.
Parking: Off-street lot.

The Pick: Yippie Ei O Springbock (which I can only assume people ask for by saying, "Springbock, please") was golden in color and smooth in body, with a broad malt character and a beautifully blended overarching hop presence, just like a well-balanced choir, where you hear music and can't really tell for sure which voice is singing which part. Very nice beer; too bad it's a seasonal.

Sweetwater Tavern, Centreville

14250 Sweetwater Lane, Centreville, VA 20121
703-449-1100
www.greatamericanrestaurants.com; Sweetwater Tavern icon

See the entry for Sweetwater Tavern, Merrifield (pages 101–105), for the main Sweetwater Tavern story.

The Sweetwater Tavern in Centreville is different from the other two brewpubs . . . but not much. It has a lighter wood interior, and the exposed-beam ceiling is in an attractive bow arch rather than the more standard peaked arches of the other two. And Jonathan Reeves is doing the day-to-day brewing here. The most basic difference, though, is not readily identifiable: It is a mirror image of the other two. So if you're used to heading for one corner to visit the little cowboy's room at Merrifield, well, don't forget to head for the opposite corner at Centreville.

You may have been wondering why I'm taking pains to say Sweetwater Tavern every time, instead of shortening it to Sweetwater. It goes back to the bottled Sweetwater Pale Ale the brewpubs contracted to have Old Dominion brew and bottle for them a few years ago. Sweetwater Brewing of Atlanta didn't think much of this idea and started legal action. The upshot of it all was that Sweetwater Tavern stopped labeling anything as Sweetwater. That's why your beer menu says Great American Restaurant Pale Ale now. Brewing may be a great industry, but marketers and lawyers rule here almost as much as they do anywhere else.

Opened: September 1996.

Owner: Great American Restaurants, Inc.

Brewers: Nick Funnell, brewmaster; Jonathan Reeves.

System: 15-barrel JV NorthWest system, 1,500 barrels annual capacity.

Production: 962 barrels in 2003.

Hours: Tuesday through Thursday, 11 A.M. to midnight; Friday and Saturday, 11 A.M. to 1 A.M.; Sunday and Monday, 11 A.M. to 11 P.M.

Tours: On request, or by appointment, or just look through the glass.

Take-out beer: Growlers available; see Sweetwater Tavern, Merrifield, listing (page 103) for details.

Food: Same as at Sweetwater Tavern, Merrifield (see page 105).

Special considerations: Kids welcome. A few vegetarian options are available. Handicapped-accessible.

Parking: Off-street lot.

Beers brewed: Year-round: Great American Restaurants Light, Great American Restaurants Pale Ale (GABF Bronze, 2002). Seasonals: Silverado Cream Ale, High Desert Imperial Stout (GABF Silver, 2001; RAF Gold, 2001, 2003; RAF Best-of-Show Bronze 2001, 2003), Pale Face Summer Wheat, Buffalo Tooth's Old Ale, Rusty Roadrunner Lager, Barking Frog Ale, Outlaw Ale, Jackalope Canyon Ale, Great American Restaurants Octoberfest, Crazy Jackass Ale, Painted Lady Lager, Hair of the Dog Lager, Yippee Ei O Springbock, Bishop's Pass Ale, St. Nick's Weizenbock, Sidewinder Holiday Bock, Chipotle Porter, Road Kill Barleywine Style Ale (RAF Silver, 2002), Boot Hill Brown Ale, Straight Shooter Stout, Iron Horse Lager, Red Tape Ale, Helles Out of Dodge, Wit's End Ale, Black Stallion Oatmeal Stout, Flying Armadillo Porter (GABF Silver, 1998), Ghost Town Pumpkin Ale, Happy Trails Christmas Ale, Kokopelli India Pale Ale, Last Chance Lager, Yellow Devil Pilzner.

The Pick: Pale Ale—whatever you call it—is the color of an old penny, with a tenacious light tan head and a bountiful hops and ester nose. It's hopped with English and American hops for what Nick calls a "Mid-Atlantic-style pale ale." It's dry, hoppy, and finishes in the same way. Very nice pint indeed.

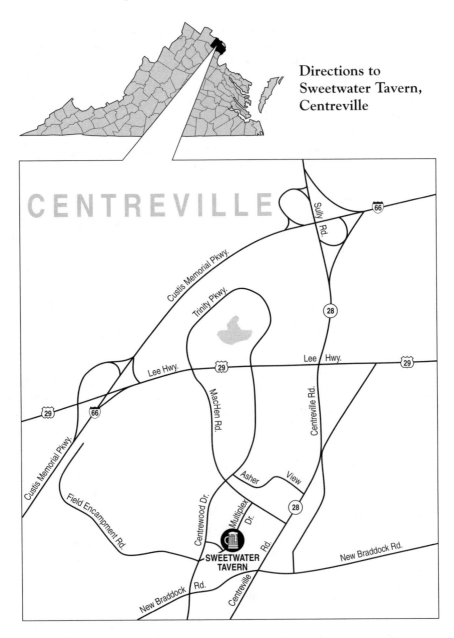

Directions to Sweetwater Tavern, Centreville

Lodging in the area: Springhill Suites, 5920 Trinity Parkway, 703-815-7800.

Area attractions: You can tour the first major battlefield of the Civil War, the **Manassas National Battlefield Park.** Start at the Henry Hill Visitor Center (6511 Sudley Road, Manassas, 703-361-1339) for a film and diorama of the battle. This was the battle where Thomas Jackson earned the sobriquet "Stonewall," and a statue commemorates his inflexible stand. Trails loop the battlefield, as does a driving tour; guide tapes and CDs are available at the center.

Other area beer sites: This is about the closest place to an area legend: *Bistrot Belgique Gourmande* (302 Poplar Alley, Occoquan, 703-494-1180) is a beloved beer bistro with phenomenal Belgian food and beer. You'll have to go, but call for directions; it can be a bit daunting to find the first time. Go hungry, go thirsty, and go prepared to want to return often.

A word about . . .

Brewing Beer

You don't need to know much about beer to enjoy it. After all, I don't understand how the electronic fuel injection on my car works, but I know that when I stomp on the accelerator, the car's gonna go!

Knowing about the brewing process can help you understand how and why beer tastes the way it does. It's like seeing the ingredients used in cooking a dish and realizing where the flavors came from. Once you understand the recipe for beer, other things become more clear.

Beer is made from four basic ingredients: water, hops, yeast, and grain, generally barley malt. Other ingredients may be added, such as sugars, spices, fruit, and vegetables, but they are extras. The oft-quoted Bavarian Reinheitsgebot (purity law), dating from 1516, limited brewers to using only water, hops, and barley malt; yeast had not yet been discovered.

In the beginning, the malt is cracked in a mill to make a grist. The grist is mixed with water and heated (or "mashed") to convert the starches in the grain to sugars (see *decoction* and *infusion* in the Glossary). Then the hot, sugary water—now called wort—is strained out of the mash. It is boiled in the brewkettle, where hops are added to balance the sweetness with their characteristic bitterness and sprightly aroma. The wort is strained, cooled, and pumped to a fermenter, where yeast is added.

A lager beer ferments slow and cool, whereas an ale ferments warmer and faster. After fermentation, the beer will be either force-carbonated or naturally carbonated and aged. When it is properly mature for its style, the beer is bottled, canned, kegged, or, in a brewpub, sent to a large serving tank. And then we drink it. Happy ending!

Naturally, it isn't quite that simple. The process varies somewhat from brewery to brewery. That's what makes beers unique. There are also major differences in the ways micro and mainstream brewers brew beer. One well-known distinction has to do with the use of nonbarley grains, specifically corn and rice, in the brewing process. Some microbrewers have made a big deal of their Reinheitsgebot, proudly displaying slogans like "Barley, hops, water, and yeast—and that's all!" Mainstream brewers such as Anheuser-Busch and SAB/Miller add significant portions of corn or rice or both; Frederick Brewing adds lots of corn syrup to their Little Kings Cream Ale. Beer geeks howl about how these adjuncts make the beer inferior. Of course, the same geeks often rave about Belgian ales, which have a regular farrago of ingredients forbidden by the Reinheitsgebot.

Mainstream brewers boast about the quality of the corn grits and brewer's rice they use, while microbrewers chide them for using "cheap" adjunct grains and "inferior" six-row barley. Truth is, they're both right . . . and they're both wrong.

Barley, like beer, comes in two main types: two-row and six-row. The names refer to the rows of kernels on the heads of the grain. Six-row grain gives a greater yield per acre but has more husks on smaller kernels, which can give beer an unpleasant astringency. Two-row gives a plumper kernel with less husk but costs significantly more. Each has its place and adherents.

When brewing began in America, farmers and brewers discovered that six-row barley did much better than two-row in our climate and soil types. Two-row barley grown the same way as it had been in Europe produced a distinctly different malt. This became especially trouble-some when the craze for pale lagers swept America in the mid-nine-teenth century. The hearty ales they replaced had broad flavors from hops and yeast that easily compensated for these differences. But pale lagers are showcases for malt character, and small differences in the malt mean big differences in beer taste.

Brewers adapted and used what they had. They soon found that a small addition of corn or brewer's rice to the mash lightened the beer, smoothed out the husky astringency of the six-row malt, and gave the beer a crispness similar to that of the European pale lagers. Even though using these grains required the purchase, operation, and maintenance of additional equipment (cookers, storage silos, and conveyors), almost every American brewer did it. Some say they overdid it, as the percent-ages of adjuncts in the beer rose over the years. Is a beer that is 30 per-cent corn still a pilsner?

Microbrewers say adjunct grains are cheap substitutes for barley malt. In terms of yield, corn and brewer's rice are less expensive than two-row barley, but they are still high-quality grains. Similarly, six-row barley is not inherently inferior to two-row; it is just not as well suited to the brewing of some styles of beer. Mainstream brewers have adapted their brewing processes to six-row barley. The difference is in the beer those processes produce.

Another difference between micro and mainstream brewers is the practice of high-gravity brewing. The alcohol content of a beer is mainly dependent on the amount of fermentable sugars in the wort, the specific gravity of the wort. A higher gravity means more alcohol.

Large commercial brewers, in their constant search for ways to peel pennies off the costs of brewing, discovered that they could save money by brewing beer at a higher alcohol content and carefully diluting it later. To do this, a brewer adds a calculated extra amount of malt, rice, corn—whatever "fuel" is used—to boost the beer to 6.5 percent alcohol by volume (ABV) or higher. When the fermented beer has been filtered, water is added to bring the ABV down to the target level of 4 to 5 percent. You may remember an ad campaign in the early 1990s, in which Anheuser-Busch accused Coors of shipping "beer concentrate" across the country in tank cars for packaging at its Virginia facility. The so-called "beer concentrate" was this high-alcohol beer prior to dilution.

How does this method save money? It saves energy and labor costs during the brewing process by effectively squeezing 1,300 barrels of beer into a 1,000-barrel brewkettle. Though 1,000 barrels are boiled, 1,300 barrels are eventually bottled. It also saves money by allowing more efficient use of fermentation tank space: 10,000-barrel fermenters produce 13,000 barrels of beer. It sounds great, so why not do that with every beer? Because the high-gravity process can produce some odd flavor and aroma notes during fermentation. That's what brewers aim for in big beers like doppelbocks and barley wines. But these characteristics are out of place in a pilsner. I also feel that beer brewed by this high-gravity method suffers from a dulling phenomenon similar to "clipping" in audio reproduction: The highs and lows are clipped off, leaving only the middle.

With a studied nonchalance, big brewers keep this part of their brewing process away from the public eye. To tell the truth, of all beer styles, American mainstream lager is probably the style least affected by this process. It is mostly a practice that just seems vaguely wrong, and you won't see any microbrewers doing it.

So now you know how beer is made and a few of the differences in how the big boys and the little guys do it. It's probably time for you to do a little field research. Have fun!

THE MOST IMPORTANT CITY
Washington, D.C.

W ashington, D.C., is, as an old Riggs Bank ad bluntly put it, the most important city in the world. New Yorkers might dispute that, and when it comes to finance, they might be right. But when it comes to power, clout, and decisions that affect people's lives around the globe, there is no need to mince words: Washington is the most important city in the world's most powerful country.

Washington has been the seat of America's government since 1800, when Congress and then-president John Adams moved to town. Washington was a "made" city. Georgetown was a small, thriving tobacco town, but where the District is today was largely bottomland; Jefferson called it "that Indian swamp in the wilderness." The French architect Pierre Charles L'Enfant famously laid out the city's broad plan of wide avenues crossing a grid of streets, with the Capitol and the White House at the center of things. The Supreme Court, supposedly an equally powerful branch of the government, was tucked in behind the Capitol.

The choice of the swamp was not popular. Mosquitoes spread yellow fever and malaria (as they had in Philadelphia, to be fair), and the government operated in crude buildings as the monumental mansion and marble Capitol were built. But when the British had the temerity to invade Washington and put it to the torch in the War of 1812, it suddenly became a symbolic capital as well as one in law. Once the Capitol dome and the Washington Monument were finished, no other city was seriously put forward to compete with Washington. It was still a relatively sleepy capital, until the massive national mobilization of Roosevelt's response to the Great Depression and then World War II transformed the city into a true national center. The Indian swamp in the wilderness had became the world's most important city.

You'd never know it in most places. With the exception of the few blocks around the Mall, the grassy strip of open space in what used to

135

be the middle of the District (take a look at a map: Arlington County, Virginia, was originally part of the District, but Virginia wanted it back, and got it, in 1847), this is a city like any other in America, although a bit more multicultural than most. There are good and bad sections, universities, shopping districts, waterfronts, parks, restaurants, a zoo, and all the things that make a city.

Actually, there is one difference: Washington is not as tall as other cities. You don't really notice it from street level, but if you view Washington from one of the river vistas or from the Anacostia Freeway, you'll notice how unmodernly flat the skyline is. You can plainly see the Capitol, the Washington Monument, the National Cathedral, all the way up to the blue dome of the National Shrine of the Immaculate Conception at Michigan Avenue and Fourth Street, NE. This view is courtesy of a law that limited the height of buildings in the District so that the Capitol and the Washington Monument would always be in sight.

That is one place where Washington differs from much bigger American cities. Yet for a city its size, over 570,000 people in 2002, it has an abnormal number of world-class museums, an accomplished and diverse cultural scene, great centers of knowledge, and a vibrant ethnic diversity, manifested in festivals and restaurants. Washington is one of the most exciting places in America.

Yet there is a price. Washington narrowly dodged the disasters of September 11, 2001. The Pentagon strike was just across the Potomac, and the fourth airplane that crashed in western Pennsylvania was believed to be headed for either the Capitol or the White House. Security is a constant concern at all government buildings, and parts of the city have been blocked off to vehicles.

There is another price that the residents have paid since the first days of the District: disenfranchisement. The democratic rights of the residents have always come second to the preservation of federal independence of the District. The District of Columbia was created to allow a capital free of the entanglements of state politics, and the result, say Washingtonians and their license plates, is taxation without representation.

Representation? D.C. residents recently gained the right to vote in presidential elections, with the District controlling three electoral votes, but they are not represented in the House or the Senate except by a nonvoting "delegate" in the House. Yet the District has more residents than the state of Wyoming. Compromises have gone nowhere, and a constitutional amendment failed to win the ratification of the states. The situation remains the same as it has for more than two hundred years.

Still, it's not something Washingtonians worry about every day. They're too busy working, playing, and thinking. If you want to remain the most important city in the world, after all, you have to stay on top of things. Meantime, we have things to do and beers to sample.

What to See

Much as when I wrote the section on New York City in *New York Breweries*, I am left with a feeling of ludicrous inadequacy when faced with the idea of compiling any kind of list, no matter how incomplete, of what to see in Washington. The Smithsonian museums alone could run to several pages, the seats of government another five to ten.

So I'll keep it very simple. If this is your first time to the capital, you should first contact the office of your senator or representative. They are your inside connection for tickets for special tours of the Capitol (including passes to the galleries of the Senate and the House), the Supreme Court, the Bureau of Engraving and Printing, the National Archives, the FBI Building, and their own offices, because you really should stop by and thank them (and make sure they're working!). They may even be able to get you a tour of the White House, though security concerns have made that one of the toughest tickets in town. Their offices are usually listed in your local telephone directory, or you can call the main congressional switchboard (202-224-3121).

Tour the monuments on and near the Mall. You'll need a ticket for the Washington Monument; you can get them for free at the kiosk on Fifteenth Street near Madison Drive (it opens at 8 A.M., and the day's tickets are usually gone by noon), or phone for advance tickets for a price of $2 per ticket by calling 800-967-2283. The other monuments are free: the Jefferson Memorial, the Lincoln Memorial, the FDR Memorial, the Vietnam Veterans Memorial, the Korean War Veterans Memorial, and the new World War II Memorial.

You must tour at least some of the Smithsonian museums. Air and Space is the most popular, and my favorite exhibit there is on the second floor directly back from the front door: Lindbergh's graceful "other" airplane, the sleekly streamlined Lockheed Tingamissartoq. The National Gallery of Art exhibits a huge collection of European and American paintings and sculpture. The National Museum of American History is the former History and Technology museum, where you can see the original "Star-Spangled Banner" as it is being restored, a full-size locomotive, and more; if the Smithsonian is "the nation's attic," as it has been called, this is the nation's garage that we've been meaning to clean out when we have the time. The National Museum of Natural History has dinosaurs, gems, stuffed and mounted animals, and anthropology exhibits. And it's all *free*.

Do all that—and to do that properly will take a week—and you've scarcely started. So get a guidebook devoted to the capital, plan, and do what *you* want to do. At the end of the day, pick this book up again, and go have a beer!

I feel similarly overwhelmed at the thought of recommending lodging in Washington. There are hundreds of hotels, motels, inns, and B&Bs, many that are quite nice. You'll probably do a better job finding a place that will suit your needs than I can.

On the other hand, I've been drinking in Washington on and off for more than twenty years, so I think I know a little bit about the best places to go. I've also been lucky enough to meet (physically or Internetly) a lot of pretty savvy beerfolk around here, who were more than happy to bring my knowledge right up-to-date.

Some suggestions: Use the Metro wherever possible; most of these bars are pretty close to Metro stops. It's clean, it's fast, it's pretty easy to figure out, although the fares can be intimidating. Make it simple: Buy a $5 one-day pass that's good all day after 9:30 A.M. (as if you'll be getting up that early anyway!). Just remember—the Metro stops running at midnight, Sunday through Thursday! (It runs till 3 A.M. on Friday and Saturday.) Luckily, cabs in Washington are pretty reasonable. Not all cabs are licensed, but I used the gypsy cabs for years without a problem.

Your particular favorite bar may not be listed here. There are, for example, a large number of Irish pubs in Washington. I've picked a few of the best; I've left out some others. If you don't see your favorite here, well, try one of these. Maybe you'll find another favorite to add to your list. Mine just keeps growing.

Capitol Hill

Four bars are very easy to reach from **Capitol City Union Station.** The first two are just a stumble away: **The Dubliner** (520 North Capitol Street, 202-737-3773) and **Kelly's Irish Times** (14 F Street NW, 202-543-5433). As my one bar source said, "You can't have one without the other," and it's true. These two pubs are the heart and soul of the legion of Irish bars in the Washington area, the core. Spend a few hours going back and forth, and you'll know what I mean. If you'd like a couple different ethnic drinking experiences, I'm happy to oblige. You can walk west to **The Flying Scotsman** (233 Second Street NW, 202-783-3848) and test the malty waters of life (the bar offers a mighty array of single malt whiskies) or you can head east to **Café Berlin** (322 Massachusetts

Avenue NE, 202-543-7656) and hoist a couple of steins while tearing into authentic sauerbraten.

Brewpub Central
There's a cluster of good bars just north of the cluster of brewpubs near the **Gallery Place** and **Metro Center** Metro stations. **RFD** (810 Seventh Street NW, 202-289-2030) is the long-awaited draft temple from Brickskeller owner David Alexander. RFD stands for Regional Food and Drink, and while Dave's taken a few shots for being a bit far-flung in his definition of "regional," there definitely are regional influences on the menu, and with thirty taps and three hundred bottles to choose from, you can pretty much make your own region. **Matchbox** (713 H Street NW, 202-289-4441) is just around the corner from RFD. It isn't really a beer bar; it's a smooth, sophisticated bar with ten real good taps . . . and a couple so-so ones, but no one's perfect. Very good brick-oven pizza and a cool vibe make this a sure stop for me the next time through town. **Café Mozart** (1331 H Street NW, 202-347-5732) is another one of Washington's solid, old German restaurants with solid, fresh German beers. **Capitol City** is the only missing brewpub in the cluster, but it isn't, really; the original **Capitol City** (1100 New York Avenue NW, 202-628-2222) is right here. The brewhouse has been taken out but Shirlington-brewed beer still flows from the taps. This is my favorite of the Capitol City pubs, a beautiful place.

Dupont Circle
The Beer Institute, a lobbying group for the industry that does great work, has its offices down here. The folks who work here have got some great places to go after work, too. Washington's most famous beer bar— arguably the country's most famous beer bar—is just two blocks west of the circle, by Embassy Row and Rock Creek Park: the fabulous **Brickskeller,** recognized by the Guinness Book of World Records as the bar with the biggest beer selection in the world (1523 Twenty-second Street NW, 202-293-1885). With well over one thousand beers on the menu (and yes, some do run out, but the menu is reprinted often, and always in teeny-tiny type), some of which Dave Alexander keeps under lock and key in the secret stash room, you're sure to find something you'll like, maybe even something you haven't had before. I know I usually do. Just don't look for taps. The Brick's obsession with different beers started as a can-collecting fetish, and it has concentrated on cans and bottles ever since. But don't fret; did you know you can get Rodenbach in cans these days?

Childe Harold (1610 Twentieth Street NW, 202-483-6700) is right off the Circle and has always been a favorite hangout of mine. The beer's not amazing, but the bar is, a comfortable place that has a real convivial feel. From here you have two choices. If you want down and dirty, with a big tap selection and a roaring crowd come nightfall, it's south on Connecticut to the **Big Hunt** for you (1345 Connecticut Avenue NW, 202-785-2333). If you'd prefer a quieter crowd with an interesting but smaller beer selection in a café atmosphere, head north on Connecticut to **Kramerbooks and Afterwards** (1517 Connecticut Avenue NW, 202-387-1462). Yes, it's a bookstore, but there's a café with beer in the back.

Adams Morgan

Adams Morgan is as Bohemian as it gets in Washington, a multiethnic neighborhood where I first enjoyed Ethiopian, Cuban, and Tex-Mex cuisine back in my college days. You can find all kinds of action here, but the beer's best at two places. The **Common Share** (2003 Eighteenth Street NW, 202-588-7180) was a bike messenger hangout and may still be; they came here for cheap good beer, and it's still here. There aren't a lot of choices, and there's not much to do except drink and talk, and what's bad about that? The other Adams Morgan place, one you won't want to miss, is **The Reef** (2446 Eighteenth Street NW, 202-518-3800). Head up the long set of steps to the barroom full of aquariums and draft beer, some very good taps. That's all they have, too; the bartender told me that "draft beer cuts down on solid waste." Tell your friends: *Draft beer can help save the planet!* Best of all, when the weather's good, you can go on up to the roof, which is killer, with a great view and vibe. I've had friends call me from the roof of The Reef just to tell me that they were there and I wasn't. It's that cool up there.

Elsewhere

There's one more German restaurant in Washington's trio of Teutonic temples: **Old Europe** (2434 Wisconsin Avenue NW, 202-333-7600) keeps the old-school lager flame burning over in the trendy streets of Georgetown. Up near what once was known as the "black Broadway," the **Bohemian Caverns** (2001 Eleventh Street NW, 202-299-0801) was a hot spot for the big jazz and swing names of the 1920s and 1930s. After long neglect, the dining room has been restored to its former glory, ornate and historical, with a *lot* of Belgian beers in bottles. But don't forget to go downstairs to the incredibly funky caverns, the live music space complete with stalactites and rough walls. Blues bands play on Thursdays, jazz groups on Friday and Saturday, and the beer's even better downstairs. This is a beer bar that has been overlooked. Finally, there's one more Irish bar of note, out in Cleveland Park. *Ireland's Four Provinces* (3412 Connecticut Avenue NW, 202-244-0860) was a bit more rowdy than the Capitol Hill pubs in my day. *Café Saint-Ex* (1847 Fourteenth Street, 202-265-7839) is an up-and-coming favorite with lovers of good beer and French aviation poetry. A solid beer menu changes regularly.

Capitol City Brewing Company, Union Station

2 Massachusetts Avenue NE, Washington, D.C. 20002
202-842-2337
www.capcitybrew.com

Welcome to the Capitol City look: high ceilings, big bar in the middle of the floor, and tall, copper-clad serving tanks in the middle of the bar. This is another old building Capitol City has successfully renovated, an old post office, and it looks grand. Its heavy walls make for a quiet, cool retreat in the worst of Washington's oppressively humid summer; the large outdoor seating area makes the most of Washington's delightful spring and fall.

The full Capitol City story is under the Shirlington Village entry (see pages 110–113), but this is a good opportunity to talk a little more about the best-selling beer they make, a beer style that's not very well understood by most people: kölsch.

Kölsch is pronounced "kooelllsch," roughly; the German "ö" is a sound we don't really use in English. You can approximate it by rolling your lips into a tight circular opening, as if you were whistling, and say "oooo." The lips give the "oooo" a kind of "ee" overtone. Do your best; I'm a beer writer, not a linguist.

Beers brewed: Year-round: Capitol Kölsch (GABF Silver, 2001; Gold, 2002), Pale Rider IPA, Amber Waves Ale (GABF Bronze, 2002), Mr. Hop's Wild Ride, Prohibition Porter. Seasonals: Cherry Blonde Ale, Belgian-style Red Ale, Hefe-Weizen, Oktoberfest, Roggen Rye Ale, Pumpkinator Ale, Wee Heavy Ale (GABF Silver, 2001; Bronze, 2002; RAF Gold and Best-of-Show Silver, 2002; Gold, 2003), Slobberknocker Barleywine.

Anyway, "Kölsch" simply means "of Köln," which is the German name for the city known as Cologne. Since it's a German city, it seems only fair to use the German name instead of the French one; besides, would you rather drink Kölsch, or cologne? Kölsch is the hometown beer in Köln, and it's a hybrid style of beer that combines characteristics of both ales and lagers.

First, check out "A Word about . . . Ales and Lagers" on page 151. Once that you get the idea of that difference, here's how Kölsch bridges the gap. Kölsch is brewed with a fairly clean ale yeast, "fairly clean" meaning that there are not a lot of the esters and other aroma and flavor components thrown off by other ale yeasts. The brewers of Köln build on that clean profile further by cold-conditioning the beer, maturing it at cold temperatures—a process that would be called "lagering" for a beer like pilsner.

The Pick: I'm almost embarrassed to pick this, with all the ranting and raving about the crazed trend to over-strength, overhopped beers I've done in the past year, but Mike McCarthy's Double IPA was Mr. Hop's Wild Ride, and no mistake about it. It's 8.5 percent, quite bright, and orange in color with a smooth, slippery malt body. You smell the esters even under the sharply piney hop aroma, but once you start sipping, the hops never ever go away. Hurt me real good, beer!

What you get is a light, golden beer with the rounded, pure malt and hops character of a lager, but with a light smear of the esters that come from an ale. It's a great beer when done right, not "light beer" at all, but with a delicate body and flavor that truly reward the thoughtful drinker. Even if you're the kind of beer drinker that screams for MORE HOPS!!!, give the Kölsch a try at Capitol City. You might learn something about subtlety.

You'll want to try the Kölsch here even if you've had it at other Capitol Citys; this Kölsch is brewed on-site. Bill Madden, until recently the head brewer for Capitol City, gave his brewers some latitude. "I encourage the guys to do their own thing," he said. "I don't want to see the brewers being automatons in the brewhouse. Within reason, of course." Of course! So belly up to the bar and start sampling nonautomaton-brewed beer.

Opened: June 1996.
Owner: David von Storch.
Brewer: Mike McCarthy.
System: 15-barrel Bohemian system, 2,000 barrels annual capacity.
Production: 1,000 barrels in 2003.
Hours: 11 A.M. to 2 A.M., seven days a week.
Tours: Upon request, brewer's schedule permitting, Monday through Friday, from opening until 5 P.M.

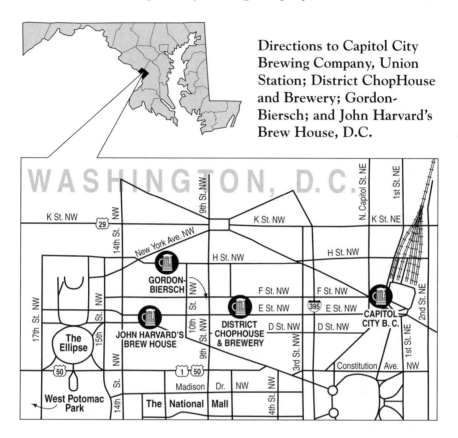

Directions to Capitol City Brewing Company, Union Station; District ChopHouse and Brewery; Gordon-Biersch; and John Harvard's Brew House, D.C.

Take-out beer: Not available. D.C. law does not allow off-site sales of brewpub beer.

Food: See page 113.

Extras: Plenty of TVs. Private back rooms for special events. Large outdoor seating area.

Special considerations: Kids welcome. Vegetarian meals available. Handicapped-accessible.

Parking: You can park here, but it's expensive. Do the smart thing: Take the Metro to Union Station; the brewpub is right across the street from the main exit.

District ChopHouse and Brewery

509 Seventh Street NW, Washington, D.C. 20004
202-347-3434
www.districtchophouse.com

Allow me to let you in on one of my pet beer peeves. There are a lot of brewpubs. There is not, however, as much difference among them as there could be.

The beers may not be as similar as they once were, the much-derided "color beer" lineup common to so many early brewpubs of gold, amber, and porter or stout. But so many of the menus are similar, to the point where you can almost predict what a brewpub will have: burgers, nachos, pizzas, a hot dip of some kind, the basic sandwiches, salmon with some kind of crust or infusion drizzle, something Asian, something southwestern, and maybe a steak or seafood. It may be good, it may be great, but I could find this kind of menu at any chain restaurant out by the mall!

Thankfully there are places like the Thai menu Typhoon in New York, Extra Billy's barbecue brewpub in Richmond, and even Franklin's in Hyattsville, which is so darned different the menu doesn't matter. And thankfully there is the District ChopHouse, because this beer geek likes to get dressed up and go to town for a real meal sometimes, and it's nice to know there's a brewpub that's ready for me.

Stepping into the ChopHouse takes you back sixty years to the Age of Swing, a refuge of sophistication in our increasingly casual world. The snazzily dressed maître d'hôtel greets you, the buoyant swing music in the air lifts your step, the solidly built bar beckons to you, and the smell of sizzling prime cuts of meat is in the air. This is an American steakhouse, and I patronize it whenever time and my wallet allow.

By the way, please don't get the idea that this is one of those aggressively themed restaurants where a wax mannequin of Count Basie sits eternally smiling behind a piano and the waitstaff breaks out in "spontaneous" dancing. The decor is understated, almost suggested, and the waitstaff is crisply outfitted and focused on one thing: serving you in a way

Beers brewed: Year-round: Light Lager, Red Ale, Nut Brown, Amber Ale, Oatmeal Stout, Bourbon Stout. The ChopHouse also runs one of the regulars as a "velvet ale" on a nitro tap for a smoother beer; worth a try. Seasonals: Copper Ale, limited number of others.

that does not intrude on your dinner. The "dinner entertainment" idea is far from this place. The ChopHouse is about fine food, drink, and service.

Let's have a seat at the bar and talk about it. Look at this bar: It's got a concrete sense of solidity to it, heavy, worn wood and a proudly showy backbar that displays the ChopHouse's excellent selection of single malts and bourbons (one thing I love about D.C. is the fine selection of bourbons you find almost everywhere; this is almost as big a bourbon town as Louisville). Get a beer, though, because you'll want to try one of the brewery's Bourbon Stouts.

The practice of aging beer in bourbon barrels is a relatively new one (or rediscovered; no one's sure), and the first modern-era brewery to do it was either Goose Island or the Rock Bottom in Denver. Former District ChopHouse brewer Jason Dorpinghaus was there in the early days of the bourbon stouts at Rock Bottom, and he brought them to Washington, a kind of transmission of beer DNA.

The beer is the ChopHouse's Oatmeal Stout, a smooth, smoky sipper of a beer even before it goes into the Jim Beam barrel. It will stay there for at least three weeks, and perhaps as long as two months. "In the early stages," Jason once told me, "you get more vanilla and coconut. As it ages, the beer picks up more of the woody notes." Once it's ready, the beer is transferred to kegs and run through the bar's handpump—completely flat.

And people love it! Cellar-cool, flat beer that just spent two months in a wooden barrel, and they drink it like mad. They'd be fools not to, because it's overwhelmingly delicious. There's such a huge bourbon nose and such a massive blast of bourbon in the mouth that it's hard to find the beer, until you realize that you're drinking synergy, the beer and bourbon together, boosting each other to new heights.

It's a beer that sets the ChopHouse apart, just another level of sophistication on this edifice of fine dining and drinking. Even the billiards room upstairs is different: two tables with their own small bar and a comfortable lounge with overstuffed leather chairs and couches.

If you're tired of an unending diet of pizza and burgers with your fresh-brewed beer, well-made though they may be, catch a cab to the ChopHouse and order up a thick steak or a couple of pork chops, paired with a big Bourbon Stout. *This* is a difference I can appreciate.

The Pick: I'm not going to talk more about the Bourbon Stout; go there, get some. But before you do, get some of the Nut Brown. I can't believe I'm saying that, because I'm just not a brown ale fan, but this dark garnet beer with the tight creamy head is surprisingly rich and complex for its typically light brown ale body. Yes, it is nutty, and the malt's plainly there too, but there's a nice hop flip at the end as well. Nicely done.

Opened: April 1997.
Owner: Rock Bottom Restaurants.
Brewer: Barrett Lauer.
System: 7-barrel JV NorthWest system, 1,400 barrels annual capacity.
Production: 934 barrels in 2003.
Hours: Monday, 11 A.M. to 10 P.M.; Tuesday through Friday, 11 A.M. to 11 P.M.; Saturday, 2 P.M. to 11:00 P.M.; Sunday, 2 P.M. to 10 P.M.
Tours: Upon request during daytime hours.
Take-out beer: Not available. D.C. law does not allow off-site sales of brewpub beer.
Food: Steaks, chops, rack of lamb, salmon, lobster, surf and turf; big honking chunks of really top-quality meat, done to your order. Do you really need to know more? There is a small "brewery fare" sandwich menu and a big appetizer menu.
Extras: Very nice bourbon and single-malt selection. Pool tables in upstairs lounge bar.
Special considerations: The ChopHouse is not really a kids' place; this is for when Mommy and Daddy get dressed up and go out on their own. It's not really for vegetarians, either, though there is a very nice roasted vegetable pizza on the appetizer menu. Handicapped-accessible.
Parking: Some metered street parking; pay garages.

Gordon-Biersch

900 F Street NW, Washington, D.C. 20004
202-783-5454
www.gordonbiersch.com

Good beer is a treasure, a valuable part of life, something to be kept from harm, not just left lying about. Maybe that's why when Gordon-Biersch came to town they put their Washington brewpub in a solidly built former Riggs bank. The thick walls, tall windows, and marble columns give you the feeling that you're walking up to the red granite bar to make a withdrawal, not just order a beer.

Okay, maybe not. But Gordon-Biersch, named for chain founders Dan Gordon and Dean Biersch, does make beer that is liquid lagered gold, helped along by the skills and patience of brewer Jason Oliver. It's kept in the vaults—sorry, in the *tanks*—for a minimum of five weeks because, you know, there's a substantial flavor penalty for early withdrawal.

Sorry, no more bank jokes! G-B is a solid brewpub, and I have no desire to deal with them lightly. Especially since they are an all German-type beer brewpub, and those are rare and wonderful things. The reason for that is explained in "A Word about . . . Ales and Lagers" on page 151, and it's all true. As Jason emphasized, "Ale styles would be faster," but it's all part of brewing the Teutonic way.

The Germans do get away with a few quicker beers. Most people don't realize it (or, more likely, don't care), but the German weizen beers are all ales, fermented at a warmer temperature by a top-fermenting yeast. Though it's true that altbiers and Kölsches are also brewed with ale yeasts, their hybrid brewing regimen then calls for a longer, cold maturation period, just like a lager.

Beers brewed: Year-round: Export, Märzen, Dunkles. Seasonals: Maibock, Hefeweizen, Festbier, Winterbock, Kölsch, Alt, Schwarzbier, Blonde Bock, Czech Pils, Pilsner.

The Pick: I could sit in this big marble hall and drink Export all day long. It's malty dry, medium in body, possessed of a smooth, well-balanced bitterness, almost perfect in its drinkability. A real quaffer, and that's what the German brewers are generally aiming at. Bull's-eye.

That's not just esoteric beer-guy stuff, either; it has a real impact on what you drink at the bar. People in Washington have been really thirsty, and Jason's production was up 25 percent for the first part of 2004. That sounds great, but when you realize that you've got to come up with a minimum of five weeks' tank time to age all that beer, you start to understand why Jason was sweating hard and running back and forth to the brewhouse when I interviewed him.

I did get a chance to ask him about brewing at G-B. I've made a big deal about the freedom brewers have at Rock Bottom and John Harvard's, at Iron Hill and Capitol City. But G-B brewers have very little leeway on what to make or how to make it. They keep three regular beers on, the Export, Märzen, and Dunkles, and one seasonal that is decreed by a calendar that comes down from corporate. Where's the freedom, where's the skill? Are these guys just brew-monkeys?

"There's not a lot of freedom," Jason admitted, "but formulation is far from the hardest part of brewing. Keeping it clean, keeping it consistent, that's difficult." I remember a dedicated lager brewer in New York telling me about it. "Ales? I could teach a chimp to make ales. You have to know what you're doing to make lagers." They're a rare, proud breed, the brewpub lager brewers.

Besides, there are the seasonals, and they keep the skills honed. Maibock, Hefeweizen, Festbier (an unfiltered version of the Märzen with a slightly different formulation), and Winterbock are the main four, with some other ones stuck in around the edges: altbier, Schwarz-bier, and Kölsch. The seasonals give the brewer a chance to show off a little, and they give the chef a chance to have fun, too. Each of the main seasonals comes with a whole specialty menu of six or seven different items, from appetizers to dessert, picked to complement or be enhanced by the beer.

Good German beer, solid food, an impressive and substantial ambience in which to enjoy it (or sidewalk tables, if you prefer), and sharp service. Everything is in order and running smoothly, just as the Germans like it.

Opened: March 2001.

Owner: Gordon-Biersch Brewery Restaurant Group.

Brewer: Jason Oliver.

System: 20-barrel Specific Mechanical, 2,500 barrels annual capacity.

Production: 1,119 barrels in 2003.

Hours: Sunday through Thursday, 11:30 A.M. to midnight; Friday and Saturday, 11:30 A.M. to 2 A.M.

Tours: On request, subject to brewer availability.

Take-out beer: Not available. D.C. law does not allow off-site sales of brewpub beer.

Food: For one thing, it's nice to see a place where as much attention is lavished on the appetizers as on the entrées. Gordon-Biersch has a large lounge and bar area, where appetizers are the main choice, often a basket of their signature garlic fries. The entrées are diverse—lamb chops, gumbo, meatloaf, tuna steaks—and there is always a separate menu, from appetizers through desserts, of dishes specially prepared to pair with the current seasonal, a very nice touch.

Extras: Sidewalk seating, weather permitting.

Special considerations: Kids welcome. Some vegetarian meals available. Handicapped-accessible.

Parking: There is street parking to be had, but it's tough to get. Either take the Metro in or bite the bullet and stash your car in one of the expensive local lots.

Area attractions: I had to throw this one in because it's right here between Gordon-Biersch and the ChopHouse. The ***International Spy Museum*** (800 F Street NW, 202-393-7798) has quickly become one of the most popular tickets in Washington, with exhibits that former spies have grudgingly admitted are "not bad."

John Harvard's Brew House, D.C.

1299 Pennsylvania Avenue NW, Washington, D.C. 20004
202-783-2739
www.johnharvards.com

See the entry for John Harvard's, Wilmington (pages 7–11), for the main John Harvard's story.

Most people don't know—or care—anymore, but John Harvard's, D.C., used to be the first Dock Street brewpub outside of Philadelphia, and Nick Funnell, now head brewer at Sweetwater Tavern, was the brewer there. It was eight years ago, and it only matters to me because I'm a total beer geek about things like that, but it's brewpub history, and we don't have much of that, so you're getting it.

It does matter a little bit, actually. Because this John Harvard's really doesn't look much like the other John Harvard's, which usually have a dark wood, gentlemen's club look to them. This place is underground, for one thing, in a fairly inconspicuous door and down a set of stairs off Pennsylvania Avenue. For another, the walls are light wood, as are the long booth dividers, not the usual darkly soothing John Harvard's tones, though I guess that's to compensate for the lack of natural light.

And then there's the ceiling. It's fairly high, done in gray and bronze-toned metals, and fairly well lit, and . . . it's wavy. Big waves. Brewer Terry Rowell thinks the architect's to blame. "I think he was going for an 'amber waves of grain effect.'" Myself, I wonder if this was the source of some of the contractor cost overruns that forced Dock Street to drop the site only months after opening.

Anyway, John Harvard's and Terry are here now, and Terry's not above a bit of avant-garde stuff himself. Check out his brewing experiment: He'd heard that yeast reacts to sound, so he brewed up an abbey-style ale and split it into two batches to experiment. "I call them St. Anger and St. Stephen," Terry explained. "I played Metallica to

Beers brewed: Nut Brown Ale (RAF Silver, 2000).

The Pick: Terry had a special batch of IPA on when I visited, hopped with Brambling Cross hops; by coincidence, a hop Nick Funnell favors. It was a delicious beer, with a complex hop flavor, an aroma of berry and pear drops, and a sturdy malt body.

St. Anger and the Dead to St. Stephen. I wanted to see if it would make a difference." I only got to taste St. Anger, so I can't give you the dope on the experiment; it tasted sweet but not cloying to me, with a background bitterness.

That's John Harvard's underground brewing experiment. Not all the data are in, but at this point the experiment looks successful.

Opened: March 1997.

Owners: Boston Culinary Group.

Brewer: Terry Rowell.

System: 10-barrel JV Northwestern system, 1,000 barrels annual capacity.

Production: 600 barrels in 2004.

Hours: Monday through Thursday, 11:30 A.M. to 11 P.M.; Friday, 11:30 A.M. to midnight; Saturday, noon to midnight; Sunday, 3 P.M. to 10 P.M.

Tours: Not available.

Take-out beer: Not available. D.C. law does not allow off-site sales of brewpub beer.

Food: The John Harvard's menu features upscale pub fare, including Asian crispadillas, chicken pot pie, steaks, Chinese chicken salad, calamari, and a few local specials.

Special considerations: Kids welcome. Some vegetarian meals available. Handicapped-accessible.

Parking: Street parking is iffy and hard to come by; take the Metro or pay for a garage.

A word about . . .

Ales and Lagers

If you're going to go to the breweries in this book, you'll have to know how to talk shop with the bartenders and tour guides and not embarrass yourself on the tour. First off, beer is any fermented beverage made from malted barley, usually with an addition of hops. The two main types of beer are ales and lagers.

What's the difference between the two? It's quite simple: two different yeasts. These have a number of small differences, the most important of which is that the optimum temperature for fermentation and aging is higher for ale yeasts (in the 60s F) than for lager yeasts (in the 40s F). That's more than just a thermostat setting. The warmer operating temperature of ale yeast encourages a faster, more vigorous fermentation that creates aromatic compounds known as phenols and esters. These can give ale-fermented beers aromas such as melon, banana, raisin, clove, and vanilla. (I call these aromas "alefruit.")

On the other hand, the cooler lager fermentation produces a very clean aroma and flavor palette. Lagers generally have purer malt and hops characteristics. A lager brewer will tell you that there's nowhere to hide when you make lager beer; the unadorned nature of the beer makes flaws stand out immediately.

I like to think of the two yeasts in terms of jungles and pine forests. Warm ale fermentations are like lush jungles—exotic arrays of flavors, splendid in their diversity. By comparison, cold lager fermentations are more like northern pine forests—intense, focused, and pure.

Among small brewers in America, ale brewers outnumber lager brewers by more than ten to one. Given that lagers are by far the most popular beers in the world, how did this come to be? Tom Pastorius of Penn Brewing once explained it to me somewhat bluntly: "More ale is being made because it's cheaper, easier, and more flexible." Hard words, perhaps, but the facts bear them out.

After lagers are fermented, they undergo an extended aging period of at least three weeks at low temperatures. The cooling and the tank time required add energy costs and decrease turnover. In the same amount of time, it would be possible to put twice as much ale through those tanks. Add the energy and labor costs of the more complicated decoction brewing process used for lagers, and you wind up with a product that costs substantially more to brew than ales but has to be priced the same. No wonder there are more ale brewers!

When it comes to lager, the Mid-Atlantic is blessed with some real pros. DeGroen's makes award-winning lager beers, as you would expect from a Weihenstephan-trained brewer with a two-century lager pedigree. Old Dominion has years of lager experience, Fordham's line is based solidly on lagers, Frederick makes some great lagers, and many of the brewpubs in the area, Ellicott Mills foremost among them, pull off lagers with great success.

Whatever your tastes—ale jungles or lager forests—you'll find something to your liking in the Mid-Atlantic.

Western Maryland

Maryland, like Caesar's Gaul, is divided into three parts: the Eastern Shore, split off by the life-filled estuary of the Chesapeake Bay; the fertile and busy central area, which runs from the Mason-Dixon line down to Washington and the Potomac, a division more of political geography than physical; and the western ridgelands, a territory roughly bordered on the east by MD Route 27 and encompassing Frederick, Hagerstown, and the largely overlooked tail to the west, almost pinched off at Hancock, where West Virginia comes within 3 miles of Pennsylvania before sliding off southwestward to allow Garrett County room to breathe.

Frederick is here, and the accident of geography left the town on this natural highway for the invading armies of the Confederacy as they made their hopeful way north to attack the breadbasket of Pennsylvania's central farmlands. The countryside around Frederick for miles was bathed in blood, horribly watered by the sacrifice of thousands for causes they likely didn't understand further than "them" and "us," "rebel" and "bluebelly."

Today Frederick stands on the front of the Catoctin Ridge, growing and prospering, still to a large degree a market town in the midst of agricultural bounty. The Civil War is not forgotten, but it is no longer a matter of "them" and "us"; rather, it is more a matter of reverence for the dead and a touristic curiosity about the past.

Little Westminster was the scene of a small but critically important Civil War skirmish right in the middle of town. J. E. B. Stuart, the cavalry commander whom Robert E. Lee referred to as "my eyes," was pacing Lee's army on the way to Gettysburg. When Stuart's cavalry army got to Westminster on June 29, 1863, their lead elements were observed by a civilian, who told Captain Corbit, the commander of about one hundred men of the 1st Delaware Cavalry.

Corbit immediately led his men at the gallop through the streets of Westminster to meet what he evidently expected to be a few troops, only to run head-on into Stuart's army of six thousand veteran cavalry troopers. Corbit and his men fought fiercely, then broke and ran—wisely—but the skirmish had had its effect. Corbit's Charge is considered one of the factors in Stuart's failure to reach Gettysburg in time to give Lee the scouting reports that could have changed the outcome of the battle . . . and U.S. history.

Westminster is still a small town on the road to Gettysburg. Some of the same trees line the streets that were there in 1863, recently saved from being cut down by an innovative Department of Transportation plan that repaved Main Street while preserving a large number of the old, beautiful trees.

West of Frederick and Westminster lies country largely untouched by the war, too mountainous for effective maneuver. This is the land of the narrows, where history was shaped into tortured paths through the ridges. The mountains here are not high, but they are abrupt and repeated and were quite daunting to horse-drawn wagons and railroads. The people of Allegany took to industry, for the natural trade routes through the area drew the National Road, the Chesapeake and Ohio Canal, and the Baltimore and Ohio railroad. The transportation was already there, and the people used it with great vigor, shipping coal, glass, bricks, and even beer from the local breweries.

The story is the same as is told in many such industrial towns: The industry left town, and the town discovered ways to exploit its past for tourism. Cumberland has created museums to celebrate its manufacturing history and organized tours of its historic homes. The proliferation of highways has passed Cumberland by as an important transportation center, but it is an interesting stop for the tourist.

Garrett County, the land west of Cumberland, is Maryland's playground, and to some degree, it has been for a long time. Wealthy industrialists had hunting and fishing camps here in the wilderness. Now it's open for everyone, with much of the land in state parks. Surprisingly, snow falls heavily here, a microclimate that quite often produces more than 200 inches of snow in a year. The summer is brief but intense, and fall is a long, lovely season.

Frederick sports four breweries, counting the U-brew setup at the Flying Barrel, and Westminster has two. Frederick Brewing is the largest brewery in the state and ships beer as far away as Oklahoma. The Flying Barrel is the smallest brewery and often "ships" its beer no farther than the other side of town. Cumberland's Uncle Tucker's is part of a rambling complex of family businesses serving travelers that once, 120 years ago, fronted on the National Road. Now, with the change of a back door to a front door, it faces onto the new "national road," I-68. Deep Creek is a resort brewpub, enhancing the Western Maryland experience.

Western Maryland has been many things over the years. At one time it was the frontier, then it was settled farmland. Men fought and died here, then made their peace and got down to work. It is a beautiful part of the Free State, with long sunlit vistas in the countryside around Frederick, the dark hollows and high ridges of Allegany County, and the deeply forested hills and rolling rivers of Garrett County.

Frederick Brewing Company

4607 Wedgewood Boulevard, Frederick, MD 21703
301-694-7899

I had this narrative all planned out as I drove to Frederick Brewing. This was my third visit to the brewery. The first was in late 1994, when I was just starting a full-time career as a beer writer and Frederick was a young company on the way up, still at the Carroll Street building where the Flying Barrel is today. Their Blue Ridge brands were catching fire, and all the talk was about how they would manage to keep brewing till the new brewery opened on the edge of town.

In 1998, I went down to see the new brewery and taste Hempen Ale, a new beer brewed with hemp seeds. The facility was astonishing, ambitiously huge with room to expand mightily. The company had bought the brands of two other Maryland breweries, well-known Eastern Shore–based Wild Goose and the much smaller Brimstone Brewing, and they were folding them into their portfolio. The company had gone public, and money was flowing like water.

Everything looked good, but I was disturbed by the way they seemed to be betting their future on the potential success of Hempen Ale . . . which seemed like a gimmick to me. I'll never forget head brewer Steve

Nordahl's response to that characterization: "It's not a gimmick," he insisted, "it's a *novelty!*"

I was right. Hempen Ale bombed, Frederick's stock crashed, and the brewery was bought by the Snyder International Brewing Group, an Ohio-based company that had bought a few small breweries and now planned to make Frederick its production base. From there, things got progressively stranger, and . . .

Well, like I said, I was planning to tell you all of this, the rise and fall, but I changed my mind once I got to the brewery and started talking to the people who are making it run today. This is the real story, not some recitation of past glories and disasters, because this is the story that's making the beer you'll be drinking at the end of your tour.

"How are we now?" said John Niziolek, brewery general manager. "Overhead is down—we had fifty people working here before; now we're running strong with eighteen. The tanks are full and quality levels are up, profit margins and production are up." The interesting thing about those claims is that they were easy to check; head brewer Daniel Maerzluft had the numbers, in four-color graphs and tank diagrams, posted in the long passageway running past the fermentation hall and the quality control lab.

Beers brewed: Frederick brews a number of brands. Wild Goose: IPA, Amber, Porter, Oatmeal Stout (GABF Bronze, 2002), Nut Brown (RAF Bronze, 1998). Seasonals: Snow Goose (RAF Gold, 1997), Wheat. Blue Ridge: Golden Ale, Amber Lager, ESB, Porter. Seasonals: HopFest, Snowball's Chance, Sublimator Doppelbock (GABF Silver, 1995, 1998). Crooked River: ESB (GABF Gold, 2002), Kölsch, Porter (GABF Silver, 2000), Select Lager. Seasonal: Yuletide Ale. Little Kings Cream Ale. Frederick also brews a number of contract beers, including Christian Moerlein Select Lager, Penn Pilsner, Terrapin, Thirsty Dog, and Highland Brewing, among others.

"Sure, the numbers are all open and available," John said. "It makes it easier for everyone to plan that way." For suppliers, too? After the troubles the brewery had gone through, suppliers insisted on cash on delivery; no more credit for Frederick. "It causes some problems," he admitted, "but it's working for us now. We've gotten used to it, and we can keep it up, and it turns out that suppliers will give you some nice breaks if you pay cash up front.

"We're the mosquito that keeps buzzing around the inside of the tent," John said with a laugh. "You know, the one that no one can kill. We stay upbeat about it and keep doing our work."

Maerzluft understands the attitude. "When we need something," he said, "if we can, we make it; if we can't, we figure out another way to do it." For example, the company brews Little Kings Cream Ale, a brand they bought back in better days. The brew requires a large container of corn syrup. How to get the corn syrup to the brewkettle, which is set up for grain delivery only?

First, shove the container in the Heatin' Hut, an insulation board shack with two space heaters and a fan inside. When the syrup is warm and free-flowing, the crew hoists the container 30-some feet on a forklift, and hooks up a long, curved piece of PVC pipe to the valve—the Hillbilly Syrup Slide. It's goofy-looking, but it works, and the whole thing cost less than $150.

That's the kind of thinking that lets Maerzluft and his crew focus on quality. It's showing in orders: Little Kings is on fire in the Midwest, selling about as fast as the crew can load the trucks. Sales of the cream ale, mostly in green 7-ounce bottles, show as a steep curve on those graphs in the hallway. Wild Goose IPA is showing similar promise as the brand reenters markets that had run dry when the cash ran out.

Daniel is thinking ahead to the day when he has some time and money to play around a little. "I'm toying with the idea of making small runs of big beers under the Brimstone label," he said, "or maybe a Wild Goose barleywine."

That surely doesn't sound like a guy who feels beaten, and I was happy to hear it. I went down to Frederick expecting to talk to people who were waiting for the hammer to fall. I came back home with a bellyful of great beer and a contact high of optimism about this big brewery with all the weird history.

The Pick: Blue Ridge Porter was the first beer at Frederick Brewing that caught my attention, and it's still true today. This is a classic: dark brown tinged with garnet, sweet chocolate malt, dry finish, just the way porter from the original days has been described. It was a grabber then, and it stuck right out of the whole line of Blue Ridge and Wild Goose beers that I sampled today. Overlooked by most; don't be one of them. And don't be too snobbish to shove a case of Little Kings deep in the ice and crack a frosty one. This is great American cream ale: sweet but clean, never cloying. It was a no-strings-attached trip back to my youth.

Opened: Original brewery, mid-1993 on Carroll Street; current brewery, February 1997.

Owners: C. David Snyder and public holdings.

Brewers: Daniel L. Maerzluft, brewmaster; Michael B. Adkins.

System: 50-barrel JV NorthWest system, 60,000 barrels annual capacity.

Production: 23,000 barrels in 2003.

Tours: 1:30 P.M. Saturdays; not available on holiday weekends.

Take-out beer: Six-packs available for sale during tours only.

Special considerations: Handicapped-accessible.

Parking: Plentiful on-site parking.

Lodging in the area: Comfort Inn, 998 West Patrick Street, 301-662-0281; Mainstay Suites, 7310 Executive Way, 301-668-4600; Hampton Inn, 5311 Buckeystown Pike, 301-698-2500; Catoctin Inn,

3619 Buckeystown Pike, Buckeystown 301-874-5555 (www.catoctin inn.com); Inn at Buckeystown, 3521 Buckeystown Pike, Buckeystown, 800-272-1190.

Area attractions: Frederick is awash in Civil War memories, and the sharpest for the town may be the one that is fuzziest in history's lens. "Barbara Fritchie," written by John Greenleaf Whittier in 1866, has been one of the country's favorite poems, the story of defiant old **Barbara Fritchie** shaking the Union flag in the face of Stonewall Jackson's troops: "Shoot if you must, this old gray head, but spare your country's flag." There was some defiance, but what it actually was is unclear; Barbara Fritchie was real, and her restored house (*really* restored; the original house was torn down after the war) is at 154 West Patrick Street (301-698-0630). Her grave is in **Mount Olivet Cemetery** (515 South Market Street, 301-662-1164), along with that of Francis Scott Key and Maryland's first governor, Thomas Johnson. There is also a memorial to unknown Confederate war dead from the nearby Antietam and Monocacy battlefields; the soldiers were buried by sympathetic Union civilians.

The area is surrounded by Civil War battlefields. To the southwest is where the prelude to the Civil War took place: **Harpers Ferry National Historical Park** (304-535-6223) commemorates (among other events) John Brown's raid on the Federal armory to seize weapons for a slave insurrection, which was foiled by the arrival of Lt. Col. Robert E. Lee of the U.S. Army (this was 1859) and a contingent of U.S. Marines. The town is also a spot of great natural beauty, one Thomas Jefferson declared to be worth crossing the Atlantic to see. To the west is **Antietam National Battlefield** (Sharpsburg, 301-432-5124), where the battle that produced the bloodiest day of the Civil War was fought. More than twenty-three thousand men died as the Union forces held against Lee's invading Virginians in 1862. The **Monocacy National Battlefield** (visitors center at 4801 Urbana Pike, which was used as a field hospital during the battle, 301-662-3515) commemorates a July 1864 battle. Confederate general Jubal Early attempted to attack a temporarily undefended Washington but was delayed by Union forces under Lew Wallace (later to gain fame as the author of *Ben Hur*) at Monocacy Junction. Wallace's forces delayed Early long enough for Washington to be reinforced. It was the Confederacy's last offensive.

Frederick itself is known for antique shops and the downtown historic district. Then go see the **Community Bridge,** a bridge that is a work of art. The bridge takes South Market Street over Carroll

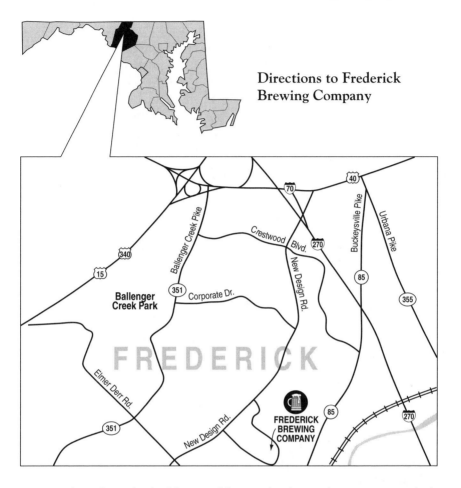

Directions to Frederick
Brewing Company

Creek and just looks like an old stone bridge with some particularly ornate carvings, until you get closer—a *lot* closer—and realize that it's actually a flat concrete span, cleverly painted to look like a stone bridge. The detail is amazing. You can see the bridge from **McCutcheon's Apple Products** (13 South Wisner Street, 800-875-3451), where you can get cider, apples, jams, and other good things.

The **National Shrine of St. Elizabeth Ann Seton** is not far away, in Emmitsburg (333 South Seton Avenue, 301-447-6606). Mother Seton was America's first saint, canonized in 1959. The shrine includes a museum and basilica church, where the saint is interred.

Other area beer sites: *Jennifer's Restaurant* (207 West Patrick Street, 301-662-0373) is a cozy place for a nice meal and a jar of Guinness (and a nip of good Irish whiskey as a nightcap), and it has a good bar, too, with a competent bartender. ***Bushwaller's*** (209 North

Market Street, 301-695-8032) is the more familiar Irish joint in town, a bit more lively than Jennifer's, and surprisingly, you'll usually find some Blue Ridge or Wild Goose beers here as well. **Firestone's** (105 North Market Street, 301-663-0330) has only four beers on draft (usually four really good ones), but has the best bottled beer selection of any bar in Frederick by far; the bartenders are usually happy to talk beer, as well. If you're in the mood for something quite a bit different, try Phil Bowers's other place, **Isabella's Taverna,** on the same side of North Market Street as Brewer's Alley (44 North Market Street, 301-698-8922). Isabella's is a tapas bar, the feast of little dishes that is so fun to do, and Phil's influence ensures that you have good beers to go with it, as well as an exceptional array of Spanish wines. Up the street is **Classic Cigars & British Goodies** (153 North Market Street, 301-682-6666), which is just what it sound like—a shop that only has cigars, HP sauce, and mushy peas, but a great selection of British and Irish beers. You can also get beer to go at **Ye Olde Spirit Shop** (1005 West Seventh Street, 301-662-4803), where you'll find a selection of Belgian, English, and craft-brewed beers, along with more than sixty single malts.

Barley and Hops Grill

5473 Urbana Pike, Frederick, MD 21704
301-668-5555
barleyhop1@aol.com

Pretty basic name, isn't it? If you don't know what to expect walking into a place called Barley and Hops, well, for one thing, you're reading the wrong book!

Look around this place. Some brewpubs hide the brewery in the back or underground; some have it right out in the open, in your face. Put Barley and Hops in the second category: The brewery wraps around a third of the pub, impossible to miss. And it's a beautiful copper-clad Bohemian system, something these Czech systems were always known for, along with the amount of work it takes to keep them clean and polished. But it makes for an appealing old world look of handcraftsmanship. "That's hand-hammered copper on the kettle," brewer Greg Curran told me. "There were over one million strikes just on the dome alone."

Neat little touches like that are all around you at Barley and Hops, though you'll probably need a little help to recognize them. For instance, when you walk in the door, note the hostess's stand: It's a 150-year-old desk from the Beeman Company, a London hops broker. The taps at the bar are Czech-made and notably different. While you're watching your beer pour from them, take a second to look up at the modernistic copper lighting fixture over the bar. It's two of a kind, and the other example is in the pub at Plzensky Prazdoj in Pilsen, the brewers of the famed Pilsner Urquell. The "tapestries" on the walls are another Pilsen link. They're painted hopsacks done by a Pilsen woman, and the only other set in the world hangs in the brewers' tasting room at Plzensky Prazdoj.

This helps explain why a brewpub has Pilsner Urquell on tap as well as their own beers! New brewer Greg Curran is okay with the guest tap; he's confident about his beers, but he admitted that he'd rather see a Mid-Atlantic-brewed beer on there. By the time you read this, he may have done something about that, and he may have done something about his beer board straitjacket as well.

Greg has shaken up this place. The beer board is indicative of why it needed it. A major part of the attraction of a brewpub, after all, is the variability, the nimble nature of an ever-changing lineup of beers. You don't have to do it that way, of course; Mark Thompson's had success with his stripped-down menu of consistently award-winning beers at Starr Hill. But ask most brewpub brewers what they like about their jobs, and near the top of the list is the creative freedom to make beers as it pleases them. Plenty of brewpub customers feel the same way and love coming in to see what's new. That's why the beer boards in most brewpubs are blackboards.

Greg came to Barley and Hops and found a beer board that was written in red paint on wood. Not quite carved in stone, but the next thing to it, complete with ABV, hopping levels, colors, a regular pigeon-hole setup for beer. "I love making big beers," Greg said, "but I toned that down. I'm doing small batches of seasonals and messing around with cask versions."

Beers brewed: Dirty Little Blonde ("DLB"), Annapolis Rocks Pale Ale, Catoctin Clear Kölsch, Tuscarora Red, Big Ben Nut Brown, Schifferstadt Stout. Seasonals: Lust for Lupulin IPA, Pilsner, Winter Warmer (a Belgian strong ale), Jack Stout (Schifferstadt aged in a bourbon barrel), Hefeweizen, Oktoberfest, Doublebock.

The Pick: I dare you to find a flaw in Schifferstadt Stout. It's smooth and smoky, just like an Irish dry stout should be, and goes down more gently than a misty day in Dublin. Does it work great in the Jack Daniel's barrel? If you doubt that, you don't know Jack!

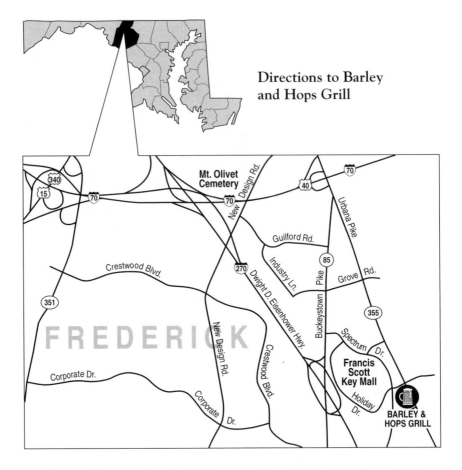

**Directions to Barley
and Hops Grill**

One of those is his Jack Stout, a dose of his Schifferstadt Stout (named for the oldest house in Frederick) that is aged in a Jack Daniel's barrel. These barrel-aged beers are the latest thing in American brewing, and Greg's right on it. His customers love the stuff, and they're always asking when the Jack Stout's going to be on.

"I have some freedom to brew the beers to the people's tastes. It's a reasonably sophisticated clientele here, beerwise," said Greg. "A lot of that's because of the Flying Barrel," a local homebrew store, brew-on-premise, and gathering point for the local homebrew club, the largest in Maryland. Greg credits Bob Frank's influence for supporting the local homebrewers and, through them, the area's beer sophistication. It's certainly not every town this far out in the country that sports four breweries, much less four breweries that get along so well.

If you do come to Barley and Hops, come hungry as well as thirsty. You can start with the Maryland Crab Soup, a house specialty, or the Smokehouse Skins: the usual potato skins, but filled with pulled pork instead of cheese. The New York strip steak is hand-cut daily and was voted Frederick's best. You'll find the beers are food-friendly, too.

Barley and Hops. It's a basic name, and the place sticks pretty close to that basic image of a brewpub: fresh-brewed beer and beer-friendly food. But when you start looking around and realize how much thought about beer went into the place, you'll remember how many different and wonderful beers you can make . . . with just barley and hops.

Opened: October 1999.
Owner: Cluster Spires Brewing Group.
Brewer: Greg Curran.
System: 15-barrel Traditional system, 1,500 barrels annual capacity.
Production: 1,048 barrels in 2003.
Hours: 11 A.M. to 11 P.M., seven days a week.
Tours: Upon request, 11 A.M. to 5 P.M.
Take-out beer: 16-ounce flip-top bottles, half-gallon growlers available; call ahead for kegs.
Food: Barley and Hops was rated as having the best steak in Frederick by a local magazine. I didn't have a steak, but my burger was an excellent piece of beef. It's a good selection of food, and everyone will find something.
Extras: There are plenty of TVs at the bar. Monday is Dollar Draft night.
Special considerations: Kids welcome. Vegetarian meals available. Handicapped-accessible.
Parking: Large on-site lot.

Brewer's Alley

124 North Market Street, Frederick, MD 21702
301-631-0089
www.brewers-alley.com

Brewer's Alley is deeply entwined in the history of Frederick town. The name Brewer's Alley refers to Frederick's brewing history. Located on what is now South Court Street, "Brewer's Alley," like Philadelphia's "Brewery Town," was the brewing center of Frederick for 150 years, taking water from the Carroll Creek. The history ended in 1901, when John Kuhn's brewery burned down, leaving Frederick without a brewery until Frederick Brewing opened on Carroll Street in 1993. Brewer's Alley would pick up the thread as Frederick's first brewpub in July 1996.

The building under the name is historic as well, nothing less than Frederick's first town hall, funded by a citizen lottery. The building was completed in 1769 and served as both the town hall and market house for 104 years, an admirable usage of government offices for essential commerce. Frederick grew up into a real market town in that century, which also saw the terrors of the Civil War as one army after another marched through the town, including, rather famously, Stonewall Jackson's, an 1862 event immortalized in the poem "Barbara Fritchie."

But the building lived on as Frederick's Opera House, and although those days were long past by the time Brewer's Alley came in, Phil Bowers decided to re-create them. Frederick is somewhat famous for tricking the eye into seeing things that aren't there, such as the Community Bridge (see Area Attractions on page 158), and that's what was done here. When you feast your eyes on the Sienna marble columns and ceilings, take a closer look, because they aren't marble. They're the work of Salyer Studio Faux, and they beautifully mimic marble. The stained glass and glass etching in the brewpub are real, however, the work of the Art in Glass Studio.

All pretty neat stuff, and worth looking at, but you're probably wondering, how's the beer? Mighty fine, have no fear. Tom Flores and his assistant, Jen Tonkin, work hard in the brewhouse, and the beer flies out of here. They're edging up against capacity, all because Brewer's Alley is such a popular spot with Frederick's citizens.

Tom had to squeeze out seven minutes to talk to me, but he does find time to make an occasional batch of New Moon Strong Ale. That's one of the things regulars know about, a little reward for being a regular. One keg of New Moon is tapped every new moon. It is, appropriately, a deep, dark brown, full of lots of hops and residual sugars as well, and strong indeed, at 7.7 percent ABV. Don't look for pints of this one; it comes in a tulip glass.

Beers brewed: Year-round: Kölsch (GABF Bronze, 1998), Nut Brown, IPA, Oatmeal Stout. Seasonals: Maibock in the spring, Hefe-Weizen in the summer, Oktoberfest in the fall, Dunkelweizen in the winter. One keg of New Moon Strong Ale is tapped on new moon every month. Owen's Ale (RAF Silver, Best-of-Show Silver, 2001), Smoked Porter, and Wedding Alt were all one-shots, but they may return if capacity is increased.

The Pick: I'm going to settle down with a big glass of that Oatmeal Stout, thank you very much. There's chocolate, malt, nuts, coffee, and some of the elusive alefruit so hard to find in some stouts. Great job, Tom; I'll have another.

Brewer's Alley has an outdoor seating area that I've only ever been able to slip into once, a number of years ago when *Ale Street News* editor Tony Forder and I drove down here to see what the scoop was on Frederick Brewing's huge new facility and their new Hempen Ale. After a long tour and sampling session, we retired to Brewer's Alley to discuss what we'd heard. Tony's smile and English accent charmed us right into the outside area, something I haven't managed before or since. It's very popular, and rightly so: Market Street is busy, tree-lined, and full of pedestrian traffic. The outdoor tables at Brewer's Alley are great for people-watching and sipping a cool one in breezy sunlight.

If you're hungry, you've come to the right place. Phil Bowers is practically a one-man Restaurant Row here in Frederick. Besides Summit Station in Gaithersburg, Bowers also owns Isabella's, up the street, and Acacia, right across from Brewer's Alley. As a local newspaper reporter said, "To say Phil Bowers and his Fountain Rock Management Group have a knack with food is like saying Rumplestiltskin had a way with straw." There's a Cajun flair to the menu: Dig into New Orleans Barbeque Shrimp (heads-on!) or an overstuffed muffuletta with a housemade tapenade, or maybe you'd like to try the Po' Boy Inspiration of the Day. You can always get crab cakes, crab and poblano cheese dip, the smokehouse macaroni and cheese, or a classic cedar-planked salmon. There's also a free Cajun buffet (and $1.50 drafts) on Wednesday nights after 8 P.M.

Whatever you get to eat, pair it with one of Tom's fine beers. The Kölsch is the best-seller, a creamy, malty, lightweight, liter-at-a-time beer. Or take the opposite end of the range, with the busy Oatmeal Stout, a beer with all kinds of good things going on inside. Just be prepared to be disappointed if you get the Hefe-Weizen when you're sitting at the bar. A wheat beer this beautifully fluffy and spicy is going to make you wish you were out there on the sidewalk in the sun enjoying it!

The beer's as skillfully made as the food, to be sure, and the whole is even greater than the sum of the parts. Brewer's Alley feels smooth, settled, well-honed, and in its place. It feels like it's been part of Frederick history for years . . . and in a way, it has.

Opened: July 1996.
Owners: Phil Bowers/Fountain Rock Management Group.
Brewers: Tom Flores, head brewer; Jen Tonkin.
System: 7-barrel DME system, 900 barrels annual capacity.
Production: 850 barrels in 2003.

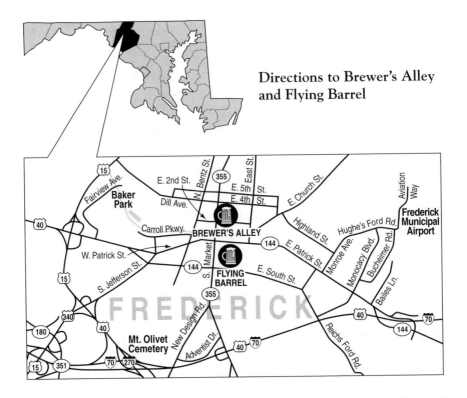

Directions to Brewer's Alley and Flying Barrel

Hours: Monday and Tuesday, 11:30 A.M. to 11:30 P.M.; Wednesday and Thursday, 11:30 A.M. to midnight; Friday and Saturday, 11:30 A.M. to 12:30 A.M.; Sunday, noon to 11:30 P.M.

Tours: By appointment, or impromptu short tours on request.

Take-out beer: 2-liter growlers; call ahead for sixtel and half kegs.

Food: Get that Cajun grub! I found it hard to duck the Po' Boy Inspiration; it's great when a chef gets excited about sandwiches. The smokehouse macaroni and cheese is rib-sticking comfort food; get it with the local ham. The cedar-planked salmon is an unexpected northwestern delight.

Extras: Second-floor banquet facility. Live music on Tuesday nights; call for schedule.

Special considerations: Kids welcome. Vegetarian meals available. Handicapped-accessible.

Parking: Plenty of on-street parking; nearby city parking garage (which is also where you can pay parking tickets . . . enforcement is swift, I'm here to tell you).

Flying Barrel

103 South Carroll Street, Frederick, MD 21701
301-663-4491
www.flyingbarrel.com

By now you've read about a number of Mid-Atlantic brewers, folks who are doing the real work: making the beer. They measure, they mash, they boil, they hop, they strain, they chill, they ferment, they package, and finally, after all their work, you drink.

To be honest, this setup suits me just fine. I enjoy the drinking part quite a bit, and the rest of it looks a lot like real work. But to hobbyists, the joy is in the making, in the effort, in the crafting. Homebrewers do just what you'd expect: They brew beer at home—all the measuring, mashing, boiling, and so on, all the way to the drinking part. Thousands of people do it; it's a big hobby, and many of them make truly good beer.

Beats there a homebrewing heart, however, that does not long to work on the big iron? Many homebrewers see pro brewing systems and think, man, what I could do with that! That's where Bob Frank at the Flying Barrel comes in. Oh, sure, the Flying Barrel's a homebrew shop, and when you walk in the door, you see the usual stuff: 5-gallon glass carboys, cans of malt extract, bins of specialty grains, bottles, caps, and a fridge full of hops and yeast.

But if you walk back into the second room, there's something else to this place. Bob's got his own big iron. Okay, it's *little* big iron, six 15-gallon kettles heated on modified wok burners, but it's more than most homebrewers have. Once you sign up for a session, you have your choice of as wide a range of malts as any pro brewer, from Germany, Belgium, England, Scotland, and America; thirty different hops from almost as many places; the full line of yeasts from WhiteLabs and Wyeast; plus live fresh cultures from Barley and Hops and Brewer's Alley.

Bob could probably get you yeast from Frederick Brewing as well, if you really wanted it. He has a kind of grandfathered arrangement with that brewery. Flying Barrel is located in the old brick building on Carroll Street where Frederick Brew-

Beers brewed: Pretty much anything you'd care to make.

The Pick: No pick here; Bob doesn't make beers for commercial consumption. If you want the best beer from Flying Barrel, you'll have to make it yourself.

ing started out, and Bob was the original treasurer of the company. "They got a lot bigger," he said, "and I wanted to stay small." Which he did, to the benefit of Frederick's homebrewers.

What's not to like? Brew up whatever kind of beer you like, in a 5-, 10-, or 15-gallon batch, throw fresh yeast of whatever type into it, and walk away. Bob cleans up your mess, stores your fermenting wort, and lets you know when it's done. Then you come in and package the beer in 12- or 22-ounce bottles, half-gallon or 2-liter growlers, regular or soda kegs, 5-liter minikegs, "party pig" fridge dispense systems . . . "We don't care what they put it in," said Bob, "as long as it ferments. All our carbonation is secondary fermentation in the package, champagne-style."

Customer service like that is the heart of the Flying Barrel, and has been since 1980, when Bob opened the store. "I took a class in homebrewing from a local adult education program," he said, "and once I started brewing, I saw a need for a homebrew shop."

After retiring from federal service, Bob took up the shop full-time, and he eventually added the brew-on-premise side. "I have no idea why we survived," he said, when I asked him how Flying Barrel survived the winnowing of homebrew shops in the mid-1990s. "Coming from the government, I didn't even realize that it was okay to make a profit!"

Making a profit these days requires a homebrew shop to diversify. Bob's got the stuff to help people make their own wine, at home or in the shop, something that's very popular with retirees. He has cidermaking equipment and instructions, and people can get the raw juice just across the way at McCutcheon's, a major family-owned cider mill.

And if the feds ever decide to make home distilling legal—"Only a matter of time," Bob says cheerfully—he's ready with books, sources for equipment, and some experienced connections. "We have arrangements with McCutcheon's to get corn sugar," Bob said with a modest grin. "And there are these boys from West Virginia who come buy it 300 pounds at a time. I'm pretty sure it's not for making Christmas cookies."

That's what the Flying Barrel is all about: customer service. If you want to make it—and it's legal—Bob and the little big iron are there for you.

Opened: July 1997.
Owner: Bob Frank.
Brewer: You.
System: Six 25-gallon brewkettles and one 15-gallon brewkettle, a SABCO system.
Production: 266 barrels in 2003.

Hours: Monday, Friday, and Saturday, 10 A.M. to 4 P.M.; Tuesday and Thursday, noon to 7 P.M.

Extras: You can make wine on-premises, too. Full homebrewing, cider-making, and home winemaking shop. You may also bring in food and drink for while you're brewing.

Special considerations: No smoking allowed. Well-behaved kids are welcome. Handicapped-accessible.

Parking: Metered street parking; free on Saturdays. Do *not* park off the street by the entrance to the Flying Barrel; it is fifteen-minute parking only.

Clay Pipe Brewing Company

1203 New Windsor Road, Westminster, MD 21157
410-871-9333
www.cpbrewing.com

Why Clay Pipe? I asked Gregg Norris. There didn't seem to be any of the old tavern heritage in Westminster that litters archeological sites in Philadelphia and New York with the remnants of these disposable smoking utensils.

"Well, I used to work for Tuchenhagen, the German brewing engineering firm," Gregg explained. "One of their big claims to fame was completely rebuilding the St. James Gate brewery for Guinness. We were there for a while doing that. One day I was working with the brewery manager, and I saw an old fellow sitting over on a bench, just sitting in the sun and watching everything while he smoked on a clay pipe.

"'Who's that?' I asked the manager. 'Oh, that's our oldest surviving retired brewmaster,' he said. 'He still comes and watches. I think he's making sure we do things right.' I was inspired by that old brewer—so inspired that I knew I had to have my own brewery, to make beer the way I wanted to, the right way," Gregg said.

Wow. I'd heard a lot of "why I did it" stories, but that one was one of the best. Gregg laughed. "No, I tell people that all the time, but it's not true."

What?! "Oh, I always tell them the truth," he said. "My son's name is Clay and my daughter's name is Piper. But that other story sounds a lot better, doesn't it?" Ouch!

His beer's a lot more straightforward, mostly. Blue Tractor Ale is a clean, easy-drinking golden ale that was something for the local market to get behind. "That backfired a little," Gregg admitted. The name was supposed to be a kind of rural joke: There are green John Deeres and red Massey-Fergusons and yellow Cats, but no solid blue tractors. The local farmers and friends of farmers couldn't wait to point that out to Gregg. "They didn't think it was funny at all," he said. "It probably would have been funnier in Manhattan!"

Backfin Pale Ale, on the other hand, was something every Marylander got: It's about crabs. "The Backfin is the tenderloin of the crab," Gregg explained. Marylanders don't need to have that explained: Backfin means the best. Brewed to be an approachable pale ale—"Not a hop bomb," Gregg hastened to explain—Backfin is in the British style, crisp, refreshing, and with a bitter, enticing finish.

Beers brewed: Year-round: Blue Tractor Ale, Backfin Pale Ale, Racers Tire Tread Porter. Seasonals: Nice Weiss, Pursuit of Happiness.

The Pick: Backfin's great and all, really, but the one I want to talk about is the Grand Reserve Porter. Gregg brews this beer for Racers Café, where they call it Tire Tread Porter. I don't care what they call it, so long as they shut up and let me drink it. This is a deep, malty porter, with recognizable hops and that roast-a-roma character brimming over every sip, almost on the edge of being a stout—which porters are, but don't get me started. Worth a trip to Racers, as if you needed convincing.

"It's subtle," Gregg said. "Subtle is very important in beer. It's what makes a good beer a great beer." Backfin is the Clay Pipe beer that's getting the most traction, so it seems to be working. Gregg learned about subtle from a well-respected source. His first brewing job, right out of college, was a job at Anheuser-Busch's pilot brewery in St. Louis. "I never homebrewed," he said. "The first beer I ever made was a märzen on the Anheuser-Busch pilot system."

He was with Anheuser-Busch for six years, then decided that small brewing looked interesting. He designed and set up breweries for Pub Systems. "I learned how to make a lot of different beers," Gregg said. "I learned brewery design, and I set up breweries all over the place. Then the market changed and things got tight, so in 1999, I went to work for Tuchenhagen. Two years later, I decided it was time to take my life in my own hands and build a brewery."

The brewery was up and running in 2002, and though Blue Tractor was out first, "Backfin was what did it," said Gregg. "I wanted to make a drinkable beer that is appealing to a broad segment of the population, distinctive but easy to drink. Backfin is it."

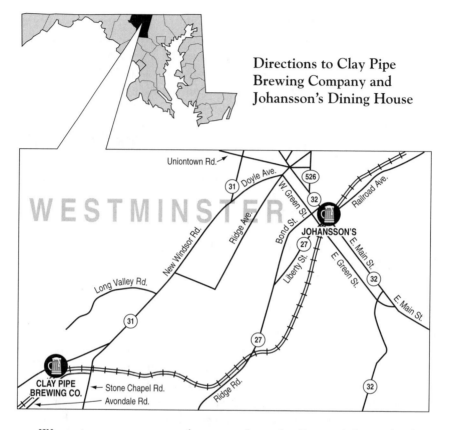

Directions to Clay Pipe Brewing Company and Johansson's Dining House

Westminster may seem a long way from the Bay and the crabs that grace Backfin tap handles. But when you wash down a hot, steamy, spicy crab with a cold glass of this subtle, distinctive beer, you'll see what Gregg means about appealing and drinkable. There's a lot to be said for it.

Opened: March 2002.
Owner: Gregg Norris.
Brewer: Gregg Norris.
System: 15-barrel Pub Brewing system, 3,000 barrels annual capacity.
Production: 500 barrels in 2003.
Tours: Drop-ins welcome; appointments preferred.
Take-out beer: Not available.
Special considerations: Handicapped-accessible.
Parking: Anywhere near the building.
Lodging in the area: Best Western, 451 WMC Drive, 410-857-1900; Westminster Inn, 5 South Center Street, 410-876-2893; Winchester Country Inn, 111 Stoner Avenue, 800-887-3950.

Area attractions: The Baltimore Ravens have their summer training camp in August at McDaniel College, on Railroad Avenue, just north of Johansson's. For camp info, call 410-654-6200 or visit the team website at www.ravens.com, but be aware that tens of thousands of other fans go to see their team practice here.

Union Mills Homestead Museum, north of Westminster (3111 Littlestown Pike, Union Mills, 410-848-2288), was the home of the Shriver family until the mid-1960s, and yes, it's *that* Shriver family, the one that keeps marrying into politics. Their home was the center of a number of businesses based on the water power from Big Pipe Creek. The main gristmill still operates, grinding flour, which is offered for sale. There are a variety of farm-life activities; call for schedules. The mills are open only from May to September.

The *Maryland Wine Festival* is held in September at the *Carroll County Farm Museum* (500 South Center Street, 410-876-2667), though I suppose there are other things to see there as well. Farm things are high on the list, with a barn, farmhouse, and outbuildings, and farm skills of bygone days are demonstrated.

Other area beer sites: *Maggie's Restaurant* (310 East Green Street, 410-876-6868) is a cozy, wood-ceilinged pub with a big malt and bourbon selection that is notably not the usual suspects. They also have Clay Pipe's Backfin on, along with the standard British and Irish beers. Cool place to hang out on an afternoon. If you're really just not happy with the beer scene here, *KClinger's* is not far away, in Hanover, Pennsylvania (304 Poplar Street, 717-633-9197). It is definitely worth the trip for the draft beer selection alone . . . but it also has a great bottled selection *and* top-notch blues acts; call for schedule.

Johansson's Dining House

4 West Main Street, Westminster, MD 21157
410-876-0101

This is a small-town brewpub. Johansson's address is 4 West Main Street; it just doesn't get much more small town than that. The front door and facade are shaded by full-branched, old Zelckova trees on the sidewalk, and just a few doors down are a bike shop and a bakery.

There's also a rail line that runs right through town, roughly parallel to MD Route 27. It crosses town at the middle of Main Street, the tracks shining silver beside the brewpub. Just how close they are isn't obvious till a slow-moving freight train rumbles through town, as they still do. I was back in the brewery with Jeff Warthen one time when it happened, and I literally could have stuck my arm out the window and touched one of the boxcars as they lurched and lumbered northward. Don't worry about missing this if you're in the brewpub; if it happens, you'll know!

The Johansson in Johansson's Dining House is David Johansson, an architectural salvager. He and his wife find old pieces of buildings that are slated for removal or demolition and pull them out for sale to new places that want to look old. There has been a brisk business in antique backbars in the past decade; that kind of wood carving is cheaper to salvage than to commission these days.

As you might expect, Johansson's is rich in such pieces. The bar, for example, with its solid wood and myriad drawers and cubbyholes, is out of an old pharmacy in Gettysburg. I'm not sure where the stuffed double-headed cock pheasant over the bar is from, or its companion piece, the motorized drinking monk. Look up and you'll see another old piece, a long paddle-type fan, tirelessly stirring the air. The dining rooms are all decorated in different styles with more period pieces.

The building itself dates from 1913. It opened as a clothing store and tailor, a tenant that lasted till 1940, then it became a department store. Mall competition put an end to that, and in 1980 it became a restaurant, which it remained for seven years. That's when David Johansson leased the basement and opened it as a sports bar, Champs. After seven years, he decided to stay. So he bought the building and put in the Dining House.

Five years later, he added a brewery while Champs was being redone and renamed it Down Under. "We were always interested in brewing," Johansson said, "and when we put an addition in, the brewery fit, so we went for it. Down Under now holds the Grundies [the brewery's fermenters], a grill, a dance floor, and seats for 200; upstairs has elegant but casual dining for about 230."

Rolfe Saunders, a kind of itinerant brewer who's been around the Mid-Atlantic area, opened things up at Johansson's in November 1998. Then Jeff Warthen, an Oxford Brewing alumnus, took over and has

Beers brewed: Year-round: Hoodlehead Pale Ale, Whistle Stop Amber, Honest Ale. Seasonals vary greatly and are rarely repeated.

The Pick: The Hoodlehead Pale Ale was named for a term of affection Dave Johansson used for his children: "You little hoodleheads!" he would call them. Hoodlehead is a golden beer with a bright white head, flavorful and estery, and whackingly bitter. To be truthful, it left my gums a bit numb. Bracing stuff.

been brewing ever since. He started out with a pretty basic brewpub lineup—golden, amber, pale ale, stout—but things have progressed from there.

Maryland once was famous for its rye whiskey, and a bottle of real rye whiskey, like Pikesville or Beam or Wild Turkey, is still (or should be) standard equipment on most Maryland bars. Jeff's done rye beers pretty regularly, including one he called Sherwood #12, named for a big rye whiskey distiller that used to be across the street from where the brewpub sits. "People asked me, 'Rye in beer?'" Jeff recalled. "I told 'em, you've been drinking rye in your whiskey for hundreds of years; it's time to get some in your beer!"

Jeff also does some big beers. I hunkered down at that big wood bar and sipped Strong Ale, a malty dessert with the power to keep me in my seat. Brewpub insiders know to keep an eye out for notice of a release of Holy Water, Jeff's strong Belgian-style ale; they also know to start campaigning for him to brew it in the summer.

David Johansson is at it again, building another bar, or restaurant, or dance hall, across the little square from the brewpub. It wasn't clear what the place was going to become when I stopped in a couple weeks ago; he seemed to be leaning toward an Irish-themed pub, but that was just the latest notion, nothing was certain. I'm sure it's going to look great inside, with plenty of neat old fixtures.

But if you want fresh-brewed brewpub beer, you'll want to be at the corner of Main Street and Railroad Avenue, parked at the big bar from the old pharmacy, under the paddle fan. I'll see you there.

Opened: Restaurant in 1996; brewery November 1998.
Owner: David Johansson.
Brewer: Jeff Warthen.
System: 7-barrel DME system, 1,500 barrels annual capacity.
Production: 500 barrels in 2003.
Hours: 11 A.M. to 1 A.M., seven days a week. No alcohol served on Sundays until noon.
Tours: By appointment, or upon request if brewer is in.
Take-out beer: Carroll County does not allow take-out of brewed-on-premises beer.
Food: Blue Crab takes pride of place on the menu; you are in Maryland, after all. Fresh seafood is delivered daily: crab, shrimp, scallops, salmon, a variety of fresh fish for daily specials, and some not-so-everyday things, like conch fritters and escargot (are they seafood or what?). Carnivores will enjoy the "turf" side of the menu, with its

filet, New York strip steaks, prime rib, and veal cutlets. Round that out with some imaginative sandwich combinations and a traditional ploughman's lunch. There are some vegetarian dishes, and the chefs will happily accommodate vegetarian requests.

Extras: Two real dart boards. Live music Friday and Saturday nights; no cover. Happy hour Monday through Friday, 3 P.M. to 7 P.M.

Special considerations: Kids welcome, but state law prohibits anyone under twenty-one from sitting at the bar. Vegetarian meals available.

Parking: Metered street parking (50¢ an hour from 8 A.M. to 5 P.M.) and town parking lot.

Uncle Tucker's

12901 Ali Gahn Road, Cumberland, MD 21502
301-777-7232
www.edmasons.com

Travelers' tales often mention wayhouses, friendly inns along the ancient trails that offered sustenance and shelter to the weary sojourner, safety in the wilderness, and a small amount of joy on a lonely road. They may be monasteries in the Brenner Pass in the Alps, caravanserais along the Great Silk Road, country inns in the Appalachians, or brewpubs along I-68. That's where you'll find Uncle Tucker's, along with your host, Ed Mason, a classic master of the house who has retired from greater responsibilities.

I've listed the usual suspects for brewpub owners before: investment banker, stockbroker, plumber, chef, developer, contractor, serial restaurateur, and a host of others. I've never before run across an active brewpub owner who was a senior politician, and Ed Mason was certainly all of that. Ed was the minority leader in the Maryland Senate, and mementos and pictures of his political career are scattered through J. B.'s Steakhouse, the upstairs part of the brewpub.

What's he doing in a brewpub? "I was in politics for twenty years," Ed said with an owlish grin. "I finally stepped on enough toes that I had more enemies than friends." So he retired to this property, which was kind of in the family.

Ed told me some of the early history of the place. The original structure was built in 1819 by Jacob Hoblitzel as a home and tavern, facing south on the Baltimore Pike, a private road from Baltimore to Cumberland. The National Road, the first federal road to the west, began up the pike in Cumberland, and the pike ran right into it. Traffic was good. But Hoblitzel died suddenly, and the land reverted to the original owner, a Revolutionary War veteran named Colonel Lemar. Lemar turned the property into a farm, worked by slaves.

Ed's father-in-law bought the property in the 1940s and changed the frontage of the home, putting the front door on the north side, which explains why the main staircase faces away from the door. Like Hoblitzel, he died intestate, and his son wound up with the property. Ed bought it from him in 1997.

"The first thing we did was to convert the cellar to Uncle Tucker's Pizza Cellar," said Ed. It wasn't as easy as that, though. There's not a square corner in the place, and no level floors! They persevered, building a stone open-fire pizza oven (it produces an excellent pizza; try the Con Funghi) and an unusual brick bar. They also added heat and air-conditioning for the first time in the house's history.

The pizza cellar opened in December 1997. Shortly after that, Ed and his son went to a restaurant convention in Chicago and got the idea of adding a brewpub. They cleared out the old laundry, an outbuilding connected to the house over the downstairs entrance to the pizza cellar. They had it up and running in June 1999. The steakhouse came next, with remodeling beginning in 2000. "We were aiming for an old tavern look," said Ed, and with the house's natural older layout, cut up into small rooms, it works quite well. The stained glass and old bricks you'll see in the upstairs barroom came out of a local monastery that was being demolished. The steaks went on the grill, and Ed was fully in business.

I was frankly concerned about Uncle Tucker's ability to sell enough beer to stay in business out here in the wide open spaces between Hagerstown and Cumberland; there's not much here for local traffic, and I was hard-pressed to conceive of a reason for travelers to hop off I-68. Ed surprised me with the news that most of the business is local.

Beers brewed: Year-round: Golden Ale, Scottish Ale, Pale Ale, Barleywine-style Ale. Seasonals: Irish Dry Stout, Oatmeal Stout, California Golden, Pilsner, Creekside Amber Ale, Scotch Chocolate Ale, Mudguppy Porter, and more.

The Pick: Ryan's Pale Ale was fruity, hoppy, and a bit busy, a bouncing puppy of a beer that seemed happy to see me. I was pretty happy to see it, too, and paid it the compliment of having another. And that biker was right: the Oatmeal Stout was really good. I couldn't wait to try it after watching him enjoy it so thoroughly!

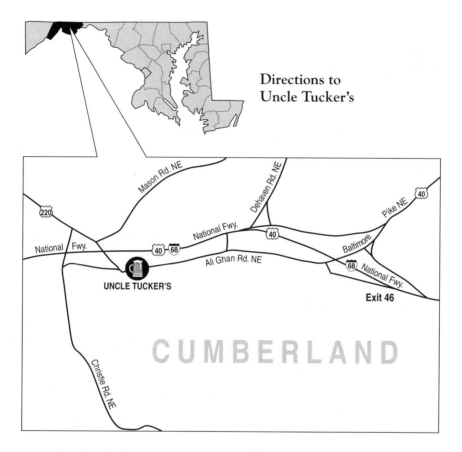

Directions to Uncle Tucker's

"We're close to Pennsylvania and West Virginia," he said, "and we do a very good business on the patio bar from May to October. The beer does okay. If you do the right volume, you can make money on it."

Brewer Ryan Miller certainly has his fans. I'll never forget my first visit to Uncle Tucker's. My dad and I stopped in on our way out to the Kentucky Bourbon Festival, weary travelers looking for simple fare of pizza and beer. As we were ordering our pizza, a big fella walked in, black shades, black hair, black leathers, black boots, and walked up to the bar. "Is the Oatmeal Stout on yet?" he asked. Assured that it was, finally, on, he ordered 2 pints. When they arrived, he put the first one up to his lips and smoothly drank the whole thing down.

"Damn," he said with real feeling, apparently speaking wholly to himself. "I've really been wantin' that." Then he picked up the second one and began to work on it more slowly.

Pretty good testimonial for a brewpub, from an obvious traveler, just off the road, still in his riding gear.

Opened: June 1999.

Owner: Ed Mason.

Brewer: Ryan Miller.

System: 7-barrel Century system, 125 barrels annual capacity.

Production: 120 barrels in 2003.

Hours: 11 A.M. to 2 A.M., seven days a week.

Tours: On request, subject to brewer availability.

Take-out beer: Growlers available.

Food: The pizza down in Uncle Tucker's is oddly shaped, kind of oblong, but quite tasty, especially the mushroom pie. The steaks upstairs smelled fantastic, and if I'd had more time—and gut room—I'd have tied into one.

Extras: Uncle Tucker's has an outdoor bar and deck overlooking Evitts Creek that is very popular in warm weather.

Special considerations: Kids welcome. Some vegetarian meals available. Handicapped-accessible.

Parking: Large off-street lot.

Lodging in the area: The Inn at Folck's Mill (301-777-7758) is part of the cluster of Ed Mason's businesses right there at the brewpub. Holiday Inn, 100 South George Street, 301-724-8800; Inn at Walnut Bottom, 120 Greene Street, 301-784-8400; Rocky Gap Lodge and Golf Resort, 16701 Lakeview Road, 800-724-0828; The Castle, MD Route 36, Mount Savage, call for directions, 301-264-4645.

Area attractions: The **Chesapeake and Ohio Canal National Historical Park** (301-724-3655) has its western terminus here in Cumberland, right where I-68 crosses the Potomac, along Mechanic Street at **Canal Place.** That's where you'll find a number of attractions, like the **Transportation and Industrial Museum** (301-777-5905), with displays on Cumberland's strong industrial past, including its breweries, and the **Western Maryland Scenic Railroad** (800-TRAIN-50), an excursion line down to Oakland that is very popular during fall foliage season. You can also ask for information on a self-guided tour of Cumberland's Victorian district at the Allegany County Visitors Bureau at Canal Place. Take a drive west on U.S. Route 40 A, the old National Road. It's quite a scenic drive, especially in the Narrows, a twisting pass through the mountains. That will take you to Frostburg, where you'll find **Thrasher's Carriage Museum** (Depot Street, directly across from the Western Maryland Scenic Railroad station, 301-689-3380), featuring a collection of fifty carriages, wagons, and sleighs, including the inaugural carriage used by Theodore Roosevelt.

Other area beer sites: The ***Schmankerl Stube*** (58 South Potomac Street, Hagerstown, 301-797-3354) is a well-known stop in these parts for German beer garden atmosphere, draft German beer, and *schmankerl* (roughly meaning "comfort food"), the rich, meaty, cheesy snacks the Germans love so well. You're also less than an hour from a hot new brewpub in Pennsylvania, ***Marzoni's Brick Oven and Brewery*** (170 Patchway Road, Duncansville, 814-695-1300), an easy drive north on U.S. Route 220 and I-99 that will net you a surprising array of good beers.

Deep Creek Brewing Company

75 Visitor Center Drive, McHenry, MD 21541
301-387-2182
www.deepcreekbrewing.com

It's winter at Deep Creek. The leaves are gone from the trees, cold winds blow through the valley, and Deep Creek Lake is frozen over. The slopes across the valley at Wisp are busy with skiers, and at night the lights on the snow glitter and sparkle as the skiers throw up clouds of tiny ice crystals. It's cold outside, but it's warm inside the brewpub, and the fireplace in the club room is roaring, a great place to enjoy a glass of malty, heavy Glen Garrett Scottish Ale. "When that fireplace is going," brewer Jason Weissberg said, "those couches in there are the best place to be."

Deep Creek Brewing is a solid lodge, rustic and welcoming. The black bear logo is everywhere; the bears "symbolize the true strength and character of the county," according to the brewery's website. Black bears? Mountain lodges? Skiing? Are we still in Maryland?

Western Maryland can be surprising to someone who's never been here. Baltimore and the Eastern Shore and even the farmland around Frederick get so much attention that people forget that there's a

Beers brewed: Year-round: Deep Creek Gold, White Dog Wheat, Holy Cow Pale Ale, Youghiogheny Red, Angry Clown Brown, Storm Peak Stout. Seasonals: Dunkelweizen, Altbier, Common, Porter, Scottish Ale.

large part of the state out past the pinched-up neck at Hancock. It's a land of ridges and cold winters, of rural meadows and old towns that haven't changed much with the passing of decades. While the rest of the state may be about commuting or sailing or crabs, out here it's about hunting, outdoor tourism, and . . . well, actually, they like crabs out here, too. Who wouldn't?

The Pick: Holy Cow IPA has a light body, but not a thin body, a distinction with an important difference. This beer slips and slides around in your mouth like hoppy spring water, light and flavorful, aromatic and estery. If it's a cow, it's a cow in tap shoes that can dance on eggshells. I could happily drink this all afternoon.

"Deep Creek is similar to some of the places I've lived, like western North Carolina," said Jason, who, like many of the young men drawn to the business, has been a bit footloose while pursuing his brewing muse. "There's the mountain biking, fishing, all the stuff you can do on state wilderness lands. It's a great little mountain town. They have four real seasons, even if summer is the shortest one. It's a real great place to live if you like the outdoors. The lake's great, the golf's great. You have the creature comforts, but you only have a weekly paper, which is kind of good in its own way, only having to read the paper once a week to get caught up!"

It's summer at Deep Creek. The hills are a lush green, thick with trees, and the grass surrounding the lake is a fresh Irish green. Boats are buzzing around the lake: speedboats, houseboats, pontoon-built "party barges," jet skis, sailboats. The deck is sunny and hot by day, all about cold beer and sunglasses. By night, the firepit glows, casting its flickering orange-yellow light on people in the cooling air with pints of Red Head Rye and Deep Creek Gold.

You can get the Deep Creek Gold to go, or at stores for about 50 miles around. Jason bottles the Gold and the Youghiogheny Red (it's "YOGCK-uh-HAY-nee," and that's the best I can do for you) in 12-ounce bottles right there at the brewery. That's how Deep Creek got started, as a contract-brewed brand, having their Deep Creek Gold and Youghiogheny Red brewed down at Frederick Brewing in 1996. Then they opened a small pub down the road, closer to Oakland, in April 1999.

This new, impressive brewpub opened in the summer of 2000; the deck and the big club room, with its stuffed black bear and overstuffed armchairs around the big fireplace, were added in 2003. It's a great place to settle in with a view of the lake through those big windows (especially if it gets too stinking hot to go outside unless you're a summer masochist) and order some lunch. Start with some crab dip or stuffed roasted red peppers, then maybe a pannini with roasted vegetables or a tangily sauced gyro, paired with a brisk glass of Holy Cow IPA.

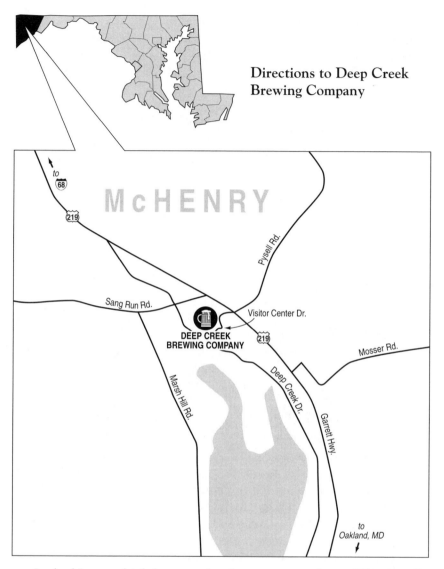

Directions to Deep Creek Brewing Company

I asked Jason which beer was his favorite one to brew. "They're all a ton of fun to brew," he said. "This Czech system's fantastic, great fun to brew on. I am partial to our pale ale. It's got a nice, citrusy nose and a smooth bitterness. The Angry Clown Brown is a bit different from most brown ales; it's an American style with a nice charge of American hops to finish it off drier, crisper, than an English brown."

It's autumn at Deep Creek. The hills are deep in the midst of the color change, and it is intense, bursts of yellow and red, bright colors moving gently in breezes that are still mild. The year is coming around to winter, but the trees have one last, glorious gift. The sunset over the ridge is giving the trees serious competition in the color contest, stirring the sky with long purple and dusky blue streaks of cloud. The firepit puts off enough heat to keep the deck pleasant, and it's time for a reflective jar of Storm Peak Stout at the end of the day.

It's great out here in western Maryland. The landscape is big and inspiring. The sky is high and blue. The newspaper, I hear, is weekly. The beer's cold, and the steaks are hot and juicy. And if you were wondering about spring, well, it's kind of muddy. Which makes it a great time to tear into a couple pints of Deep Creek Gold and a big plate of slow-roasted Grecian Lamb with the piquant sauce they use here at Deep Creek.

Opened: November 1996.

Owners: Gregg and Sherri Mortimer.

Brewer: Jason Weissberg.

System: 10-barrel Traditional Brewing system, 1,200 barrels annual capacity.

Production: 329 barrels in 2003.

Hours: Monday through Saturday, 11:30 A.M. to 10 P.M.; Sunday, 10 A.M. to 10 P.M. Open later on weekends if business allows.

Tours: Monday through Saturday, 11:30 A.M. to 4 P.M., as requested; or by appointment.

Take-out beer: Six-packs, cases, growlers, kegs.

Food: Even here on the far side of the Blue Ridge, Marylanders want seafood, and the menu offers crab dip, crab cakes, mussels Provençal, shrimp imperial . . . But there's an interesting Greek influence as well: Try the Grecian Lamb Pannini (one of five such toothsome grilled sandwiches on the menu) or Scallops Grecian style. Some nice steaks are also available, and there's a big Sunday brunch. Vegetarians will enjoy the salads and vegetable sandwiches.

Extras: Deck with fire pit and great view of ski slopes and lake. Sports TVs always on in bar. Fireplaces. Occasional live music; call for schedule.

Special considerations: Kids welcome. Vegetarian foods available. Handicapped-accessible.

Parking: Free on-site parking.

Lodging in the area: Wisp Mountain Resort, 290 Marsh Hill Road, McHenry, 301-387-5581; Comfort Inn, 2704 Deep Creek Drive, McHenry, 301-387-4200; Innlet Motor Lodge, 2001 Deep Creek Drive, McHenry, 800-540-0763.

Area attractions: Garrett County is covered with state parks, including **Deep Creek Lake State Park** (898 State Park Road, Swanton, 301-387-5563), which offers fishing, boating, swimming, camping, and hiking trails. If fly fishing is more your passion, hook up with **Around the Bend Troutfitters** (800-477-3723) for a guided trip to the area's hot spots. If you'd like to learn fly fishing, **Streams and Dreams** (301-3-TROUT-1) offers lessons and lodging on the Youghiogheny. There are a number of boat rental places around the lake; ask at the brewpub. Deep Creek is a large lake; what you see from the brewpub is just the tip. You can also see the **Wisp Ski Area Resort** across the lake from the brewpub (290 Marsh Hill Road, 800-462-WISP). There are twenty-three slopes at Wisp, and believe it or not, a lot of the snow is natural. The mountains make for an enclave of heavy snow here in western Maryland; winters with more than two hundred inches are not uncommon. Whitewater rafting on Youghiogheny River is a favorite and well-known recreation in the area. Two outfitters in nearby Ohiopyle, Pennsylvania, can get you soaking wet in style: **Mountain Streams** (800-723-8669) and **White Water Adventurers** (800-WWA-RAFT). Remember: Beer and white water *do not mix.* Save the drinking till after the ride, because outfitters simply will not take you on the river if you have been drinking. You can certainly drink at the brewpub's **Annual Western Maryland Bikes, Brews, and Blues Fest;** call the brewpub for details on this fall festival.

Other area beer sites: The **Mighty Oaks Pub** at Oakland Golf Course (433 North Bradley Lane, 301-387-4343) was started up by two guys who used to be at Deep Creek. They intended to start a brewpub, but for now they're having beers brewed for them at Old Dominion—pretty good beers, too. The place itself isn't much: a padded bar in a low-ceilinged basement room with a big-screen TV. But it's the best beer you'll get in Oakland. You can also take a short trip to Morgantown, West Virginia, to try the acclaimed beers at the **West Virginia Brewing Co.** (1291 University Avenue, 304-296-BREW); I was next to these guys at a beer festival a couple years ago, and the beers are definitely worth the detour.

A word about . . .

Bars

Sometimes the pint is not the point. I've been collecting great bars for more than twenty years, and that's one thing I've learned. There are more bars all the time that have a good selection of beer. But not all of them are great bars, because it takes more than beer to make a bar, a tavern, a saloon, a joint. Beer is a social drink, and you've got to have that socializing for a great bar.

I don't like nightclubs and big chain bars. The Nazis had a slogan, *Kraft durch Freude* ("strength through joy"), which referred to the nightclubs where soldiers and sailors were sent with orders to have a good time. All too often I get that same feeling of enforced enjoyment at nightclubs. It's all about selling the next beer and shoving you off the stool to make room for the next big tipper.

But it's not always about twenty taps and great hops bouquet, either. There's a bar on Capitol Hill, the **Tune Inn** (3331½ Pennsylvania Avenue SE, 202-543-2725), where the beer selection's nothing, the jukebox is full of Hank Williams Sr., and stuffed deer hindquarters are mounted over the restroom doors to identify the gender. Get a two-buck fried-egg sandwich and a ration of abuse from your waitress. She's not snarly because that's the "theme" here; she's working a long shift, putting up with legislative assistants all day, and now she's got to deal with *you*?

I try to get here every time I go to Washington. It's a great "bar bar," as a now-defunct group called the Bar Tourists used to describe them. What is it? I don't know, but I feel it. I feel like part of life when I'm there. I can feel the vibe, and it says "reality." There's no pretension here.

I like places like Mahaffey's Pub and Growlers in Baltimore, where the people that run the places are really jazzed about beer, they're nuts about it. They really care about what they're selling. That comes through—the staff get it, and they care about the beer, too, sometimes fiercely. Wayne Mahaffey called Tom Cizauskas, the beer representative that had gotten him started on transforming his corner bar into a beer bar, and shouted, "I did it, Tom! I got rid of Miller Lite! It's the last one; now it's all great beer!" He was as excited as if he'd won an Olympic medal. Wayne gets it.

I like bars like McGarvey's, in Annapolis, where they don't care at all about the beer, as long as it's cold, it's selling, and the lines are clean.

They're more concerned about making sure you've got what you want, that you're having a good time, that the food's hot and on time. That comes through as well, and the staff at McGarvey's make a game of it and have a blast.

I like places like the Gravity Lounge in Charlottesville, where they're doing something really different, a bookstore that's a constant performance space, and the beer is good enough to be part of that. It's a place that's not prissed out about drinking, but it doesn't focus on the drinking either, and that's a valuable part of the mix that some bars never do get.

I like places like Max's on Broadway. Max's is all about getting the most great beers on tap and getting them to the people who want them. That's all, and they're great at it, and that's cool.

So just what is it that makes a great bar? It's hard to say. Good beer is part of it, and I don't mean this IPA or that helles, I mean fresh beer served through clean lines into a clean glass (and not a frosted one, *please!*). But it's also about bartenders that see you, not through you, and who keep things moving without losing their personality. It's about a look that didn't come out of a box that someone else will open in another town six months later. There's enough light to see the person you're talking to, and not so much volume on the sound system that you can't hear the conversation. The regulars are good people, and you can feel like a regular quickly. The beer and the food (and there doesn't even have to be food) are reasonably priced and well presented. And even when it's full, everything still feels right.

It's not that tough to do it. As I wrote that last paragraph, I was smiling to myself, thinking yeah, like RFD and The Reef, like Racers Café and Sean Bolan's, like Capital Ale House, and the Brickhouse Run, like Cogan's Instant Art Bar, like . . . There are plenty of great bars.

And sometimes it's something very personal. My old college roommate, Dave Nalle, lived around the corner from the Brickskeller and took me there when I was first getting excited about beer. I was awestruck. These people were living my dream. When I moved to the area, I went to the monthly tastings at the Brick religiously, and I learned a lot about beer from Bob Tupper, the Brick's resident beer instructor. I met Dick Yuengling there on his very first public-speaking appearance and got him to sign a Porter bottle. I ate mussels with the Belgian ambassador there. I saw Michael Jackson there. Later, whenever I visited the area, I went to the Brick to touch those roots again. One night I was with a gang of librarians who teamed up with a bachelor party to sing songs from *The Student Prince*, and we made the walls ring. And in 2002, I was the guy up on the little stage of beer, hosting a Smithsonian-sponsored panel discussion of the future of regional breweries. I'd come full circle, and the Brick was an intrinsic part of my journey. There will never be another bar like that for me.

Sometimes it's about great beer. But it always tastes better in a great bar.

Blue Ridge

The Blue Ridge is the detached front of the Appalachians. Slip behind it—and there aren't many easy ways, short of heading up to Front Royal and going around the northern end—and you find the Shenandoah Valley, a broad, fertile area that was the breadbasket of Virginia for years, and still is. Orchards, poultry farms, vineyards—the harvest is varied and large.

The harvest was blood and death during much of the Civil War. The Shenandoah was some of the richest farm country in the Confederacy, and the Blue Ridge was a perfect screen for troop movements that could suddenly cross the ridge and be only two days' march from Washington . . . or Richmond. This was a strategic target for both sides, though for the Confederacy to lose it would mean a much greater loss than for the Union.

Stonewall Jackson defended the Valley for much of the early part of the war, and his Valley Campaign was a classic of maneuver. The Valley was safe until 1864, when Lincoln realized the need for a knockout punch to end the war. Sherman marched through Georgia; Grant sent Phil Sheridan into the Valley with forty thousand men with orders to burn and wreck everything he saw, so thoroughly "that crows flying over it for the balance of the season will have to carry their provender with them." Sheridan carried out the orders in a businesslike trail of fire and destruction that was known in the Valley for years as "the Burning." The Confederacy would collapse in a few short months.

The Valley recovered, as farmers always do—because they have no choice—and once again became Virginia's breadbasket. Farm markets hug every medium-size town in the Valley, farm stands dot the roads, and the scent of apple blossoms in the spring can make you dizzy. War truly *is* hell, but the Valley has come out the other side.

Harrisonburg and Staunton are the brewery towns in the Valley. Harrisonburg is still a quiet town, with a deep vein of artistic and cultural richness flowing from James Madison University. Staunton is almost unique in the Valley, a town largely untouched by the Civil War, not destroyed in "the Burning," and so home to five separate National Historic Districts of historically significant homes and buildings. Good thing Phil missed this one.

Above the Valley is the Shenandoah National Park, 300 square miles of landscape, the high heart of the Blue Ridge, lined down the middle by the Skyline Drive. Pollution has dimmed the views in the summer, but the drive is still intensely gorgeous—and much more enjoyable during the week. The park is also home to a section of the Appalachian Trail (info on this section is available at www.patc.org) and hundreds of miles of other hiking trails. Milepost 51 marks Big Meadows, a large clearing with a visitors center, facilities, frequent deer herds, and a very relaxing atmosphere.

Down in the jumbled hills just east of the Blue Ridge is where you'll find Charlottesville, Thomas Jefferson's beloved home. The town is still fairly small, though an ugly commercial sprawl is developing up U.S. Route 29 that I don't recall from previous visits. The pedestrian mall down West Main Street is a step toward regaining and retaining that small-town feel, and it has been quite successful, more so than similar steps have been in other towns. Just one small quibble: I wish the truncated side streets had been more clearly marked as dead ends for the visiting beer writer!

Charlottesville is home to Jefferson's equally beloved University of Virginia. I've known several UVA graduates, and the loyalty they feel toward their school, as well as the natural feeling of the superiority of the education they gained there compared with any other, is deep and honest. Jefferson seemed to feel the same way, placing his role in creating UVA on his tombstone with what he felt were equally important accomplishments: "Here was buried Thomas Jefferson, author of the Declaration of Independence, of the Virginia Statute of Religious Freedom, and father of the University of Virginia." Proud parent.

The beer in this region is almost all from brewpubs; tiny Queen City plans commercial production along with its brew-on-premise output, and the medal-bedecked Starr Hill is looking to break out of central Virginia with a bigger facility. Starr Hill and South Street present an interesting study in opposing philosophies: beer minimalism vs. beer liberalism. Calhoun's is all about drinkable, interesting beer with top-notch casual food. And Kegler's, for now, is about getting back into brewing again before the pin-setting machines break down.

That's life on the Ridge, over in the Valley, and down in Charlottesville. It's a gorgeous piece of Virginia—of America—and it's a blessing to be at peace there.

Calhoun's Restaurant and Brewery

41 Court Square, Harrisonburg, VA 22801
540-434-8777
www.calhounsbrewing.com

When I start working on these books, the first thing I do is send out a questionnaire to all the breweries, asking for all the obvious information—website, owners, founding date, brewhouse data, hours—and the not so obvious, the questions about nearby lodgings, attractions, and great local bars. Most people get it, but some of the questionnaires fall into the hands of marketers who get the bright idea of telling me there are *no* other local watering holes worth visiting, as if that will curb my curiosity to the point that I'll write, "Oh, and don't bother looking for other places to drink, just stay at the Fullabeer Brewpub and spend your money." As if.

So I was somewhat surprised when I got the questionnaire back from Eric Plowman at Calhoun's with the notation "N/A" for that question. Harrisonburg is a college town, after all, and though students aren't generally known for spending their money on upscale beers, preferring to go for quantity over quality, the faculty usually supports such places. Yet I couldn't imagine that Eric was attempting to pull the wool over my eyes; he is one of the most plainly honest persons I've ever met in this business, open and transparent almost to a fault.

When I got to Harrisonburg, my faith in Eric's honesty was vindicated; there just aren't that many places to drink in this town! There's Calhoun's, of course, and there's a funky little place called The Little Grill Collective, which has pitchers of Old Dominion Black & Tan at the same price as pitch-

Beers brewed: Calhoun's does not have year-round beers, as such. They have a series of beers that come on as Eric brews them: Smokin' Scottish, Plowman Porter, Golden Light, Downtown Amber, Honey Blonde Ale, Bad Dog ESB, Hefe-Weizen, Bombay India Pale Ale, Kölsch, Czech Pils, Oatmeal Stout.

ers of carrot juice, but that's really about it except for a few definitively student swill troughs. That's about when it hit me: Eastern Mennonite University is in Harrisonburg, and they're generally not big drinkers. The James Madison University students are evidently satisfied with what they have access to (and also agree with the Mennonite students that there's a lot to be said for the great ice cream at Kline's Dairy Bar).

Calhoun's, therefore, pretty much has the "better beer" gig in Harrisonburg all to itself, and that works out well for everyone involved. When the weather's warm—and it does get warm here, I can tell you—the pub's patio seating balloons its capacity to over 300, and Eric can make enough beer to keep everyone happy. The quality of the beer keeps people happy, too; when beer lovers found out I was headed for Calhoun's, the most common reaction was "Get the Smokin' Scottish!"

The Pick: I'm not sure how often Eric makes it, but he had a Czech Pilsner on that was beautifully suited to his style of brewing. It was briskly bitter from start to finish, clean as a whistle, and a dead-on ringer for the lagers of Bohemia. Just the thing for lounging on the patio when it's really just a little bit too hot to be out there but you can't bear to stop watching the action on Court Square. Otherwise, you can't go wrong with the Smokin' Scottish or the crisp, solid Bombay India Pale Ale.

That's a mainstay beer here at Calhoun's, proving that brewpub crowds can always surprise you. Oh, the lighter beers are usually the most popular, but a lot of brewpub brewers will tell me of odd beers that somehow strike their customers' fancy. Often it's a spiced pumpkin beer. At the Porter House near my home in Pennsylvania, the locals demanded that the 8 percent Belgian-style Triple become a regular tap, and at Calhoun's, it's this malty ale touched with a distinctive smoky flavor. Most people try beers made with smoked malt and may charitably say, "Well, that's . . . different," but these brave Virginians made the Smokin' Scottish a favorite. Maybe it's the popularity of barbecue in Harrisonburg.

Whatever the reason, if they like it, that means it will be there for them. "What I brew is very demand-oriented," said Eric. "I brew the brewpub standards: one or two lighter beers, something dark, something hoppy. And the Smokin' Scottish. It is fun to experiment, though. That's the fun thing about a brewpub."

Eric grins a lot—even the day I visited for the book, which was the day after a big beer dinner at the pub at which Taylor Smack from South Street brewpub in Charlottesville had joined the fun, fun that wound up in the brewery cold room at 2 A.M., thoroughly sampling Eric's new IPA. But Eric kept smiling, and his sunny exterior could fool you into thinking he's more in this game for the fun of it, not the heavy brewing side of it.

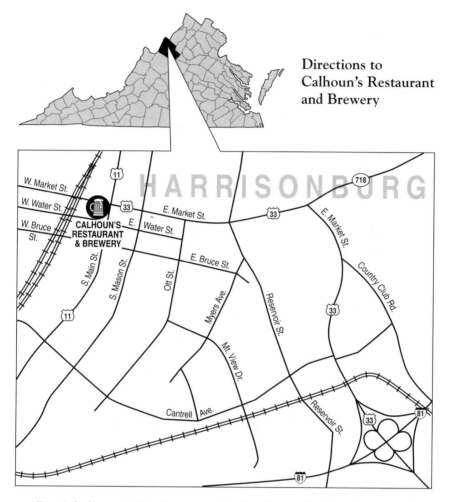

Don't believe it. Eric keeps an absolutely spotless brewhouse: "I like it clean," he said. He is Siebel-trained, and I've seen him go toe-to-toe with some of the most technical brewers in Virginia and more than hold his own with talk of fermentation regimens and oxygen uptake. His beers are beautifully clean, clearly representative of style, and absolutely dialed in on consistency.

You've got a big, airy place to enjoy them in, too. Calhoun's manages to look summery inside even when it's gray outside, with its high ceilings and big windows, and plenty of potted plants. In warm weather, the people-watching out on Court Square is great entertainment: attractive students in their summer clothes, confused tourists like me, and circling traffic cops looking for parking offenders. All free, and you can have a cold, clean beer while you watch.

I can remember spending a long weekend in Harrisonburg back in the early 1990s, before Calhoun's opened. It was hot, in the high 90s, and we were staying with my brother-in-law in his un-air-conditioned apartment. We literally drank every bottle of better beer in Harrisonburg that weekend (there weren't any good bars then, either), and ran out with a day and a half to go. If only Eric had opened Calhoun's a few years earlier, we could have enjoyed Smokin' Scottish in cool splendor. Don't miss the opportunity today brings you.

Opened: June 1998.

Owners: Eric Plowman, Mike Comfort.

Brewer: Eric Plowman.

System: 10-barrel JV NorthWest system, 550 barrels annual capacity.

Production: 550 barrels in 2003.

Hours: 11 A.M. to midnight, seven days a week.

Tours: Tours are available for groups, by appointment.

Take-out beer: 2-liter growlers available.

Food: Calhoun's has the usual run of steaks, seafood, appetizers, and all that jazz, but what really gets me going is the variety of wraps and grilled sandwiches that indicate some mad genius in the kitchen. I'm a big fan of the fried oyster po' boy, and the sauce and trimmings are excellent.

Extras: Live jazz Tuesday and Friday nights; no cover. Calhoun's also has a large outdoor beer garden with a fountain that's very nice in the twilight hours.

Special considerations: Kids welcome. Vegetarian meals available. Handicapped-accessible.

Parking: You can try parking on Court Square and watch your meter every second, or you can be smart and park on Graham Street, beside Calhoun's.

Lodging in the area: Joshua Wilton House B&B, 412 South Main Street, 540-434-4464; By the Side of the Road B&B, 491 Garbers Church Road, 540-801-0430.

Area attractions: I already mentioned *Kline's Dairy Bar;* time to stop teasing you and let you know that it's at 58 East Wolfe Street (540-434-6980), right next to the *Smokin' Pig* barbecue joint (540-433-3917). The Smokin' Pig and the *Bar-BQ Ranch* (3311 North Valley Pike/U.S. Route 11, 540-434-3296) both serve excellent Virginia-style chopped barbecue. Harrisonburg is the market town for a large agricultural area that's a major producer of turkeys, among other goods. Head south on U.S. Route 11 to get to the *Shenandoah Her-*

itage Farmer's Market (call for seasonal hours, 540-433-3929), which has plenty of crafts, antiques, and doodads, as well as fresh produce and meats.

A quick run east on U.S. Route 33 will bring you to the **Skyline Drive,** the little brother to the more famous Blue Ridge Parkway. The Skyline Drive drives through the heart of the **Shenandoah National Park,** 105 miles along the top of the Blue Ridge, twisting and turning through some of the most beautiful scenery in Virginia. If you can, wait for a clear day, and one that's a weekday, to escape the other tourists. The reward is tremendous.

Massanutten Ski Resort (VA Route 644, follow the signs, 800-207-6277) boasts the longest vertical drop in Virginia—or Maryland and Pennsylvania, for that matter—more than one thousand feet. You'll find fourteen trails, with night skiing, a snowboard park, and a snowtubing park.

The famous and fabulous **Luray Caverns** are not far from Harrisonburg (970 Route 211 West, Luray, 540-743-6551). This is a year-round attraction. As in all caves, the air is a constant comfortable temperature in the low 50s, making it warm in the winter and cool in the summer, kind of like what Colonel Crockett famously said about the effects of drinking rye whiskey. Your tour will include the playing of the "Stalacpipe Organ," a keyboard-controlled arrangement of specially tuned stalactites that is the world's largest musical instrument of any type. Closer, though not quite as grand—yet, because they're still being explored—are **Endless Caverns** (south on U.S. Route 11 from exit 264 off I-81, 540-896-2283), which you should find pretty easily; their billboard on the western slope of the mountains is the largest in the East. Endless Caverns are not as polished as Luray, and some people, like my geologist father, prefer it that way.

Other area beer sites: Eric was right—there's not much. But the **Little Grill Collective** (621 North Main Street, 540-434-3594) is employee-owned and decidedly different. Lots of places try to do the hippie groove restaurant thing; these guys just lay back and let it happen. Not a lot of beer here, but there is a small selection of good bottles, and where else can you get a pitcher of draft Old Dominion Black & Tan *or* a pitcher of carrot juice . . . for the same price? There's live entertainment, too; call for the schedule.

South Street Brewery

106 South Street, Charlottesville, VA 22902
434-293-6550

Here we are at South Street, just off the Main Street pedestrian mall in Charlottesville. If it looks like an old brick warehouse, well, it is, dating from the 1850s, and the fading painted sign on the outside is authentic. Go on inside and see how the place opens up, high ceiling and spacious room. Now take a look at the longest bar in town. Nice copper top, too. Check out that double-sided free-standing fireplace, real nice in the winter. Take a glance at the colorful decorations, maybe order some food from South Street's eclectic menu. Settle into a stool at that long, long bar. Okay? Comfy? Good, maybe we can get a beer now. I didn't think you'd ever get down to business!

Beer is the business at South Street; people come here and groove on it, and Taylor Smack is brewing it. I had stopped in some years ago when his boss, owner Jacque Landry, was brewing, and I was pretty impressed with the beers he had on. No slight on Jacque, but I can see why he lets Taylor do the brewing. This guy's good.

Jacque's philosophy that guides the tap selection is different from Mark Thompson's minimalist concept across town at Starr Hill, as different as this part of town, with its small streets and big pedestrian mall, is from the broad avenues closer to the UVA campus. Here at South Street, things take a broader approach to brewing: some truly big beers, some real different beers, and just more beers. Which do I like better? Depends on how I'm feeling when you ask; right now I'm sitting at that long, copper-top bar, and the variety is looking pretty good.

Taylor Smack is originally from Lynchburg, Virginia. "Coming back here to Virginia and brewing is like a dream for me," he said happily. He went away and learned how to brew at Goose Island in Chicago. He learned well, which shouldn't surprise

Beers brewed: Year-round: Hogwaller Kölsch, Satan's Pony Amber Ale, JPAle (RAF Silver, 2002). Mostly year-round: Absolution Old Ale, Porter's Porter. Seasonals: South Street Pilsner, Marguerita's Wrecking Ball Oktoberfest Lager, SummerBock, Maibock, Special Pale Ale, IPA, ESB, Olde 420 Foreign Stout, Aisling Stout, Nut Brown Ale, Belgian Golden, Wit, Trippel, El Hefe's Hefeweizen, Dunkelweizen, Altbier, Aged Barleywine, Old Elijah Bourbon Stout, Ultimate Sin, Golden Promise Rye PA.

anyone; John Hall and company know their way around a brewkettle.

Now he's here at South Street, brewing up a storm on his John Mallet–customized Saaz brewhouse. Mallet is a bit of a legend around here, a former Old Dominion brewer who went independent, doing brewing engineering, building, customizing, and salvaging brewhouses while also spreading brewing tips all through the Mid-Atlantic. "I love this brewery," Taylor told me. It's easy to see why. This baby's got all the gadgetry: a wort sample chiller, a steam-heated filter, a mineral dump system. It's a bells-and-whistles showcase, and Taylor uses them all.

The Pick: It doesn't happen often, but here at South Street I'm picking the most popular beer: Satan's Pony. This is simply a fantastic beer that has realized its potential under Taylor's hand, a real tour de force of bright, fruity yeast character, solid malt underpinning, and tempting hop finish. Steal this pony and ride him to heaven.

That would be one thing if the beer was just okay, but the gadgets obviously are not getting in the way of Taylor's abilities at all. It's funny—brewers who work on manual systems often talk about the merits of hands-on brewing, but the few I've known who have gone to more fully tricked-out systems never complain.

Let's get down to it. The big seller here is Satan's Pony, a malty amber ale done with the house British ale yeast and British malt. Taylor brews it with lots of bright esters and a solid malt underpinning. The JPAle is a heavily Cascaded pale ale brewed with South Street's English yeast; the very American citrusy character of the Cascades and the esters from the English yeast make for a hybrid pale ale unlike most brewpubs' interpretations. Taylor didn't have a hefeweizen on yet—it was still spring—but these spritzy, fluffy beers are very popular at South Street, and you can believe that warm weather will see at least one on tap.

But look at these cool-weather seasonals! Golden Promise Rye PA, an unfiltered rye beer that's sweet and spicy; a swaggering no-nonsense tripel that's not at all delicate; the Special Pale, JPAle's big brother, which rings all the hops and malt bells; and Absolution Old Ale, a 6.7 percent old ale that is sticky with malt but surprises you with a backfill of hops in the finish. Then Taylor started pulling out the scary beers: Bourbon Stout, Strong Ale, Aisling Stout. It was a great tasting session.

Too bad it wasn't a Monday. Taylor throws a cask on every Monday, and some of these beers just ached to be on cask. That's one of the great things about using British yeasts over the more common American-type ale yeasts: The British yeasts were bred and evolved for cask ales. They create the esters and aromas that make it wonderful, and they drop out of the beer to leave it bright. I tasted Taylor's beers and knew how good they could be in their natural habitat.

Monday and Wednesday nights are also live music nights at South Street, a steal with the no-cover policy. Sandwiched between is an even bigger bargain, Two-Dollar Tuesday, with all pints of Taylor's beer priced at two bucks, an understandably popular event in a college town. Heck, be honest—with these beers, you'd like it, too.

The worn brick facade of South Street doesn't show you much, it's true. That's what this book is for, that's why I went to every single one of these breweries, that's why I drank all those beers—it's for you, so you'll know about great places like South Street, and the longest bar in town. Don't let all that work go to waste.

Opened: October 1998.

Owners: Fred Greenewalt, Jacque Landry.

Brewer: Taylor Smack.

System: 7-barrel Saaz system, 700 barrels annual capacity.

Production: 625 barrels in 2003.

Hours: Monday through Saturday, 4:30 P.M. to 2 A.M.

Tours: By appointment only.

Take-out beer: One-liter growlers available; call ahead for kegs. Take-out available only from April through October.

Food: The food at South Street is the closest thing I've ever seen to fusion cuisine at a brewpub. There are familiar favorites, but there is also a definite and interesting Eurasian slant to things. Go prepared to enjoy.

Extras: Live music Monday and Wednesday nights; no cover. Tuesday is $2 draft night.

Special considerations: Cigars not allowed. Kids welcome. Vegetarian meals available. Handicapped-accessible.

Parking: Extensive lot across the street from the brewpub; no charge after 6 P.M.

Lodging in the area: 200 South Street Inn, beside brewpub, 800-979-0200; Red Roof Inn, 1309 West Main Street, 434-295-4333; Omni Hotel Charlottesville, 235 West Main Street, 434-971-5500; The Inn at Monticello, 1188 Scottsville Road, 434-979-3593.

Area attractions: Do tour the grounds at the **University of Virginia** (not the campus, "the grounds"), which were planned with loving care by Thomas Jefferson. The ubiquitous Edgar Allan Poe was a student here. Tours are available with student guides (park in the lot by Emmet Street and Ivy Road, 434-924-7969). Then you'll want to go see Jefferson's home, **Monticello** (on VA Route 53, about a mile and a half east of VA Route 20, 434-984-9822); after all, you've been looking at it on the backs of nickels all your life. Monticello represents a look into Jefferson's mind: elegant, a bit cluttered, and open to many influences. The house is filled with Jefferson's inventions and collections: mastodon bones, the seven-day clock, relics of the Lewis and Clark expedition.

Don't miss the **Michie Tavern** ("MICK-ee") on VA Route 53 on your way to Monticello (434-977-1234). The tavern was built in 1784 in Earlysville. It was moved in 1927 to Charlottesville, where it was restored to its current robust condition, giving a view of the early American taverns that served as gathering places for the people. The tavern, gristmill, smokehouse, root cellar, and general store are all real and functional. You can get lunch in this tavern museum.

There also are twenty vineyards near Charlottesville. Virginia wine is advancing quickly in quality and sophistication, and the state's hospitality takes a backseat to none found in California. Take a look at www.virginiawines.org to make your choices.

My dad made me promise to warn you: The pedestrian mall on West Main Street is beautiful, with trees and benches and fountains, but it can make driving in this end of town a "can't get there from here" proposition. You've been warned.

Other area beer sites: Taylor Smack steered me to **Ludwig's Schnitzelhouse** (2208 Fontaine Avenue, 434-293-7185), and he's a genius: Ludwig's has that *gasthaus* feel and a great selection of German *and* Belgian beers (which I would think would drive a Reinheitsgeboten German nuts), as well as spot-on German food. **Court Square Tavern** (500 East Jefferson Street, 434-296-6111) has a small, import-slanted tapline, but a deep bottle selection of both imports and craft brews. It's a small place, and half underground, but nicely decorated and the food smelled great. The **Gravity Lounge** (103 South First Street, off the Main Street mall, 434-977-5590) is a bookstore, a performance space with live music three or four nights a week (very up-to-date calendar at www.gravity-lounge.com), a café with pastries and coffee, a Wi-Fi wireless hot spot, and a beer and wine bar, with impressive bottle selections of both. Can't get hipper than that. Pizza and beer are the deal at the **Mellow Mushroom** (1309 West Main Street, right under the Red Roof Inn, 434-972-9366), and if this sounds simplistic, it's not: this place offered the best selection of taps in town by far, thirty-four of them, and some pretty wild ones. Not outrageously priced, either. Walk up the stairs to **Michael's Bistro and Taphouse** (1427 University Avenue, 434-

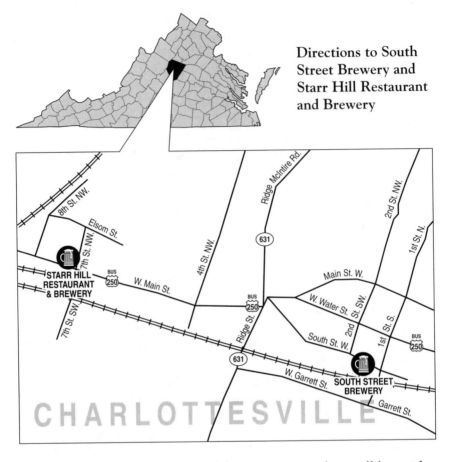

Directions to South Street Brewery and Starr Hill Restaurant and Brewery

977-3697), and you'll find a delicious menu and a small bar with a small but wonderful tap selection, with one handpump. It's a quiet oasis of calm appreciation, and boy, did I ever appreciate it. If you're out late and need a place for coffee and good greasy eats (admit it, you've been *there* before), drop in to the **White Spot** (1407 University Avenue, 434-295-9899) for a Gusburger.

Starr Hill Restaurant and Brewery

709 West Main Street, Charlottesville, VA 22901
434-977-0017
www.starrhill.com

"I'm a beer minimalist," Mark Thompson says by way of explaining Starr Hill's relatively small lineup of beers. He has four regular beers—Mojo Lager, Amber Ale, Pale Ale, and Dark Star Stout—and one seasonal on at any one time. He's got a very simple reason for wanting it that way: passion for perfection. "I'd rather have four A+ beers on than eight B– beers," he said.

He's got them, too: Mark Thompson has been the most medal-winning brewer in the Mid-Atlantic since he started at Starr Hill, and every one of those four regular beers has won at least one GABF or World Beer Cup medal. His Dark Star has won, by Mark's count, more medals than any other dry stout in the country. This brewer is sharp as a laser, and his passion shines through his earnest love for beer. He says things like "It's not about us, it's not about the beer, it's about The Gift Of Beer," and you hear the capital letters and you can see that he really believes what he's saying, believes it with real fire.

That's at the heart of one of Mark's better ideas, Open Door Mondays. The brewpub is closed on Mondays, but the door is open. "We let the people come right in and brew," said Mark, gesturing expansively. "Beer making is inherently exciting, and when they make the beer, they *own the beer*. That *is* the gift of beer. And the beer is a vehicle to people, meeting them, talking to them, getting to know them."

He's not worried about someone walking through the door and screwing up the beer somehow by adding too much hops or overhydrating the grist. "We *want* the beer to be different every day; we want it to evolve." He also said that at least one time an accident like that turned out to be benefi-

Beers brewed: Year-round: Mojo Lager (GABF Bronze, 2003), Amber Ale (GABF Bronze, 2001) (both also brewed at Old Dominion), Pale Ale (GABF Gold, 2003), Dark Star Stout (GABF Gold, 1999; Bronze, 2000–2001). Seasonals: Porter, The Love Hefeweizen, Fest Beer, and The Gift, a changing winter beer.

cial enough that it became part of the regular regimen for that beer.

If people do come in and brew, they're learning at the base level. Starr Hill has one of the first five brewhouses made by JV NorthWest, now considered a top-of-the-line fabricator. Back in the day when Starr Hill's predecessor, Blue Ridge Brewing, bought the system, well, things were a bit rougher. The welds are a bit ragged, there isn't any automation at all, and it's not pretty. "Brewing beer on this system," Mark admitted, "is like rubbing sticks together to make fire. It's a lot more work than striking a match, but if you know what you're doing, the fire's just as warm."

The Pick: Dark Star Stout. I don't always go against the grain! Dark Star is the bitterest, darkest, and lightest-bodied beer Starr Hill makes, and that seemingly contradictory knot is appealing to me. I love lightweight beers with plenty of flavor, and Dark Star's got it, in deep black spades: bitter, smooth, drinkable, and just on the low side of rich. This is beautiful stuff.

Rough and ready brewhouse, only a few beers on tap, and Mark is a minimalist in his beer formulation as well. He was trained that way by one of the real pioneers of the microbrewery movement, Karl Ockert, who started brewing at BridgePort Brewing in Portland, Oregon, in 1984. "Karl taught me the 3-2-1 method of formulation," said Mark. "No more than 3 malts, no more than 2 hops, and 1 yeast. If you use more than that, you don't know what you want to achieve, and you're just muddling up the end results."

These beers are the products of that philosophy, and their simplicity is nothing short of brilliant. Mojo, which the ale-loving Mark had to be persuaded to make by his assistant, Matt Reich, is clean and easy to drink. The Amber is a beautifully rounded malt-side ale, nothing fancy. The Pale Ale, Mark's favorite—"I just reach for it every time," he said—is a Brit-style pale with plenty of fresh hop flavor, and Dark Star is just about perfect; those medals are no lie.

Passionate as Mark is, he gets the whole picture in a way some brewers don't seem to grasp. "Making the devil's juice is easy," he said. "Getting someone to buy *your* beer instead of their favorite beer is the hard part." One of the first things Mark did was to get the infrastructure in place. He took a hard look at Virginia's wholesaler-friendly beer laws, and put his wife in charge of Starr Distributing, a separate wholesaling company that handles Starr Hill's beers, along with a few other micro lines. "We're playing by the rules," he said. "We're just playing by the rules our way."

Having their own wholesale channel gave Starr Hill the freedom to cut deals that got them into big music venues in the Mid-Atlantic area, following up on the success of the pub's own big music program. The heart of the pub is the upstairs stage, a 250-plus-seat space that has seen big-name acts booked in on early weekdays when the acts would normally be traveling. Not only does that pack in people in Charlottesville, but it also made the connections with the musicians and managers that helped get Starr Hill into the big stages where those same performers played: the Nissan Center, the Virginia Beach Amphitheater, the huge annual Bonnaroo Festival in Tennessee.

Those music connections worked so well that Starr Hill's little 5-barrel JVNW system couldn't keep up. If you see Starr Hill beer outside of the pub, chances are it was made at Old Dominion; all the bottles are made there.

But Mark's passion is in every drop of Starr Hill beer. Listen to him as his eyes gleam with it, and he makes you believe him: "There's malt, and hops, and yeast, and water in the beer. And the fifth ingredient is . . . The Love." Anywhere else it would sound corny. From Mark, it sounds like a revival meeting at its sweating, fervent peak. Preach on, Mark.

Note: Just in time to catch final edits, I learned that Starr Hill seized their future. They purchased the brewhouse of the former Native Brewing in Alexandria and moved it to their new production brewery just outside Charlottesville, at 3391 Three Notch Road, Crozet (434-823-5671). It's a 25-barrel brewhouse with enough tanks for around 9,000 barrels annual capacity, plus a barely used high-end bottling line. No decision has been made on the fate of the brewpub's small brewery. This is going to put all of Starr Hill's beer back under Mark's control, and he's ecstatic. More brewery, more beer, more Love.

Opened: September 1999.
Owner: John Spagnola.
Brewers: Mark Thompson, master brewer; Matt Reich, assistant.
System: 5-barrel JV NorthWest system, 350 barrels annual capacity.
Production: 2,000 barrels in 2003 (majority of production at Old Dominion).
Hours: Tuesday through Sunday, 5 P.M. to 2 A.M.
Tours: By appointment, or just come in on Open Door Monday.
Take-out beer: Call ahead for kegs.
Food: Starr Hill proudly uses local or organic foods as much as possible in its kitchen. It also has one of the best selections of vegetarian food that I've seen in a brewpub: black bean fritters, vegetarian chili, nachos, pizza, vegetable kabobs, a blackened sweet potato sandwich, and more. If you're looking for something a bit more beefy, how about the prime rib sandwich or half rack of ribs, or maybe the nice-looking barbecue pork burrito? There truly is some-

thing here for everyone, and the kids' menu is served till midnight, for the sophisticated youngster out on the town.

Extras: Excellent live music in the hall upstairs; call for schedule or check the constantly updated and detailed website for lots of details and online ticket sales. Starr Hill carries one guest beer tap, usually something really good, and they have an excellent bourbon selection.

Special considerations: Kids are welcome. Some excellent vegetarian meals. Handicapped-accessible.

Parking: Plenty of on-street parking.

Kegler's

2000 Seminole Trail, Charlottesville, VA
434-978-3999

The best thing I got out of my visit to Kegler's was a rare back-of-the-alley tour of the pin-setting machinery at this huge forty-eight-lane bowling alley. Brewer and maintenance man Dave Brockner took my dad and me back there to see the big, automated pin-setting machines. They had a great time talking pulleys and gears and such; my dad had been a pin setter when he was a boy and has always had a deep interest in clever mechanical gadgets.

"When we've got league bowling going," Dave said, "we get a maintenance call about every ten minutes." Every ten minutes? For five hours at a stretch? "That's why we have the microwave and the bathroom back here," Dave said, grinning.

Why are we talking bowling? Because when I visited, Dave hadn't brewed on Kegler's little Micropub system since Hurricane Isabel in the fall of 2003. "We lost the last batch when the power went out during the hurricane," Dave said. "I haven't brewed since then; I've just been too busy." He is kept quite busy working on the rebuilt pin-return equipment ("The old stuff is the best," he told me) and the waxing and maintenance on the alley's real wood lanes, which Kegler's owners like better than the more modern composite materials.

Beers brewed: Golden ale, pale ale, brown ale.

The Pick: No beer, no pick! I'll have to come back when Dave's stolen some time to brew.

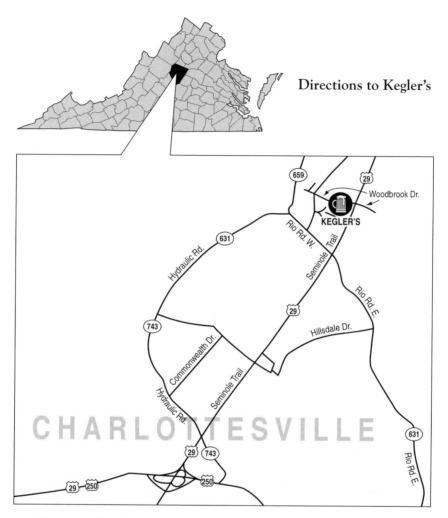

Directions to Kegler's

There evidently hasn't been a lot of incentive to brew, either. "Bowlers have a strong sense of brand loyalty," Dave explained. "If they drink Bud, they drink Bud. It's not easy to get them to try something different. Our beer didn't sell all that well; we never sold out a full batch. It was a pilot idea for AMF, and they didn't do any more of them." Brunswick tried the same idea, with about the same results.

Successful or not, Dave intends to get back to brewing. "I have ordered more of the ingredients, and I'm going to brew some more beers," he said. "I just like it because it's unique." He's not intimidated by the quality of the local competition, either. "Oh, I know," he said, "Starr Hill is the award-winning brewery in town. But every micro-brewery has its own flavor." And brewers have always marched to their own drummers, a tradition that Dave Brockner is upholding in fine fashion at Kegler's.

Opened: Brewery installed August 2000.
Owners: Private investors.
Brewer: Dave Brockner.
System: 2-barrel Micropub system, 150 barrels annual capacity.
Production: Not available.
Hours: Monday, 11 A.M. to midnight; Sunday, Tuesday through Thursday, 9 A.M. to midnight; Friday, 11 A.M. to 2 A.M.; Saturday, 9 A.M. to 2 A.M.
Tours: On request, subject to brewer availability.
Take-out beer: Not available.
Food: Kegler's has the usual gamut of bowling-alley food: burgers, hot dogs, sandwiches, pizza, and snacks.
Extras: Forty-eight lanes of bowling with automated scoring, "extreme bowling" nights, league play.
Special considerations: Kids welcome. Pizza for vegetarians. Handicapped-accessible.
Parking: Large on-site lot.

Queen City Brewing, Ltd.

834 Springhill Road, Staunton, VA 24401
540-213-8014

If you were ever curious about how I go about researching these entries, this one's a classic. Follow along as I discover and explore a new brewery.

I heard about Queen City through the hopvine as I was making one of my last trips for this book. Anning Smith at Shenandoah mentioned something about a brew-on-premise in Staunton (that's pronounced "STANT'ihn," and you'd better get it right if you want to get along down here) when I stopped in to talk to him. The next day, I was in Richmond at the April meeting of the Rubber Boot Society, an informal Virginia brewers' association that meets monthly to discuss technical points of brewing and drink each other's beer, to talk about the whys and wherefores of creating a flagship brand. The guys from over in the Valley confirmed it: The BOP was called Queen City, and it had been up since October.

Well, nothing would do but that I saddle up two days later and head west, past Charlottesville and over the Blue Ridge into Staunton. Staunton is the birthplace of Woodrow Wilson, and his home, along with a number of other historic build-

Beers brewed: As you like it.

The Pick: Queen City didn't have beer available for sampling yet, but the root beer was very assertive. My son and I thought it was pretty strong stuff, and it went great with vanilla ice cream.

ings, is still standing pretty much as it was back in his time. Staunton was largely missed by the Civil War and is one of the few towns in the Shenandoah Valley to retain its historic buildings. About the only evidence of the Civil War I could see was the large, old sign for the Stonewall Jackson Hotel down by the Wharf District historic area.

But I wasn't in Staunton to do Civil War archeological research, learn about Woodrow Wilson, or even eat Mrs. Rowe's fried chicken. I was there to find Queen City Brewing, and after a pleasant little drive through town, I did. It was closed.

Just till 4 P.M.! Luckily, the telephone number was posted on the door, so I made a quick call, left a message on the answering machine, and went back into town to track down some bars for your thirsty moments. I had made it down to the Edelweiss German restaurant south of town—and with six taps and more than forty-five bottled German and Austrian beers, it was well worth the trip, believe me— when my pocket started ringing. It was Travis Smithdeal, calling me from the brewery.

Twenty minutes later, I pulled into the lot of what looks suspiciously like an old convenience store—and it is, a converted 7-11—and greeted Travis, a small, relatively quiet man with an easy, friendly smile. He let me into the shop and showed me around. It's a wide-open area with the piped and polished BOP equipment right in the middle of the floor, five 30-gallon kettles and one 45-gallon kettle, all Canadian-made, as most BOP equipment is. This is a top-of-the-line model, with steam heat and stainless piping.

We went back to the cold room, where he showed me all the fermenting beer in its plastic cylinders. Travis smiled again and said, "I have some people who come in between brewing and when it's time to bottle, and they just come in this room and look at their beer like it was a baby in a nursery." When it's time to bottle the baby, Queen City offers 12- and 22-ounce bottles, half-gallon growlers, and Party Pigs; the brewery will also keg for you if you have your own keg.

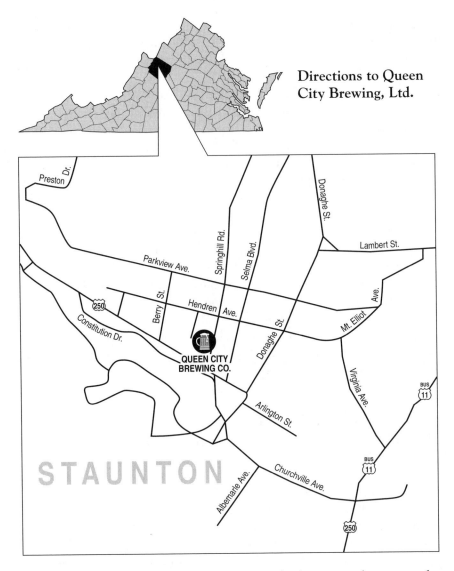

Directions to Queen City Brewing, Ltd.

Travis told me that he and his partner had gotten a leg up on the business from Kevin Yeaton, who used to run the Monticello BOP and brewery down in Charlottesville, where Travis had made some batches of beer. I was wondering why Kevin had closed Monticello. Turns out Kevin had developed celiac sprue and became highly allergic to the gluten in beer. He closed the brewery but gave a lot of advice and all his recipes to the guys at Queen City.

I was scribbling away furiously, trying to get all this down (and obviously getting a fair amount), and I asked him what else the brewery had. They also offer soda-making (Travis gave me a bottle of root beer for my son, a budding root beer snob) and a selection of cigars. "We try to cover all the vices," Travis said with a chuckle. Queen City is also working on getting a commercial brewer's license so they can make beer for sale to local tavern accounts. The ATTTB works slowly, but they should have the license by the time you read this.

That was about that, so I thanked Travis, gave him a couple of the exquisitely fresh samples Andy Rathmann at St. George had given me the day before (had to make room in the cooler for that root beer), and motored back over the ridge, down into western Richmond, and stopped at Hops to sample some beers . . . but that's another entry.

Now you know how it's done. Just remember: If it were as easy as it sounds, everyone would be doing it!

Opened: October 2003.
Owners: Travis Smithdeal, Greg Ridenour.
Brewer: You.
System: The Brew Store system: five 30-gallon kettles, one 45-gallon kettle.
Production: Not available.
Hours: Tuesday through Friday, 3 P.M. to 8 P.M.; Saturday, 10 A.M. to 6 P.M.
Take-out beer: You can package your beer in a number of ways.
Special considerations: Kids welcome. Handicapped-accessible.
Parking: Off-street lot and easy street parking.
Lodging in the area: Thornrose House, 531 Thornrose Avenue, 540-885-7026; Sampson Eagon Inn, 238 East Beverly Street, 800-597-9722; Ashton Country House, 1205 Middlebrook Avenue, 800-296-7819; Super 8, 1015 Richmond Avenue, 540-886-2888.
Area attractions: Staunton was largely left untouched by the Civil War and is home to five National Historic Districts. Walk the town to see the Victorian and older homes, or visit the Wharf District to see the old train depot, mills, and warehouses, which now house shops and antique markets. The **Woodrow Wilson Birthplace and Museum** (Coalter Street and Frederick Street, 540-885-0897) is in Wilson's actual home, not a re-creation. The tour includes the gardens and Wilson's Pierce-Arrow limo. Country-western singers the **Statler Brothers** are also from Staunton, and there is a small museum and gift shop (501 Thornrose Avenue, 540-885-7927) where they once went to school.

The Shenandoah Shakespeare Company performs regularly at **Blackfriars Playhouse** (11 East Beverly Street, 540-885-5588), their new home, where Shakespeare is produced in authentic, "natural" fashion, with natural lighting. The playhouse also hosts musical and other theatrical events; call for the schedule.

Just off I-81 is the *Frontier Culture Museum* (U.S. Route 250, west of exit 222 off I-81, 540-332-7850), a working farm that brings together homes and cultures of different ethnic groups that settled the Shenandoah Valley. Actual original buildings were moved from Europe to represent where these settlers came from: a German wattle and daub farmhouse, a Scotch-Irish stone cottage, and an English two-story wood frame house. The fourth home on the farm is an American log house from near Roanoke. The homes are real, the cattle and pigs are real, the hay is real, and all those smells are real. The staff, dressed in authentic costume, is really working the farms and is there to answer questions. Call about the scheduled demonstrations.

Now go on out to **Mrs. Rowe's** (just east of exit 222 on U.S. Route 250, 540-886-1833) and get some fried chicken.

Other area beer sites: *The Baja Bean* (9 West Beverly Street, 540-885-9988), a very good Mexican restaurant, has four solid rotating taps that will have at least one beer to please you and the usual suspects in bottles; the bottle selection is slanted toward Mexicans, of course. *The Clock Tower Tavern* (27 West Beverly Street, 540-213-2403) is a pretty happening music spot (Staunton was the home of the Statler Brothers, and it's rubbed off), and about it for nonmainstream bars in town. It usually has one of the Starr Hill beers on. I would assume that these two are going to be targets for Queen City's beer. *The Wine Cellar* (8 Byers Street, 540-213-WINE), a wine and spirits store, has a decent selection of beer as well, as is often the case in Virginia. South of town, you'll find the *Edelweiss* (19 Edelweiss Lane, just off exit 213 of I-81, 540-337-1203), a German restaurant with no bar but six taps of German beer, a very good German and Austrian bottle selection, lots of German wines, and a ton of great German food; well worth a stop.

I had done some visits down in Blacksburg before Blacksburg Brewing closed, and I was going to leave those places out, but what the heck, I'll throw them in here. Blacksburg's not too far down I-81. *The Cellar* (302 North Main Street, 540-953-0651) may look like just a little pizza restaurant with eight so-so taps, but go downstairs, into the *cellar*, and you'll find a big ankh-shaped bar with a column of taps in the middle, with a drain watered by . . . well, you'll recognize it. Very good beers and a good bottle selection come across the concrete bar (that's high-tech concrete, stained with espresso and sealed, very hip right now). I had a good ol' time at the **Rivermill Map Company** (212 Draper Road, 540-951-2483), enjoying college-town prices: a 20-ounce Tupper's Hop Pocket Pils for $2.25! Great small tap selection, a menu full of cheap good eats, and really fresh taps of New River Pale Ale. Don't pass up the **London Underground** (112 North Main Street, 540-552-9044) as just a storefront bar; it's a lot deeper than that. There's a beat-up old bar in the back, a funky old bar, with 20-ounce dimple mugs of beers like Blackhook Porter on nitro, Guinness, and Sierra Nevada Pale Ale. Kind of frat-house at night, but real nice on an afternoon. Beware the chili: It comes with a daily heat rating, and no whining or handwringing is allowed. The stop that really makes a drive to Blacksburg worthwhile is **Vintage Cellar** (1340 South Main Street, 540-953-2675), an absolutely awesome beer store. Okay, it's mainly a wine store, but you'll never notice it. Three aisles of beer grab your eye, deep selections of British, Belgian, German, and craft brews, and a small but very high-end cider selection, something you don't see often enough. There are beer tastings on Fridays; call for a schedule. This great store with excellent service also offers home-brew supplies and beer books.

A word about . . .

Regional Foods

"Now, you're eating the whole menu . . . is that just the sandwiches, or does that include the Maryland fried chicken?"
—Paul Reiser, playing Modell, in *Diner.*

People in the Mid-Atlantic take their food seriously. Yes, I know all about regional foods—I grew up in Pennsylvania Dutch country eating stuffed pig stomach, scrapple, and chicken gravy on waffles, and I got a full-immersion course in New York's regional foods two years ago when I wrote *New York Breweries;* there are still leftover bottles of wing sauce in the pantry and hot dogs in the freezer. (They're Zweigle's. Red hots. Because that's important to some people.)

But even New York's love affair with the tube steak pales beside Maryland's fascination with blue crabs, Virginia's obsession with country-cured ham, and D.C.'s guilty love affair with the half-smoke (Delaware is happy eating Maryland's crabs and Pennsylvania's scrapple). These are widespread passions, too. It's no surprise to see crabs along the Chesapeake, where they are caught, but cross the Appalachian Front into western Maryland, and the menu is still heavily laden with the sweet, white flesh of the beautiful swimmers. Virginia's well-known "Virginia is for lovers" tourism campaign was hijacked early on by Free Staters: Maryland is for crabs.

You'd have to be crazy not to feel that way, though. Blue crabs are delicious, a sweet succulence that takes so well to any number of companion flavors: sharp cheeses and mild ones, cream, hot sauce, garlic, spinach and artichoke (because crab turns that ubiquitous appetizer dip into something special), tomato . . . and Old Bay Seasoning.

Old Bay is a Baltimore secret that has finally gotten out, a blend of spices prepared and sold by Baltimore-based McCormick. What is Old Bay? It's a blend. Gustav Brunn arrived in Baltimore in 1939 from Germany (smart move!) with a spice grinder and soon developed his secret mix of more than a dozen spices and herbs. McCormick will name only eleven—including celery, bay leaves, mustard, red and black pepper, cloves, allspice, cardamom, paprika, and ginger—which gives you an idea of what Old Bay has going on in that big yellow metal box. It goes well on chicken, potato chips, and steamed vegetables, and it makes a great "boil" for shrimp. But steamed crabs take so well to Old Bay that it's odd to think of them without it. How did they season crabs before Herr Brunn? How could they have?

Eating steamed crabs is a bare-hands operation, breaking off legs, cracking the shell, and teasing out the white flesh. It makes eating a lobster look positively simple, but most Marylanders would turn down a 2-pound Maine lobster for a dozen #1 crabs, the big ones.

Where can you get them? Perhaps the best-known crab joint in Baltimore is **Obrycki's** (1727 East Pratt Street, 410-732-6399), which has a host of other seafood delights, including crab imperial, crab soup, deviled crab balls, crab dip, crab cakes, deviled crab cakes, sauteed lump crab meat (my favorite way to eat crab, other than hand-cracked), and shrimp stuffed with crab. You could also travel over to the Eastern Shore to one of the shore towns and find a dockside restaurant.

But I believe the best way to eat crabs is to get down and dirty with 'em at a roadside crab shack, like our old family favorite, **Hopkins Crab House** (on U.S. Route 222, north of Port Deposit, 410-378-5250), where I made the family take me the day after I moved home from California. Or you can pick up a dozen and take them home. Put a couple thicknesses of newspaper down on the table, get your hammer, and start cracking. Every so often, cut through the Old Bay with a chunk of well-buttered bread, then go back at it. By the way, the *very best* thing to drink with steamed crabs is, by general acclamation, beer. Even wine people admit it. So get a couple cases of Backfin or McHenry on ice and live it up. And when you're done, just roll up the newspapers and throw them in the trash.

We've been talking about hardshell crabs, of course. Softshells are something completely different. These are crabs that have just molted, and their shells are still soft from the process. The fat that they've built up to fuel the molting makes them delicious. You take the whole crab, clean it, and fry it up in butter. You eat everything, shell and all, and they are simply fantastic. People get silly about softshells, they're so good.

What's a half-smoke? That's kind of a mystery, because half-smokes are hard to find in stores, wrapped in carefully labeled plastic wrap. They're so hard to find outside their natural habitat of street carts and chili houses that it brings to mind the Texas joke that armadillos are born dead by the side of the road. You haven't really been to Washington until you've gone native and wolfed one of these by a food cart. And then got another because the first one was so good.

The classic place for half-smokes in D.C. ("classic" because food critics have "discovered" it) is **Ben's Chili Bowl** (1213 U Street, 202-

667-0909). Ben and Virginia Ali's chili house is a D.C. landmark and a favorite of Bill Cosby's, who is said to stop in for three chili half-smokes whenever he's in town. The mahogany-colored chili, full of black beans and smoky meat, is laid on with mustard and onions.

I've got a different place to go for my chili half-smokes. Bill Cosby may or may not know about the **Weenie Beanie** in Arlington (2680 South Shirlington Road, 703-671-6661), but it's a favorite of mine, and of the day laborers who wait on the street corner there. And it's just down the hill from the Shirlington Village Capitol City Brewing Company, so you can guess how I found it. They have a real good fish sandwich here, too.

But what *is* a half-smoke? Washington's favorite hand meal is a little bit bigger than a hot dog, and a whole lot tastier. It's a half-pork, half-beef smoked sausage, and the best ones, maybe the originals, come from Esskay meats, a Baltimore company that is now owned by Smithfield, a company with a pretty good pork pedigree of its own. You can find them, by the way; you just have to know where to look. Try www. wholesomefoodsinc.com, a mail-order outfit in, of all places, Edinburg, Virginia, in the Shenandoah Valley.

Virginia is quite partial to its pork as well, only the locals like to cure it to the point of petrification. Smithfield hams come from Smithfield, Virginia, and they classically are cut from hogs fattened on acorns and peanuts, and salt- and smoke-cured to a dense hardness. They will keep for months unrefrigerated, tightly wrapped and sewn up in cloth.

When you're ready to eat your ham, it's a simple, easy-to-follow process. Cut off the cloth and fully immerse the ham in water to soak. After four hours, change the water. Continue the four-hour changes for at least twenty-four hours. Then scrub the ham with a stiff brush to remove the pepper and any mold. Really, it says this right in the instructions. To bake the ham, wrap it in heavy aluminum foil, with 5 cups of water packaged right in the foil with the ham. Put it in a 500-degree oven for fifteen minutes, then turn the oven off for three hours. Bring it back up to 500 degrees for ten minutes, then turn it off for eight hours. Do not open the oven door at any time.

Can any ham possibly be *worth* all this trouble? You bet. Thinly sliced Smithfield ham is incredibly flavorful, but it must be thinly sliced, or the salt is overwhelming. In the words of Henri Charpentier, John D. Rockefeller's personal chef, "Carve a ham as if you were shaving the face of a friend." The most popular way to eat it is just thin slices of ham on a Parker House roll or "beaten biscuit" (and I am *not* going to get into the whole beaten biscuit issue; maybe next book). These ham biscuits are very popular at gatherings and at **Padow's,** a chain of ham delis based in Richmond that has spread as far west as Roanoke, which is the location of the Padow's where I got my Smithfield ham. I cheated and got the fully cooked one, with the soaking and cooking already taken care of. I got some **Hub's** peanuts, too, the long, sleek Virginia peanuts that are the choice goobers when you're going uptown.

Padow's also carries "Virginia hams," less salty hams that have almost the intensity of flavor of the Smithfield hams, but not quite. If you ask, they may also have some sugar-cured "country hams" from North Carolina, but . . . well, you're just asking for trouble.

What else can you do with your Smithfield ham? I made a very easy and delicious ham and oyster pie, a dish I'd enjoyed some years ago at the **King's Arms** in Williamsburg. Take about half a pound of thinly sliced Smithfield ham, cut up into pieces about the size of a quarter, and a dozen Chincoteague oysters. Make a double piecrust recipe, and line a 9-inch pie pan with one crust. Mix up the oysters and ham in a white sauce, and pour it all in the pan. Cover it with the other crust, crimp the edges, and cut some vents in the top. Bake it in a 400-degree oven for about twenty minutes, or till the crust is golden. Eat immediately. Share if you must.

Oh, there's so much more here in the borderlands between the solid eaters of Pennsylvania and New York and the hungry traditionalists of the South. We haven't really talked about peanuts, or Baltimore's beloved pit beef, or the fried pies of the Shenandoah Valley, or Virginia's idiosyncratic take on barbecue (chop it up and bury it in funky sweet tomato-vinegar sauce, then serve it on white-bread burger rolls with a big topping of cole slaw), or the "waterman's chowder" of the Chesapeake that puts Manhattan and New England chowders to shame, or the glories of Washington's ethnic restaurants. So much to eat, so few pages to put it on. But Paul Reiser mentioned a beauty: Get yourself some Maryland fried chicken, a hearty fried chicken breaded with cracker crumbs and served with cream gravy. That's chicken-fried chicken, my friend. Some people like it almost as much as crabs. Almost.

Richmond and Tidewater

Richmond—along with Houston, Texas; Kailua-Kona, Hawaii; and Sonoma, California—holds the distinction of once having been the capital of a country within the current borders of the United States. All of these countries ended quickly, but none in so violent an end as the Confederate States of America. Richmond burned in self-inflicted agony as the Confederacy came to an end, torching her own commercial buildings to deny anything to the advancing Union troops—a hard lesson the Confederates had learned in Sherman's infamous March to the Sea.

Richmond burned, but Richmond had too long a history to disappear. The area was first explored by Capt. John Smith in 1607, shortly after he landed at Jamestown with the colonists. By 1609, commerce was taking place at the spot that came to be known as Shockoe Slip, and a community named None Such was growing.

Downriver, the Jamestown community had taken hold, and all along the James, tobacco plantations began to operate. The New World was not brimming over with gold, as popularly thought in England, but planters grew rich once England stuck their weed in a pipe and smoked it. Tobacco was practically the currency in the Tidewater area, stretching all along the James up to the falls at Richmond.

This wealth from agriculture started a Southern culture that would bring huge fortunes to the area, bring slaves to America and start a controversy that would boil over into rebellion and war, and sow the seeds of defeat in that war by relying on agriculture and honor to such an extent that "mechanics" were despised and dishonored. The first "slaves" in America were probably European indentured servants; the first African slaves came to America in 1619.

The plantation system built itself further on slavery, and solid citizens like the founding fathers kept slaves. Jefferson had more than two hundred slaves on his estate at Monticello; Washington owned more than three hundred, but freed his slaves in his will.

As the Northern states grew in industrial might and population, they looked south and saw only misery. Abolitionists raised the banner of emancipation; slaveowners returned cries of the rights of the states to enact their own laws.

When matters came to a head and the Southern states seceded to form the Confederacy, they chose Richmond as the capital, a spare 100 miles from the Union capital in Washington. The Tidewater region was right in the thick of things throughout the war, including the Guantá-namo-like Union outpost at Fortress Monroe, which remained a thorn in the Confederate side throughout the war and served as the start point for George McClellan's ill-fated Peninsular Campaign. When Ulysses S. Grant finally put the pressure of Union manpower and logistics to bear on the Confederate capital, Richmond burned.

But the South—or at least, Richmond—had learned. Richmond became one of the leading industrial centers of America. Iron foundries, cigarette factories, aluminum foundries, all flourished in the River City. The Hampton Roads took to shipbuilding in a major way, but also stuck to the trade for which it had been known since tobacco days, a large part of which passed over Richmond's railroads. The James became a busy highway of barges carrying goods from ocean to inland and vice versa.

Manufacturing in Richmond, as in many American cities, has declined, though the city still has sizable foundries and the big tobacco factories. Newport News still builds ships, and Norfolk is one of the largest naval bases in the world. The whole area pulses with military power, with three army posts, the marines' Camp Allen, Langley Air Force Base, and Oceana Naval Air Station. Richmond has grown as the state capital and become a financial center as well. The entire area has experienced a growth of tourism from historical sites, beaches and state parks, amusement and entertainment centers, and even the local breweries.

Through it all, Richmond has remained a beautiful city, noted for tree-lined streets, public statuary, and gracious hospitality. Restoration of the train station in downtown, a landmark stranded and surrounded by interstate flyovers, is continuing as the city realizes a vision for the future that will present the best face to the rest of the area.

Tidewater has retained its close links to the sea and the land. The James remains a highway to the sea and a favorite of pleasure boaters. Hampton Roads and the lower Chesapeake Bay are just as awe-inspiring as ever. Virginia Beach has reinvigorated itself as a family destination with a bigger beach and a cleaned-up boardwalk.

The area's breweries range from small brewpubs like the Hops pubs, to thriving brewpub–production breweries like Legend, all the way up to the huge Anheuser-Busch brewery in Williamsburg. Until Mobjack Bay recently ceased brewing operations to go to contract brewing, Richmond had as many breweries as Philadelphia, a city seven times its size and one generally regarded as a top American beer town.

With the long history of this region, it's bound to stay interesting. The strong traditions of Tidewater and Richmond make for interesting stories (and museums) and a solid base for their culture; the intense drive for improvement and the future will make for great new excitement in the years to come.

Blue and Gray Brewing Company

The Courage to be The Best

3321 Dill Smith Drive, Fredericksburg, VA 22408
540-538-2379
www.blueandgraybrewingco.com

Brewers are usually a fun bunch. Sometimes it gets boring, looking at tanks and hearing about crash-cooling and grist hydration, but most of these guys are willing to relax and have a couple, and then things get looser. I've been hanging out with brewers since the late 1980s, and I've had a lot of laughs.

The prize, however, goes to the crew at Blue and Gray Brewing, and the brewers weren't even there the day I stopped in. Jeff Fitzpatrick had a crew of brewery investors there, guys who volunteer on weekends and take their "pay" in beer, and we were laughing out loud before I even had my first sample of Fred Red. As the afternoon passed, I learned that they were all retired military, U.S. Navy and Marine Corps, and that they had eight advanced degrees among the three of them.

Happy people must make good beer, because Blue and Gray turns out some superior brews. You'd never think it to look at the place, though that's

Beers brewed: Year-round: Fred Red Ale, Falmouth American Pale Ale, Blue & Gray Classic Lager, Stonewall Stout. Seasonal: Christmas Cranberry Ale, Spiced Winter Ale.

true of a number of breweries. Blue and Gray is housed in a plain, old brick warehouse, one huge room that holds everything: the 25-barrel Newlands brewhouse, the tanks, the tasting area, and the cold room. You may not recognize the cold room as such right away; it's an old Hershey's ice cream truck up on blocks with most of the cab cut away.

The Pick: I could easily Pick any of these beers; they're all very good and hit me right in the sweet spot. But let's focus on Fred Red, because this kind of beer is not common. Fred Red is a dark garnet, with a fruity nose; a malty, juicy mouth; and a finish that leaves you thinking about your next sip. It's a beer that tastes just as good ice cold or at cellar temperature, and that's not easy.

"I saw it sitting in a field," said Jeff, "and asked the owner what he wanted for it. He said 'Oh, you don't want it, the motor's blown and you'd have to replace that before you could drive it.' I finally got it as is for $125." He laughed. "I spent more than that on having it towed here!" The refrigeration equipment still works fine, and it makes a great place to hang banners. If you think that's funny, ask to see the Franken-filler, a perfectly functional counterpressure filler that was ginned up by one of those overeducated navy guys. It looks like a cartoon in a plumber's magazine, but it does the job.

All this stuff is done on the cheap because what really matters at Blue and Gray is the beer. Jeff has sacrificed a lot to live this dream, and he's not going to let a few dollars get in his way. "I had a master's degree in public administration," he said. "I was working on government performance measures, but I wanted a change. About the same time, I had started homebrewing, and good beer got to me. Once you've had Starbuck's, you can't go back to regular coffee!"

Jeff went to working part-time in Washington while working full-time on building the brewery. Once it was built, he has been tireless in selling and promoting the beer. "If we're able to publicize that we're on tap in a place, so that people know to ask for our beer, the beer does well," he said. "Working with accounts that way is the best way I can spend my time. I know I'm never going to sell the beer outside of Virginia, so my time is best spent getting to know all my local accounts on a first-name basis."

He never misses a trick, either. When I asked Jeff for recommendations on bars in Fredericksburg, he named a few, then asked if I would mind asking for his beer when I went in, telling the bartender that I'd been to the brewery and they'd sent me to his bar. Not at all, Jeff, not at all; anything I can do for beer this good is a pleasure.

After I finished up with Jeff and got ready to leave, I stopped and chatted with the "volunteers" outside. They were nailing up trellises to the side of the building for the hop vines Jeff had planted. He's also talked

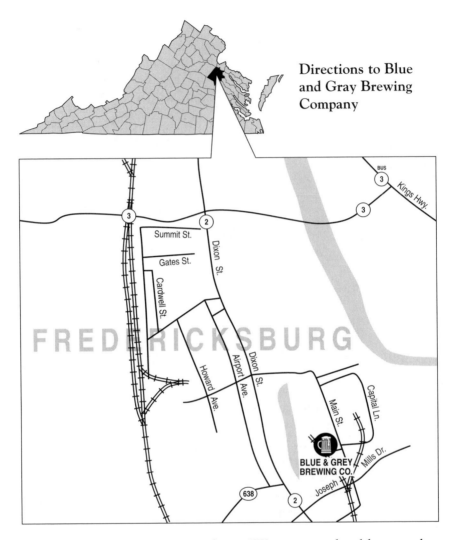

Directions to Blue and Gray Brewing Company

some local farmers into growing hops. "We use more local hops as they grow more," Jeff said. "Virginia used to be the hop capital of the colonies."

Local knowledge and local loyalty have taken Blue and Gray this far. Jeff's persistence and enthusiasm will continue to carry them into the future. And if that isn't quite enough, the inspired humor that comes up with slogans like "I'd give my right arm for a Stonewall Stout" might just do the trick.

Opened: St. Patrick's Day 2002.
Owner: Jeff Fitzpatrick.
Brewer: Jim Moeller.
System: 25-barrel Newlands system, 1,500 barrels annual capacity.

Production: 800 barrels in 2003.

Tours: Wednesday, 3 P.M. to 6 P.M.; Saturday, 10 A.M. to 1 P.M.

Take-out beer: 22-ounce bottles, cases, growlers; call ahead for kegs.

Special considerations: No smoking allowed in brewery. Kids welcome. Handicapped-accessible.

Parking: Free lot.

Lodging in the area: Kenmore Inn, 1200 Princess Anne Street, 800-327-7622; Holiday Inn, 564 Warrenton Road, 540-371-5550; Best Western Central Plaza, 3000 Plank Road, 540-786-7404.

Area attractions: George Washington grew up near Fredericksburg on his father's *Ferry Farm,* now an archeological site east of town (268 King's Highway, 540-370-0732). But unlucky Fredericksburg is more famous for its unwilling participation in the Civil War, a fate destined by its position between Richmond and Washington. Four major battles were fought near here: Chancellorsville, where Stonewall Jackson was shot by his own men; Fredericksburg; Spotsylvania Court House; and the Wilderness. These battlefields, which saw a brilliant victory by Robert E. Lee and the start of Grant's grinding assault on Richmond, are preserved in the *Fredericksburg and Spotsylvania National Military Park* (visitors center is at 1013 Lafayette Boulevard, 540-373-6122). Self-guided tour materials are available for rental or purchase at the visitors center.

    The brewery is across the street from 1 Bowman Drive, the home of the *A. Smith Bowman Distillery,* distillers of Virginia Gentleman bourbon, which was recently purchased by the Sazerac company. Sazerac has announced its intent to greatly increase the visibility of the distillery, including a visitors center and tours. Call 703-373-4555 for more information about this bourbon distillery in Virginia.

    Historic Fredericksburg is a good place for walking and shopping, a pleasantly shaded and pretty town.

Other area beer sites: The *Hard Times Café* (314 Jefferson Davis Highway, 540-899-6555) has a jiving bunch of guys behind the bar and grill, and some Blue and Gray taps in there with the crafts and imports; check out the bottles, too. *J. Brian's Taproom* (200 Hanover Street, 540-373-0738) has some kind of weird vibe going on: a hangout for Irish parrothead Republican Red Sox–lovin' Packers fans, it looks like. But it's a nice old place with a small bar and great beers in historic downtown Fredericksburg. Jeff also recommended *Sammy T's* (801 Caroline Street, 540-371-2008), which has a menu sure to appeal to vegetarians, and *Spanky's* (917 Caroline Street, 540-372-9999), which is a bit more than a deli. Quite a bit more, evidently.

Richbrau Brewing Company and Restaurant

1214 East Cary Street, Richmond, VA 23219
804-644-3018
www.richbrau.com

Shockoe Slip is one of the oldest commercial neighborhoods in the United States, dating back to 1609. See the canal running by the James? George Washington was the president of the company that built it. See the State Capitol building up the hill? Thomas Jefferson designed it. See St. John's Church up the opposite hill? That's where Patrick Henry made his famous declaration. This isn't just Virginia history, this is one of the very birthplaces of America.

The buildings here in the Slip don't date from that long ago, though. The oldest ones only go back as far as 1866. When the Union Army finally closed in on the Confederate capitol in April 1865, desperate Richmond residents set fire to the warehouses to keep the supplies from falling into Yankee hands. The war over, they rebuilt, and those brick warehouses are what you see in the Slip today. As Richbrau owner Mike Byrne says, "This isn't a mall. It's real. The neighborhood's been here, and it's staying."

Byrne ought to know. He's been working on this cobblestoned stretch of Cary Street for the past twenty-five years. "I tended bar up at Sam Miller's," he said. "Believe me; I know my customers by now!" He knows them, and he strongly believes in giving them what they want.

"Look," Mike said, "you don't go to a seafood place and order steak, right? Well, turn it around. If my customers want fruit beers, I'm not going to make fun of them and offer them something else; I'm going to provide them with fruit beers . . . along with our other beers. Our brewers take the customer's tastes into account and translate that into good beermaking. That's what a brewpub is about: regional tastes."

Mike saved this place. He bought it in 1995, when it had been foreclosed after a 1993 opening. "We changed everything," said Mike, and I'll back him on that. It was a different place; you could tell

Beers brewed: Year-round: Griffin Golden Ale, Big Nasty Porter, Old Nick Pale Ale. Seasonals: Alley Oop Ale, Hefeweizen, Maibock, Hogwash Ale, Oatmeal Stout, Barleywine, Special Belgian Ale, and more.

right away. "I think I fired thirty people in seventy-two hours," he recalled. "Not because they weren't good people, but they were just bodies in slots; they weren't picked for the jobs they were supposed to be doing. You have to embrace the customer, the food, the beer, not just do a job. Take that element out, and all you've got is chairs and equipment."

Richbrau has been growing since that time, "a slow evolution," said Mike. No longer is it just the brewery in the window and the dark wood-trimmed bar. There's a large dining room, an even larger pool hall upstairs, a dance club for weekends, and the Taphouse, a lighter, brighter addition on the uphill side of the building that has become my favorite part of the brewpub.

The Pick: Richbrau's Barleywine has always been excellent; I have heard of some people traveling to Richmond in December just to get some. Come to think of it, I did that one year. It's a big ol' glass of beer candy, sugar-rich and sweet but fenced and spiked with a trenchant bitterness. This is a mouthful, no doubt, and you'll savor every drop. But don't overlook the Griffin Golden. It's tasting fantastic lately, and that's a big feather in Mike Banks's cap.

Head brewer Mike Banks likes it here, too, and he sat with me while I had lunch. "I really love this job," he said. "I feel lucky. Mike gives us a lot of freedom." He shared an aged bottle of his Special Belgian Ale with me, a deliciously balanced beer spiked with orange peel and candy sugar.

After a slow run at the market, Richbrau is going to try the bottle game again, and given how great the Griffin Golden tasted on my last visit, the brewery is definitely ready for it. "You'll see our product growing in the market soon," Mike Byrne told me. More slow evolution.

Next time you stop in at Richbrau, come on over to the Taphouse. Rest your elbows on the one-hundred-year-old loblolly pine bar, and if you think that's old, take a look at the service bar over by the kitchen; it's four-hundred-year-old pine, milled out of beams they found in the basement that survived the Civil War fires. Survey your choices: Griffin Golden, Old Nick Pale Ale, the Big Nasty Porter, three or four seasonals, and a broad selection of spirits. Now, order up, settle in, and take off your watch. Turn off your cell phone. Relax. This neighborhood's not going anywhere, and while you're enjoying the beer, neither are you.

Opened: Originally in 1993; new owner reopened in July 1995.
Owner: Mike Byrne.
Brewers: Mike Banks, brewer; Arec Leinen, assistant.
System: 14-barrel Pub Brewing system, 1,200 barrels annual capacity.
Production: 695 barrels in 2003.
Hours: 11:30 A.M. to midnight (or later), seven days a week.

Tours: On request, limited by brewer availability, and by appointment for groups or individuals.

Take-out beer: Growlers, six-packs, and 22-ounce bottles available; call ahead for kegs.

Food: It's a brewpub menu in the dining room and the pub, with steaks, burgers, seafood, pasta, and the like. You can also order from the stripped-down pub menu everywhere but in the TapHouse Grill. The Grill has its own menu: shrimp and cheese grits, mouth-watering grilled sandwiches, cowboy steak, grilled salmon . . . a more upscale menu, but still casual and reasonably priced.

Extras: Where to start? This place is huge! Richbrau has dart boards and eleven pool tables on the second floor, along with a bunch of tuned-permanently-to-sports TVs. It also sponsors cultural nights, with local authors having frank, beer-driven discussions of their work. There's Club Richbrau, a full-featured dance floor, and live music every Friday; call for schedule.

Special considerations: Kids welcome. Vegetarian meals available; better selection in the TapHouse Grill. Handicapped-accessible.

Parking: Street parking can be dicey; there are pay garages in the area.

Lodging in the area: Linden Row Inn, 100 East Franklin Street, 804-783-7000; William Catlin House, 2304 East Broad Street, 804-780-3746; Massad House Hotel,11 North Fourth Street, 804-648-2893. The Jefferson Hotel (101 West Franklin Street, 804-788-8000) is steeply more expensive than most hotels I've mentioned, but it is a beautifully restored wonder. If you don't stay here, at least stop in at *T. J.'s Grill and Bar* for a beer and look around.

Area attractions: See the *Virginia State Capitol* (Capitol Square, 804-698-1788), a historic building that, like much else in this city, has surprising depth. Aaron Burr was tried for treason here in 1807, the Confederate Congress met here, and the only statue of George Washington done from life is in the rotunda. *The Museum of the Confederacy,* 91201 East Clay Street, 804-649-1861 (gotta like that phone number!), holds military artifacts, more than five hundred political and military flags of the Confederacy, exhibits on free and enslaved African Americans, and artwork related to the Confederacy. Right next door is the *White House of the Confederacy,* the executive mansion of Jefferson Davis, the only president of the Confederacy. The *Edgar Allan Poe Museum* (1914 East Main Street, 804-648-5523) is not in Poe's Richmond home, though he lived longer in Richmond than anywhere else. It is the oldest home in Richmond, dating from 1737. Exhibits include first editions and Poe-abilia.

Had enough museums? Take a walk along the **Richmond Flood-wall,** a mile-long levee that runs along the James River. Walk out to Belle Isle and Brown's Island on the foot bridge under the Lee Bridge (Seventh Street and Tredegar Streets), and tour the earthwork fortifications on the island—or just look at the water and the waterbirds.

The **17th Street Farmers' Market** in Shockoe Bottom is open every day but Sunday and has been since 1779, one of the oldest in the country. It's a real farmers' market, so don't expect costumed interpreters, just produce and meats.

Catch the **Richmond Braves** at the Diamond (3001 North Boulevard, 804-359-4444), an aging but beautiful minor-league ballpark, and just down the street from Zippy's Ba-Ba (see page 225).

And if you want to get a bit crazy, you have some options. Hop in the James and shoot the rapids with the **Richmond Raft Company** (4400 East Main Street, 800-540-7238). There are some serious Class IV and V rapids at the falls, and these guys will take you. Or you can get your thrills in neater packages at **Paramount's King's Dominion** (exit 98 off I-95, Doswell, 804-876-5000), a very popular amusement park north of town with a water park and an even dozen roller coasters. They used to have a brewpub, too, but all things pass.

Other area beer sites: Richmond's premier beer bar has become **Capital Ale House** (623 East Main Street, 804-643-ALES), by virtue of . . . well, of everything. The Ale House has a great tap selection, not just in sheer numbers, but also in the range and rarity of the selections. The bottle range is equally deep and includes special bottlings. The food is beyond pub grub. The decor is stunning for beer drinkers used to dive bars or tarted-up fern bars: dark wood, high ceiling, well lit, and the oh-so ice rail down the center of the bar to keep your beer cold. The new **Capital Ale House at Innsbrook** (4024-A Cox Road, Glen Allen, 804-780-ALES) is, if possible, even more so, a huge space that can accommodate seven hundred people, with seventy-seven total taps. It has a nonsmoking bar, an outdoor bar with additional seating and a patio with pools and ducks, a fireplace room, and even more cooler space. It's magnificent. I still like going to the **Commercial Tap House and Grill** (111 North Robinson Street, 804-359-6544) for a couple good reasons. First, you never know what's going to happen at the Tap. My brother-in-law Carl and I recently walked in on a transsexual murder mystery night of performance art that was hysterical. Second, the Tap is making a great beer comeback after a bit of a slump, and it's had some great beers on. And the Tap was first, and that counts.

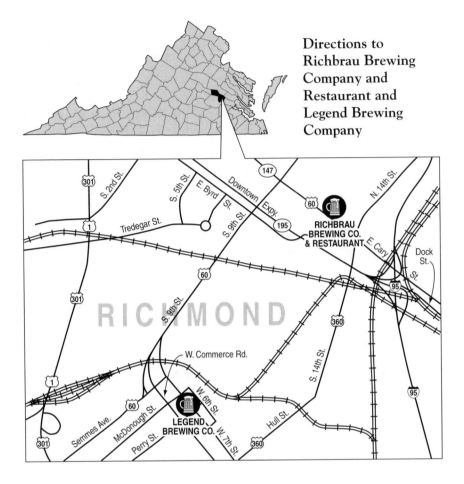

Directions to Richbrau Brewing Company and Restaurant and Legend Brewing Company

Bottoms Up Pizza (1700 Dock Street, 804-644-4400) is right down in Shockoe Bottom, beside the big parking lot under the I-95 flyovers and the old train station; it feels a bit *Blade Runner*-ish down here at twilight. The beer's good, pizza's great, but service can be glacial. Take a tip: Sit at the bar. Not far away is **Julep's** (1721 East Franklin Street, 804-377-3968), where, as you might expect from the name, you will find not beer but an excellent bourbon selection at a beautiful high-end bar and restaurant. The food is top-rate; Richmond reviewers called Julep's the best new restaurant in town.

Penny Lane Pub (421 East Franklin Street, 804-780-1682) is a real-deal English-style pub, of the urban persuasion. The owner, Terry O'Neill, purportedly worked in Liverpool as a bouncer at a club where the Beatles played in their early years, and Penny Lane is covered in Beatles memorabilia as well as football memorabilia. It's fun, the beer's well kept, and the malts and Irish whiskey selection is quite good. The **Fox and Hounds British Pub** (10455 Midlothian Turnpike, 804-272-8309) is nowhere near as authentic, but it's a refuge from the world, a slightly worn bar with billiards, old pinball games, a serious darts scene, and a surprising selection of draft and bottled beer. No one will ever know you're here. Not far from the Fox and Hounds is a completely different place: **Mekong** (6004 West Broad Street, 804-288-8929), which looks like a bleak storefront from the outside but is a palatial Vietnamese restaurant inside, with a startling selection of Belgian and American specialty beers in 750-milliliter and 22-ounce bottles. The rare combination of top-rate Vietnamese cuisine and nonmundane beers is too good to pass up. The **Sidewalk Café** (2101 West Main Street, 804-358-0645) is just a representative example of the many small, good, friendly restaurant bars in The Fan area, seemingly one on every corner. Wander in, wander out, on to the next one, it's a Richmond thing. One that's really out there and should not be missed is **Zippy's Ba Ba** (3336 North Boulevard, 804-359-5673), out by the Richmond Diamond. Zippy's looks like a garage that someone backed a restaurant into, and left it running. And Zippy's motorcycles are sitting around the place. The beer is top-notch: great drafts, great bottles, great attitude. These guys have beer in their Greek restaurant (with fantastic burger bar and Greek food, too) because they really, really dig beer. I'm way behind that kind of guy. And don't forget: "We are closed Saturdays, so I can race my motorcycles. Zippy."

One more. Carl told me that Richmond people never ever go to Petersburg, so he took me there, to **The Brickhouse Run** (409 Cockade Alley, 804-862-1815). It was phenomenal, one of my favorite bars of this whole book, a beautiful small bar with a stone floor, brick walls, a low ceiling, and a great bartender. We had St. George IPA on cask, in perfect condition. The owner, Steve Dickinson, said he didn't want the forced Britishness of some "pubs" in America. "I tried to envision what a Virginia pub would look like if Virginia were part of England." Odd twist, but it sure worked. Ask him to see the pictures of his wife's grandfather. Highly recommended.

Hops Restaurant and Brewery, Richmond

9498 West Broad Street, Richmond, VA 23294
804-934-0303

1570 Koger Center Boulevard, Richmond, VA 23235
804-794-2727

www.hopsonline.com

This was the first Hops I ever visited. This chain is a big one, with more than fifty Hops brewpubs. I had been told terrible things about Hops—that the beer was awful and I shouldn't bother going, because they're "not really brewpubs," whatever that means.

Well, that just didn't do it for me; I had to go and see it and make up my own mind. What I found made me curious. There were five beers on tap, all brewed in-house on the plainly visible brewing system in the back of the dining room. At least, I'm pretty sure that's where it was. The major difference once I got inside these places was the bartender. I remember this one had the brunette with the pierced eyebrow, but I'm not sure where the brewhouse was located. The eyebrow distracted me, I guess.

But the beer was just fine. They were all clean and tasted fresh, and the Alligator Ale was a dark brown beer on the border between brown ale and porter, with a medium body and hints of chocolate. Something odd was going on here; maybe people were just overtaken with chain hatred? I confess to more than a touch of it myself, but there's no denying that these beers were better than I'd been led to expect.

I called Dave Richter, the director of brewing operations for the whole chain, at his office in Tampa, and asked him to tell me the story. "Back in the day," Dave began, "the original owners were Coors Light drinkers and just wanted to be able to say that they made everything in-house, like the food. 'We don't really need to get involved with brewers; here's the recipe, boom.'" The beers were

Beers brewed: Year-round: Clearwater Light, Lightning Bold Gold, Thoroughbred Red, Alligator Ale. Seasonals: Flying Squirrel Nut Brown Ale, Love Handles Low Carb, Powder Horn Pilsner, Big 'Skeeter Pale Ale, Lumberjack Oatmeal Stout, Beat the Heat Wheat, Single Hop Ale, Royal English Amber, Star Spangled Ale, Hoptoberfest.

formulated using a lot of corn syrup and brewed with dry yeast, two procedures that would raise the hackles of most beer lovers.

Dave's changed that. "I've been able to upgrade the malts," he said. "No more corn syrup. We use liquid yeast instead of dry yeast. As much as I'd like to brew things like Belgian tripels and barleywines, it just doesn't fit in the concept. So we try to put out a consistent set of beers. I've made my guys very paranoid about cross-contamination of yeast and ramped up our cleaning regime. That's where we are."

Dave knows what he's talking about, and surprise, he's from Virginia. He grew up in Alexandria and started homebrewing in high school. That expe-

The Pick: Alligator Ale is the biggest flavor in the four core beers, but my Pick is the Lightning Bold Gold. This beer caught me off guard. It's Coors Light light in color, but it has more body than the Silver Bullet and real malt flavor behind it. It's not going to wean you off something like Old Dominion's Millennium, but it is a stealth mainstreamer, one that could easily be a stepping-stone to better beer for your light beer–swilling buddies.

Directions to Hops Restaurant and Brewery, West Broad Street, Richmond

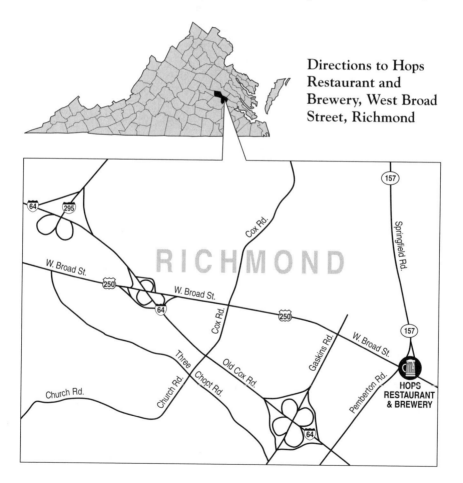

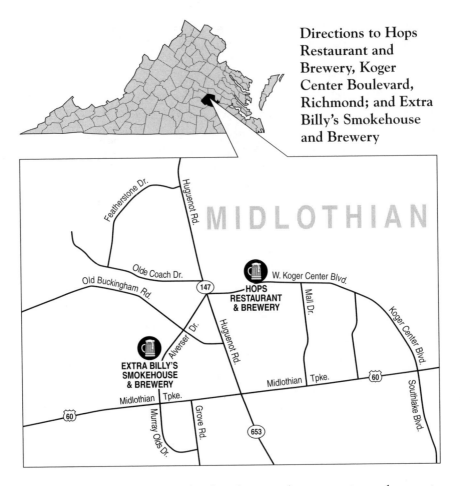

Directions to Hops Restaurant and Brewery, Koger Center Boulevard, Richmond; and Extra Billy's Smokehouse and Brewery

rience eventually wound up landing him a job as an assistant brewer in Tampa, and from there he studied brewing at the Siebel Institute and UC Davis, the country's top two schools. "That's not a requirement at our brewpubs," said Dave of the education. "But it's not at most others, either." True enough.

"We're trying to put out some more interesting beers," Dave told me. "We keep the four core beers on, and then the seasonal. Our summer seasonal is a filtered American wheat with Florida orange blossom honey and a little coriander. A lot of the brewers prefer to stick to the hoppier beers. The Big 'Skeeter Pale Ale has 52 IBU." That's a lot more than I expected from Hops, I have to admit!

"It's a challenge, getting all the ingredients out to all the breweries," Dave said. "Half of them are in Florida, but we've got breweries in Colorado, Minnesota, Connecticut . . . It's hard getting a seasonal out there that everyone's happy with, but it's still fun. It's beer; it's supposed to be fun."

John Evans is a very helpful and considerate fellow, and someone who obviously had taken to Dave's cleaning and yeast orders. The beers were clean as a whistle, and even the Clearwater Light was surprisingly tasty, despite being as pale as Michelob Ultra.

Beer quality like that has to help, but it's not easy to overcome the image of Hops as beer-in-a-box. Dave Richter's aware of that. "You can't change public opinion overnight," he agreed, "so we just keep our heads down and keep swinging." There's not much else to do. Why not stop in and see how Dave's efforts are coming along? You won't find a barleywine or a Belgian tripel, but I can almost guarantee you'll find four clean beers and a seasonal that just might surprise you.

Opened: May 2000.

Owner: Avado Brands.

Brewer: John Evans.

System: 3.5-barrel Pub Brewing system, 800 barrel annual capacity.

Production: About 340 barrels in 2003.

Hours: 11 A.M. to 11 P.M., seven days a week.

Tours: On request or by appointment.

Take-out beer: Growlers available.

Food: As at Hops Alexandria (see page 119). The Pot Stickers were really good, too.

Special considerations: Kids welcome. Some vegetarian meals available. Handicapped-accessible.

Parking: Large lot.

Legend Brewing Company

321 West Seventh Street, Richmond, VA 23224
804-232-8871
www.legendbrewing.com

Picture it: a mild, shirt-sleeve New Year's Eve twilight. I've been bar-hopping with my family and my brother-in-law Carl Childs's family in Richmond: lunch at Capital Ale House, a couple small bottle shops in Carytown, a quick pint in The Fan, and now it's sunset on the deck at Legend. We're enjoying the view over the James River while sipping glasses of briskly hoppy pilsner and sweet root beer.

This is the biggest outdoor drinking area in town, with that broad view of the river and downtown. We're dining on a real variety of stuff, too: steamed mussels, a bratwurst platter, a crab quesadilla with Legend's own salsa, and the ubiquitous big juicy brewpub burger. Inside, where Carl and I manage to coordinate our visits to the men's room in such a way that we wind up at the bar for a short sampling session away from our wives' eagle eyes, there's another large dining area, though it's largely deserted because of the lure of the deck in this unseasonably mild weather. We rejoin our families on the deck, and it's a great ending to a truly good day.

Now picture this: Years before that New Year's Eve, Carl and I arrive at Legend on a hot summer afternoon. There is no deck, there is no view of the James, there is no upstairs. There is only the downstairs area just outside the cast-iron gates of the brewhouse, an L-shaped bar wrapped around a small grill with two tables and a window bar with stools, seating for about sixteen. The menu is simple: You can have omelettes, you can have chili, or you can have a chili omelette. There is no table service; you just call out what you need, and then go to the bar and pick it up. But the beer is already quite good, and Carl and I are swapping around glasses of Doppelbock, Pilsner, and the Legend Brown, which will become the brewery's mainstay.

That was Legend in the old days, when chances were good on the weekends that owner Tom Martin

Beers brewed: Year-round: Lager, Pilsner, Brown Ale, Porter, Golden IPA. Seasonals: Doppelbock, Pale Ale, Oktoberfest, Chocolate Porter, Tripel, Barleywine, Hefeweizen, Stout, plus numerous one-offs like Rye, Wit, Alt, Imperial Stout, Hefemalzen, and more to come.

would be sitting at one of those three tables having a beer with you. The beers today are more varied, the menu has expanded greatly, the old downstairs bar is a prep kitchen, and the deck is great, especially on the summer nights when they haul out the 16-millimeter movie projector and show classic films on a portable screen, or during the Sunday-night bluegrass jams. But I don't know anyone who was there in the old days that doesn't miss that tiny downstairs bar—well, any customer, that is.

The Pick: The first time I had Legend's Golden Ale, I thought I was just being thorough—oh, well, might as well have the Golden while I'm on my way to the Porter; it's my job, after all. I almost broke my neck double-taking at this beer. Golden Ale is what Legend calls their deceptively light-colored IPA, and it's a brisk one, an IPA in light's clothing. This relatively light-framed IPA is so hoppy it almost burns, in that good way properly hopped IPAs have. Consider this fair warning.

Let's all heave a sigh for the old days of brewpubs, then, and move on. Legend is doing about 4,000 barrels a year these days, which may not sound like a lot, but they're doing almost all of that themselves, through their own distributing company or through the pub. They move about 1,000 barrels a year through the pub and most of the rest within 20 miles of there. They've moved into Fredericksburg recently, and tried the Virginia beaches, but that just didn't work out.

Still, 3,000 barrels within 20 miles makes Legend a real presence in Richmond, the local beer. Walk into most bars in the city, and you'll find the distinctive white cylindrical taphandle with its unicorn decal. They're just starting to break into the chain restaurants, too. Chances are if you just tell a Richmond bartender "I'll have a Legend," you'll get Legend Brown Ale, the sweet, easy, smooth beer that is the brewery's best-seller. Just be forewarned that it's a 6 percent beer you're drinking.

Some breweries would call Legend's growth small, but the crew there is happy with it. Four thousand barrels a year's not such a bad place to be. They haven't borrowed a lot of money to get there. Tom had a good chunk of money to start with from family investors.

They got a good deal on the next step, too. I got a look at Legend's new brewhouse—new to them, anyway. The brewkettle is a 30-barrel reworked lauter tun from Old Dominion, and three 25-barrel vessels came from Steamship Brewing, a defunct Newport News brewery, including a lauter tun that may have originally been at the old Chesbay brewery, an early Tidewater pioneer in microbrewing. That's going to make it a lot easier for Legend's brewers, who are currently brewing two or three times a day on a 10-barrel system to keep up with demand.

This used to be a bad neighborhood. Now things are improving; they're turning the old warehouses into loft apartments and art galleries. I like to think that at least part of the credit should go to Legend.

Brewpubs have proved to be excellent seeds for strong neighborhoods, even when they're tiny seeds that serve only chili and omelettes. As they grow, they bring the neighborhood right along.

The last time I went to Legend was for a brewers' meeting. All the brewers gathered back in the brewery, talking, drinking. I took the opportunity to pour myself a quiet pint of absolutely exceptional Tenth Anniversary Ale, sneaked out to the prep kitchen, and sat in my old spot by the window. I'd go up to the deck later and enjoy the view. But for now I was enjoying the old days . . . the Legendary ones.

Opened: December 1993.

Owner: Tom Martin.

Brewers: John Wampler, Alex Coppola, Sean Overbey.

System: 10-barrel Bohemian system, 4,500 barrels annual capacity.

Production: 4,000 barrels in 2003.

Hours: Monday through Thursday, 11:30 A.M. to 11 P.M.; Friday and Saturday, 11:30 A.M. to midnight; Sunday, 10:30 to 11 P.M.

Tours: 1 P.M. Saturday.

Take-out beer: 1-liter growlers, 22-ounce bottles, cases of twelve 22-ounce bottles.

Food: How about that crab quesadilla? The homemade salsa really is good, too. I'm always happy to see the traditional English ploughman's lunch on a brewpub menu, and Legend does it right, with pickle and bread and strong cheese. Don't overlook the mussels and the bratwurst platter, or the Cajun-style goodies.

Extras: The deck overlooking the James River and downtown Richmond is the best in the city, and a major draw almost year-round. Four dart boards give the brewpub a more British feel. Check out the free movies on the deck Tuesday nights in the summer; the audience participation is a hoot. There's a Sunday brunch, and bluegrass music Sunday nights, no cover, and you might see the Legend manager jamming with one or two of the groups.

Special considerations: Kids welcome. Vegetarian meals available. Handicapped-accessible.

Parking: Off-street lot and unmetered street parking.

Extra Billy's Smokehouse and Brewery

1110 Alverser Drive, Midlothian, VA 23113
804-379-8727

William "Extra Billy" Smith was a classic Southern politician. Born in 1796, he began practicing law in Culpeper County in 1818 and soon got involved in politics. Defeated in a congressional election in 1842, he retired to Fauquier County to rusticate. He was surprised to learn in 1845 that he had been chosen governor by the legislature. He served in Congress from 1853 to 1861, then was elected to the Confederate Congress, but resigned to command the 49th Virginia Infantry. After being severely wounded at Antietam ("As a soldier he was noted for valor rather than tactical skill," notes one biographical website), he resigned and was reelected governor of Virginia, a post he held until the fall of Richmond. He was elected to the House of Delegates again in 1877, at the age of eighty.

Impressive, but . . . why "Extra Billy"? Young William Smith started a mail-coach service in 1827 that ran from Washington to Georgia. As Smith expanded the service, he made so many claims for "extra" payments for mail delivery—history is a bit cloudy on whether the claims were wholly justified—that he gained the nickname "Extra Billy," a tag that followed him through his government and military service.

That's just the kind of historically sentimental, tongue-in-cheek name to endear a barbecue place to Richmond residents, and the original Extra Billy's, at 5205 West Broad Street, has been serving up great authentic barbecue to them for years. But the late Bob Harr, who was running things back when I made my first visit to the as-yet-unfinished brewpub in Midlothian, had his eyes set on the rapidly growing Richmond suburbs. "There's five times the people out there," he said matter-of-factly.

Beers brewed: Year-round: American Ale, Red Ale, Pilsner. Seasonals: Java Bock, IPA, Brown Ale, and others as Bill decides to brew them.

The Pick: Bill's Red Ale is the best-seller, and it's easy to see why. This malty, creamy ale, with caramel notes and a hint of roastiness, picks up all those flavors in the barbecue. Bill also had a weird one on when I visited, Java Bock, a blond bock infused with Viennese and Tanzanian coffee. It was floating with real coffee flavor and propped up with real bock body. Odd, but it worked well.

The new Extra Billy's, with a used JV NorthWest brewhouse out of a brewery in Charlotte, North Carolina, opened in 2000 on Alverser Drive, a rapidly growing area itself, cheek-by-jowl with plazas and big-box stores like the Circuit City across the way. Like the original, the place is permeated with the sweet, raunchy smell of hickory smoke and pork. The meat cooks in the low-temperature smoky hickory fire for upward of seven hours, and it is toothsome.

I asked Bob at the time why he decided to add a brewery to the tried-and-true barbecue formula. He told me of a man who drove down from just outside Washington, a ninety-minute haul, to arrive at Extra Billy's ten minutes before the 11 P.M. closing time, only to find that they were out of barbecue. "He said, 'How'm I going to go back home without any barbecue? I gotta have some of your barbecue!' Well, we found him some somewhere. I realized that good beer and good barbecue both have what you call cult followings." Bob chuckled. "That is, you get crazy people looking for both of them!"

It sounded like a good idea to me, but things haven't been quite as rosy as they could have been at the new Extra Billy's. Brewer Bill Ehlert blames it on the James River. "Around here," he said, "the James River might as well be the Great Wall of China. People from here don't go to Richmond, people from Richmond don't come here. The reputation of the original Extra Billy's should have filled this place, but no one out here knows about the original place—not when it's across the James." You can feel how it frustrated him. "I'm from Buffalo," he said with a laugh. "When I cross a river, I'm in another *country!*"

He can't even get any crossover sales going. Virginia laws make it problematic to get the house beers to the Richmond restaurant. The brewpub can't afford to advertise much, and there are other, more established barbecue joints on this side of the river. "I still think it's a good concept," said Bill, and I have to agree. Of course, barbecue and brewpub beer are two of my favorite things, so naturally I think it's a good concept!

All you have to do is get out there to Alverser Drive and roll down your car window. The mouth-watering smell will draw you in (worked for me). Then you can drop anchor at the bar, where the beer taps come out of the side of a big pink pig (Bill hates this, but I think it's classic!), and warm up with some barbecue beans and cornbread, and a couple of Bill's beers, before tackling the smoked sausage, pulled pork, or ribs. Dang. I'm drooling. Barbecue in a brewpub, and crazy people looking for them. That's us!

Opened: April 2000.

Owners: Harr family.

Brewer: Bill Ehlert.

System: 7-barrel JV NorthWest system, 750 barrels annual capacity.

Production: 210 barrels in 2003.

Hours: Tuesday through Thursday, 11:30 A.M. to 9:30 P.M.; Friday and Saturday, 11:30 A.M. to 10:30 P.M.; Sunday, noon to 9 P.M.; closed Monday.

Tours: As brewer is available.

Take-out beer: Growlers available.

Food: Delicious, smoky, mouth-watering, sense-obliteratingly good barbecue, buddy, that's what's for eating here. Pork, beef, chicken, sausage, beans, all the sides (it's Virginia, so you've got to have cole slaw for your pulled pork sandwich)—it's all here, and it's real good.

Special considerations: Kids welcome. Very little vegetarian food. Handicapped accessible.

Parking: Large lot.

Williamsburg Brewing Company

189B Ewell Road, Williamsburg, VA 23188
757-253-1577
www.williamsburgbrewing.com

Brewers start in lots of places. Some were plumbers, some were college admissions counselors. Fritz Maytag, rather famously, was the heir to an appliance fortune. A fair number came from the restaurant business or government service. I've known guys who were bouncers, pool salesmen, graphic artists, investment bankers, or schoolteachers before opening their breweries. Some guys just like starting businesses: Alan Newman of Magic Hat was described as "a serial entrepreneur." There are more than fourteen hundred breweries in the United States, and the men and women who started them came from all walks of life.

But I'll bet that Hugh Burns is the only brewery owner who used to be a Stealth fighter pilot. That's right—the owner of Williamsburg Brewing has logged hours in the cockpit of the F-117 Nighthawk, the most sophisticated combat aircraft in the U.S. Air Force (that we know about). As you might suspect, it was a long, strange trail that brought him to this historic town in Tidewater Virginia.

"Let's see," Hugh said. "We were living in Austin, Texas, where the Whole Foods supermarkets started. They had all kinds of great foods, and then I was walking down the beer aisle, just looking, when I saw a bottle of Chimay Belgian ale for $8. Eight dollars? I gotta try that! I really enjoyed it, and then Michael Jackson's *The Beerhunter* show was on the Discovery channel, and I watched all of that. I wanted to learn more."

Hugh got his chance when he was posted to a squadron in New Mexico. "The squadron commander was a homebrewer," he said with a wicked grin, "and some of the other pilots had started homebrewing. Well, fighter pilots are by nature competitive, so we started seeing who could brew the best beer. We'd get together for what we called ATF parties; we'd go skeet shooting, then break out the cigars and homebrew."

As retirement time started to come around, Hugh and his wife, Nadia, started looking at opportunities. "Opening a brewery" started as a joke. "But then we took a serious look at it," said Hugh, "and the more we looked, the more feasible it seemed. I had a biology degree with a minor in chemistry, so that helped. We drove around and looked at populations and demographics. Two major factors in craft beer consumption are education level and income level. Williamsburg had high levels of those two, and a strong tourist flow as well."

They opened the brewery as a draft-only operation and kept it that way for the first three years. "We were in Williamsburg," Hugh said, "so we do traditional American-style ales. We started with the pale ale and porter; there was a strong history of porter in Williamsburg. We did our wheat ale as a summer beer, and it sold so strongly we kept it on as a year-rounder. The stock ale was one we added as a traditional favorite in early America. We also regularly brew a *saison*-style we call ColoniAle for the Colonial Williamsburg taverns—Chowning's goes through a lot of it—and a steam beer that we do for Berret's seafood restaurant." They're doing bottles now, and every-

Beers brewed: Year-round: Williamsburg Pale Ale, Porter, Wheat Ale, Stock Ale, Amber Lager, ColoniAle. Seasonal: Grand Illumination Ale.

The Pick: Make mine the Porter. This is big, substantial beer, chock-full of flavor: roasty coffee notes, chocolate, malt. At 6.8 percent, it's riding the Baltic porter line, but the ale fermentation keeps it in the strong English territory. Not a simple supping beer. You'd better know what you're intending when you tear into one of these.

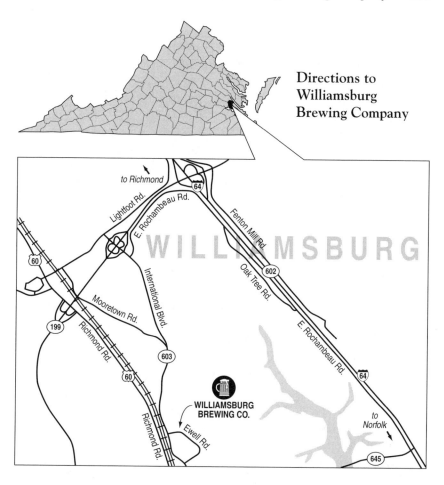

Directions to Williamsburg Brewing Company

thing is bottle-conditioned. "It's a little more work," Hugh said, "but the beer stays fresher longer."

Those beers, and seasonals like Williamsburg's popular Grand Illumination Ale, are brewed on a "very manual" 20-barrel Specific brewhouse. Everything in the brewhouse is on wheels (the brewing "platform" is a big stepladder) and gets moved around at bottling time. "Space is tight," Hugh told me. The seasonals are brewed to different recipes every year. It's more fun, more exciting that way, and "we get a chance to use ingredients that might happen to be really good that year," said Hugh.

Hugh and Nadia's six children help out in the brewery and in the store next door. The store sells the usual brewery merchandise—shirts, hats, glassware—as well as homebrew equipment and supplies, in a nod to Hugh's origins. "It was our first profit center," Hugh admits.

Things were tough for a while, as Nadia opened and ran an independent wholesale company to market the beer to customer accounts. "We almost went under twice because of the tough Virginia wholesale franchise laws," Hugh said, a song whose melody twines through the story of most breweries in this state, home to some of the least brewer-friendly wholesale laws in the country.

But the wholesale company, Nadia's sales efforts, and the improving quality of the beer are turning the tide. "We're brewing balls to the wall now," Hugh said, sounding like the jet jockey he used to be; right up against the firewall is probably pretty familiar territory for a guy hot enough to fly the Nighthawk. Just a bit more time and a little more luck, and Williamsburg Brewing will be flying high.

Opened: November 1996.

Owner: Hugh Burns.

Brewer: Hugh Burns.

System: 20-barrel Specific Mechanical system, 2,000 barrels annual capacity.

Production: 1,025 barrels in 2003.

Tours: Saturdays, 1 P.M. and 3 P.M.

Take-out beer: Six-packs, cases, growlers; half, quarter, and sixtel kegs. "Yes, we will refill growlers from other breweries!" says Hugh.

Special considerations: Handicapped-accessible.

Parking: Free lot at the brewery.

Lodging in the area: The Cedars B&B, 616 Jamestown Road, 757-229-3591; Williamsburg KOA Resorts Campground, 4000 Newman Road, 757-565-2907. Colonial Williamsburg lodgings are available at the Williamsburg Inn, Williamsburg Lodge, and the Governor's Inn and Guest Houses (757-229-1000).

Area attractions: *Colonial Williamsburg* is right here, and it's awesome, a wholly re-created colonial town. But note that most of the buildings have been *re-created*, not *restored*. Almost ninety of the buildings are restorations, but more than five hundred are re-creations. That's not to take away from the value, but it comes as a shock to some people. Get the details on what to see and what to do at www.colonialwilliamsburg.org or call 800-447-8679. There are no "don't miss" notes here. Try not to miss *anything* . . . which will take a few years, and do engage the guides in conversation; they love to be in character.

The *Colonial National Historical Park* (visitors centers at the western terminus of the Colonial Parkway, 757-229-1733, and the eastern terminus, 757-898-2410) encompasses two hundred years of colonial history. The **Jamestown Settlement** is the site of the first settlers in Virginia, who landed here in 1607. There are replicas of the ships that brought the settlers, typical buildings, a fort, and an Indian village. The **Yorktown Battlefield** commemorates the final battle of the Revolutionary War, where Washington's long campaign of maneuver finally came to a victorious end as his forces marched from New York to combine with Lafayette's forces (and a successful French naval blockade of the Chesapeake Bay) to besiege and defeat the British Army under Cornwallis. The battlefield site includes reconstructed redoubts and siegeworks.

Okay, time to shop. Go to the **Williamsburg Pottery Factory** in Lightfoot (just follow the signs that are everywhere, 757-564-3326) for a little bit of everything, then you're off to **Merchants' Square** on Colonial Williamsburg's Duke of Gloucester Street for the really neat stuff (with the big price tags).

Other area beer sites: The Colonial Taverns along Duke of Gloucester Street are regular restaurants and bars, and you don't have to be on a Freedom Pass to get into them. I've enjoyed eating at **The King's Arms** (opposite the Raleigh Tavern; call 800-TAVERNS for reservations, which are recommended, and for information on all the Colonial Taverns) since I was a young man; it's expensive, but the food is excellent, and happily the beer is as well. **Chowning's** (next to the Courthouse, and it's pronounced "CHOON-ings") is known for its Gambols, a "lively" nightly entertainment that's a lot of fun if you're in that colonial (or ColoniAle) mood. Beware, there are no reservations for the Gambols, and the line forms early. When you're ready to rejoin the twenty-first century, the **Green Leafe Café** (765 Scotland Street, 757-220-3405) has had a long line of taps for quite a while. **Berret's Taphouse and Grill** is the less formal side of Berret's Seafood Restaurant (199 South Boundary Street, in Merchant's Square, 757-253-1847). It does a good job of keeping Virginia beers on tap and Virginia wines in the cellar, and the seafood is top of the line. See the listings for St. George Brewing Company (page 243) as well; you're not that far away.

Anheuser-Busch

7801 Pocahontas Trail, Williamsburg, VA 23185
www.budweiser.com (all Anheuser-Busch website links are collected at
www.anheuserbusch.com/misc/links.html, a fascinating page)

Anheuser-Busch is the world's largest brewer, with approximately half the U.S. market and 8 percent of the world's market. The brewery in Williamsburg is only one of its twelve breweries in the United States, a diversified production plan that allows Anheuser-Busch to deliver beer across the country, as fresh as possible.

Some people will ask, inevitably, why put an Anheuser-Busch brewery in a book about microbreweries and brewpubs? Well, it's my book, and I say it's about *breweries,* so I'm including it, case closed. I also have very fond memories of this particular Anheuser-Busch brewery. I toured here with my father back in the summer of 1978, and it was an important time in our relationship; for the first time, we traveled as two adults, rather than as parent and child. It was a great weekend. But there is another reason: The truth needs to be told about Anheuser-Busch (A-B).

The truth? Yes, truth, because there's a lot of silliness out there. Because Bud Light and Budweiser are the world's two largest-selling beers, A-B is often the whipping boy of the microbrewers. A-B has taken its share of shots at the micros as well, to be sure; that's business.

The truth is, A-B has more than one hundred highly trained and qualified brewmasters who are fanatical about quality in ingredients and process. I've met some of them. They're nice guys, but just between you and me, they're nuts. One of them talked to me for an hour about their yeast; it was as if he couldn't stop himself. Because A-B is so huge, and so profitable, they can afford to do their own research on barley strains (they have a barley research institute), and malting (they have three of their

Beers brewed: Budweiser, Bud Light, Bud Ice, Michelob, Michelob Light, Natural Light, Natural Ice, Busch, Busch Light, King Cobra, Hurricane Malt Liquor, Budweiser-Sweden, Bud NA.

The Pick: If I'm in a mainstream beer situation, I'll take Busch over most others. Just a bit more body than Bud, just a bit different in taste, and I don't really mind drinking it from a can at all.

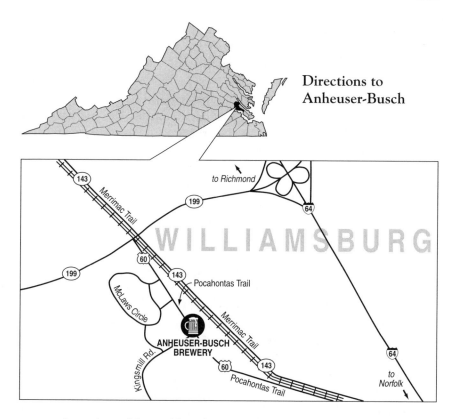

**Directions to
Anheuser-Busch**

own maltings), and hops (they have several hops farms), and rice (two rice mills), and yeast (they have . . . well, you get the picture).

Why so much research, why so much fanaticism? Trace it back to the true founder of the business, Adolphus Busch. After marrying Bavarian Brewery owner Eberhard Anheuser's daughter, Adolphus bought into the business in 1865. He took it from a penny-ante operation to a strong regional brewery. Part of the reason for this success was his superb salesmanship abilities. Adolphus was reputed to use every trick in the book, and some unpublished ones to boot.

But another large component was his obsession with quality. Adolphus traveled widely in Europe and America, sampling beers, studying brewing processes, and evaluating malts and hops. He wrote long letters with detailed instructions on purchasing the finest malt and how to best use it to make excellent beer. "You cannot make a fine beer with inferior malt," he said in one letter I've seen.

This obsession continues today. A-B buys only the finest hops they can find; I've talked to independent hops brokers who confirm it. Their maltings are top-notch operations, their rice operations are so high-quality that they are actually able to export rice to Japan. They buy the best equipment and maintain it perfectly.

That's why I laugh when earnest beer geeks say, "If Anheuser-Busch wanted to, with their talent and equipment and quality control they could make the best beer in the world." As far as A-B is concerned, they already do make the best beer in the world. It's called Budweiser.

The "chip tanks" are the lagering tanks, where the famous beech-wood aging takes place. I've seen it, I've held the beechwood. Thin strips of beechwood, about 18 inches long and 1.5 inches wide, are boiled numerous times, then spread in the bottom of the chip tanks by hand. They provide a settling place for the yeast in the beer. The chips are used three times, then dumped.

This is "beechwood aging"? The theory is that without the chips, the yeast would be crushed. A-B brewers have told me that they've done batches without the beechwood, and they could taste the difference. I believe them, because this *has* to be an expensive process, with lots of labor involved in handling the chips and the purchase and process of the chips themselves. (They come from Tennessee and south Missouri, by the way.) A-B wouldn't do something that expensive if there weren't a good reason.

The chip tanks are huge, with specialized equipment you won't find anywhere else. They're expensive and exacting, all in the service of consistency of product. This is the heart of A-B's story and of their success. They do things their own way, they are unafraid to spend on fanatical stretches of quality, and they plan for the future. I have a lot of respect for that.

Opened: December 1972.
Owners: Anheuser-Busch Companies, Inc., Patrick T. Stokes, President and CEO.
Brewers: Daniel L. Driskill, senior brewmaster.
Production: 9.4 million barrels in 2003.
Tours: No longer available.
Extras: The hospitality room at the end of the tour offers two free samples, a snack bar, and a gift shop.
Special considerations: Handicapped-accessible.
Area attractions: It only seems fair to put **Busch Gardens** (exit 242A off I-64, 800-343-7946) amusement park here. The idea is that this is "the Old Country," and the sections of the park are themed to

European countries. So you have the Loch Ness Monster roller coaster in Scotland, Da Vinci's Cradle in Italy, and the Alpengeist coaster in Germany. It's actually a beautiful amusement park, with lots of trees and water, plenty of good food, and even beers with your food; better take it easy on the beer unless you're a veteran of the rides at the Oktoberfest! **Water Country USA** (800-343-7946) is next door, a full-size water park with rides for the fearless teenager and the little ones alike. "Bounce" tickets are available that give a discounted entrance to both parks.

St. George Brewing Company

204 Challenger Way, Hampton, VA 23666
757-865-7781
www.stgeorgebrewingco.com

Anybody wanna buy a hot dog stand? Andy Rathmann's got one sitting up on his roof.

It's just a little memento of this brewery's checkered career up till now. Let's go back to the beginning, and you'll see how it fits in. Ron Walkup started up a brew-on-premise in Virginia Beach back in 1996, a place called B. A. Brewmeister. You'll still see the name crop up on some out-of-date websites. The beers were getting good reviews, so he decided to open a small microbrewery and focus on production.

St. George Brewing opened in 1999 in an old ice plant on Kecoughtan Street. That's pronounced "KICK-a-tan," and I know because I used to live just down the street from where the brewery opened . . . unfortunately, about twelve years too soon. The brewhouse came from DME, and Andy Rathmann came with it. "I was doing contract work for DME," he said, "and I was tired of traveling. I liked the water, and Hampton's surrounded by it, so I settled here."

It looked smart. "Things were doing well at the brewery on Kecoughtan," Andy continued, "and we had an expansion coming up in December. But we decided to put it off till after Christmas, so the tanks weren't on-site. It was a good thing; the brewery burned on Christmas Eve." Bad wiring in another business in the building was the likely cause, but it was immaterial. St. George had lost everything but the paperwork in the office.

"We actually weren't in bad shape," said Andy, a big smile on his face. "We had pushed hard to have beer stored up for when we were down for the expansion, and we had a refrigerated truck stuffed full of kegs. We had the new brewery planned out on paper within a week, and in the meantime, we brewed at Clipper City, we brewed at Rock Creek, and we made an arrangement to brew at the Atlanta Beer Garden."

Atlanta Beer Garden was a semifailed brewpub in Newport News, in that it hadn't made it but hadn't been broken up yet. Andy and the gang weren't interested in running a brewpub, just using the brewhouse. Virginia had other ideas. Atlanta Beer Garden's brewing license was a brewpub license, and that meant that in order to brew, they had to sell food.

"Well, we just wanted to keep it simple," said Andy. "We needed to sell food, right? So we bought a hot dog stand." But don't you have to make a fairly good percentage of your income from food with a brewpub license? Andy just smiled. Okay!

They found the new building in Poquoson (and that one's pronounced "puh-KOE-sen"), just down the road from the roar of NASA's massive wind tunnels, and moved in over the summer of 2001 (the hot dog stand took up its new home on the roof sometime after that), buying more land and expanding the building to hold the new 30-barrel brewhouse, bought used from Tabernash Brewing in Colorado, and the bottling line, and finally, those new tanks. Ron Walkup left about this time to become a schoolteacher. Andy runs the production side of the brewery, Conor Halfpenny does sales, "and we all do marketing," said Andy.

St. George has won some awards, including a gold medal for their IPA in the British-based "Beauty of Hops" contest, and their beers are clean and crisp, especially their Pilsner, the round lager peg in the square-hole ale brewery. Blame Rathmann: He did his brewing apprenticeship in Germany, "two and a half years of it, one month at a time going from brewery to brewery," he said. He came back to America and

Beers brewed: Year-round: St. George Golden Ale, IPA, Porter, Pilsner. Draft-only: American Brown Ale, Tavern Ale.

The Pick: Andy's Pilsner is good stuff, smooth, not too heavy, and crisply hoppy. But the Pick is the IPA, a solidly malty entry in this popular class. The malt gives this one a serious foundation, fires up the ale yeast to produce a beautifully fruity crop of esters, and buoys the earthy, spicy bounty of a whopping dose of Fuggles hops. A thumping good example of how you can make an American-style IPA with British hops.

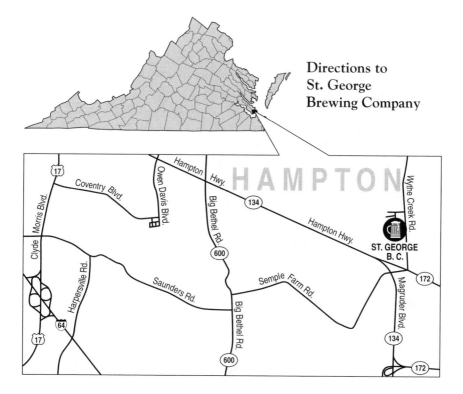

Directions to St. George Brewing Company

did the program at UC–Davis. "I was very excited and proud," he said, "but I still loved lagers. I almost didn't get hired here because of that."

One sip of the St. George Porter or Golden Ale shows that Rathmann certainly knows his way around an ale yeast. This is a small but well-made portfolio of beers that are selling from Virginia Beach to western Virginia, and up to the D.C. Metro area. "We're too limited on personnel to do sales right at this point," Rathmann said, and you get the feeling he realizes that they may have spread themselves too wide. "We're looking to build on our base, around here and up in Richmond."

If they can come back from that disastrous Christmas Eve fire, then shuffle through brewing in an abandoned brewery while building a beautiful new brewery and selling hot dogs on the side, I'll give St. George a pretty good chance at success. Such persistence should not go unrewarded.

Opened: August 1999.
Owners: BA Brewmeisters, Inc.; Bill Spence, major stockholder.
Brewer: Andy Rathmann.

System: 30-barrel Newlands/DME system, 5,000 barrels annual capacity.
Production: 1,209 barrels in 2003.
Tours: On request.
Take-out beer: Six-packs, cases, and sixtel and half kegs available.
Special considerations: Handicapped-accessible.
Parking: Off-street lot.
Lodging in the area: I have to mention the Hotel Chamberlin (888-729-7705), on the grounds of Fortress Monroe, because I spent so many happy hours here . . . and I do mean happy hours, down in the bar, because of the free buffet! The view of Hampton Roads is great. Victoria House B&B, 4501 Victoria Boulevard, 757-722-2658; La Quinta Inn, 2138 West Mercury Boulevard, 757-827-8680.
Area attractions: The **Virginia Air and Space Center** (600 Settlers Landing Road, 800-296-0800) celebrates Hampton's link to space; the original astronaut training station was at Langley AFB, still a very active base, and you can often see F-15s circling in to land there. The Space Center has the command module from Apollo 12, a moon rock, an IMAX theater, interactive exhibits on the physics of flight, and a variety of NASA aircraft. **Fortress Monroe** (on the Fort Monroe army post, 757-788-3391) is the largest stone fort in America, with a moat that I crossed every day when I worked at the post library there. The **Casemate Museum** was where Confederate president Jefferson Davis was confined after the war; his cell is preserved. The fort was also the army's Coast Artillery School, and the museum has an electronic map exhibit demonstrating how these mighty guns once defended the Chesapeake and Washington against invasion or naval bombardment.
Other area beer sites: We got a lucky tip from a very kind woman on **Harpoon Larry's** (2000 Armistead Avenue, Hampton, 757-827-0600). Carl and I were just looking for lunch, which we found: Harpoon Larry's motto, "Killer seafood," isn't just hot air. It was great, and I'd go there right now for more, but we also found a surprising tap selection that I'd venture to say is probably the best in Hampton.

Cross the water to Norfolk, though, and let the beer fun begin. The top two were easily **Cogan's Instant Art Bar** (1901 Colonial Avenue, 757-627-6428) and **The Taphouse Grill at Ghent** (931 West Twenty-first Street, 757-627-9172). Cogan's has thirty-three taps, including two house beers: Onemore and Gorilla Piss. The gorilla theme is all over Cogan's, in colorful pulp age science-fiction illustrative glory, and it is loose and vibed-up, as you would expect from a place with a name like this! The pizza's great, too. The Taphouse is a branch of Richmond's Commercial Taphouse, and it is just as determinedly rough-hewn, and perhaps even more tap-happy; there are some outstanding beers here. Up Colonial Avenue from Cogan's is **The New Belmont** (2117 Colonial Avenue, 757-623-4477), a restaurant and bar; head upstairs, where the bar is really happening. You'll find decent taps, a very good selection of malts, okay bourbons, and a lot of wine in a setting of polished wood and brick sophistication. You'll feel a bit better if you're dressed a bit better here, and it's a chance to observe wine geeks.

The **Bier Garden** (438 High Street, Portsmouth, 757-393-6022) is a Euro-beer mecca, both draft and bottle, in a great setting, especially when the outdoor patio is open. The **German Pantry** (5329 Virginia Beach Boulevard, Norfolk, 757-461-5100) is a deli with tables, taps, bottles, a mug club, and a German grocery; remember to "Ask Wallace for password!"

On down into Virginia Beach, you'll find **PJ Baggan** (960 Laskin Road, not far from Hilltop Brewing, 757-491-8900), where the beer's kept in the back (gotta keep that wine out front!), but that's where the comfy chairs and the bar are, too, so that's okay. It's a liquor store, it's a cigar shop with a walk-in humidor, it's a bar! There's a **Harpoon Larry's** in Virginia Beach, too (Twenty-fourth Street and Pacific Avenue); mmmmm, more killer seafood! **Hometown Heroes** (3717 Tiffany Lane, 757-471-5201) was recommended by Mike Pensinger at Hilltop; it's a sports bar with lots of TVs and lots of taps. The **Farm Fresh Supermarket** (2058 South Independence Boulevard, 757-416-9832) also has a surprisingly good beer selection; the beer manager there is very motivated.

Hilltop Brewing Company and Restaurant

1556 Laskin Road, Virginia Beach, VA 23451
757-422-5652
www.hilltopbrewery.com

Let's get the laughing over with. Yes, the brewpub's called Hilltop, and yes, the roof of the building *might* be 50 feet above sea level. After all, you could see the ocean from the roof if not for the high-rise hotels in Virginia Beach, which is pretty much flat as a pancake. Okay, got that over with? It's named for the Hilltop shopping plaza where it's located, and no, I have no idea why the developer called it Hilltop. Ambition, maybe.

Be that as it may, Hilltop is the only brewpub in all of Hampton Roads, and it has been here since 1997, so laugh *that* off. That could easily be the response of contracted brewer Mike Pensinger, a pleasantly pugnacious fellow who's been known to get right in the online face of people who give his beer what he considers unfair or uninformed reviews on the beer and bar–rating websites. Pensinger, an active-duty navy chief petty officer (due for retirement in September 2004) who also owns the local homebrew shop, Homebrew Hobbies (www.homebrewusa.com), shares brewing duties with Peter Goebel.

"Pete brews the Frog Grog Kölsch and any beer with wheat in it," Mike explained, "and I brew everything else." It's an odd division of duties, but not unknown in brewpub circles. It's even more understandable when you consider Pensinger and Goebel's arrangement with owner Kurt Furith. At the end of the year, they get 1099s, not W-2s: The men are contract workers, not employees of Hilltop.

"All I do is brew," said Mike, with evident satisfaction. They brew as they see fit, and it looks like everyone's happy with the arrangement. Mike's particularly happy with the free license to brew whatever he wants: "within reason," he adds, though even that seems pretty broad when you learn that it apparently encompasses Mike's Over the Top IPA, a 7.5 percent ABV hopmonster that Mike claims rings in at a terrifying

Beers brewed: Year-round: Frog Grog, Pale Rider. Seasonals: IPA, Maibock, Over the Top, Witbier, Porter, Alt, Hefeweizen, Sweet Stout, Oktoberfest, ESB, Irish Red, Brown Ale, Barleywine (one keg released at one-year intervals).

147 IBU. "Arrogant Bastard has nothing on me," he proudly stated, naming a famously hoppy beer from Stone Brewing of San Diego.

It may seem hard to believe that a lone brewpub in an East Coast beach town can make beers like that on a regular basis. East Coast beach towns, unlike the western ones, which support such famously experimental brewpubs as Oggi and Pizza Port, are generally places where people drink the lightest beer they can find in the heat, although there is Dogfish Head to consider. Mike allowed that the regular customers at Hilltop did drink a lot of the lightweight Frog Grog, "but they also drink some weird stuff, and they do like draft beer."

The Pick: I liked the Irish Red, a mild, sweet, somewhat light-bodied beer that was gutsy enough to hold my interest and smooth enough to be massively drinkable. With a nod to Pete, I also liked the Hefeweizen, a clean, zesty classic of this Bavarian-style wheat beer.

The guest taps backed him up. There are twenty taps at Hilltop, and whatever they don't fill with their own beers, they fill with guest beers. The day I was there, I saw Old Dominion Oak Barrel Stout, two St. George beers, Murphy's stout, and some Weeping Radish taps, along with some more mainstream beers. "Nothing from Anheuser-Busch," Mike said. "We don't put them on."

So how does a brewpub survive in a beach town? "We're not easy to find," Mike offered, and met my quizzical follow-up look with an explanation. "The people who come here found us on the net or through word of mouth. We get a lot of locals in here because we're not on the beach. They work down there; they don't want to drink there. It's also good because we're not as affected by the ebb and flow of the beach season; it's more steady business."

Furith and his partner, Dianne Dukes, originally planned Hilltop as a fine-dining restaurant that would match good food with good beer. It turned out that Americans weren't up to speed with that idea, and they went to a sports bar format in 2000. That's been a success, and the menu has changed to match it, though it's still not the basic pub grub.

Come to think of it, Hilltop's just not your basic brewpub. With its division of brewer labor, and sauerkraut pizzas, and that whopping big IPA, Hilltop's a bit different. And when you're a beer lover in a beach town, usually that's just what you're looking for.

Opened: June 1997.
Owners: Kurt Furith, Dianne Dukes.
Brewers: Peter Goebel. (Michael Pensinger left Hilltop in late 2004.)
System: 8.5-barrel Saaz system, 1,000 barrels annual capacity.
Production: 350 barrels in 2003.

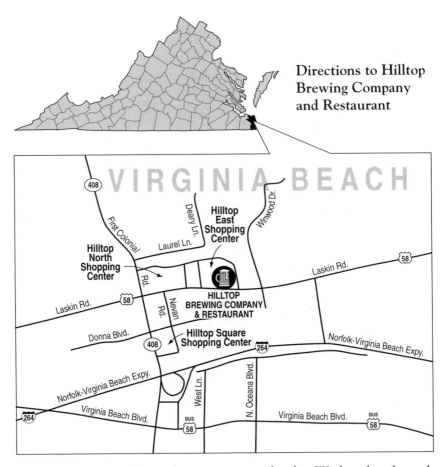

Directions to Hilltop Brewing Company and Restaurant

Hours: Monday and Tuesday, 4 P.M. to midnight; Wednesday through Sunday, 11 A.M. to 2 A.M.

Tours: On request, subject to brewer availability.

Take-out beer: Growlers available.

Food: There's the standard pub grub, but the thing to go for at Hilltop is the "eclectic pizzas," like the Crazy Kraut, with sauerkraut, bacon, and onions; She Crab, with spinach, sweet corn, and garlic; Thai Chicken; Philly Cheesesteak; and the classic Hawaiian, with ham and pineapples. If you're just looking for a quick snack, you can't go wrong with the fried dill pickles.

Extras: Live entertainment Tuesday, Friday, and Saturday; call for schedule. Open mike nights on Thursdays. Frog Grog Wednesdays feature a fresh keg of Frog Grog, and until it kicks, it's 50¢ a pint. There are guest taps of beers, including Virginia and local beers like St. George, Old Dominion, and Weeping Radish.

Special considerations: Kids welcome. Vegetarian meals available. Handicapped-accessible.

Parking: Large on-site lot.

Lodging in the area: Belvedere Motel, 3603 Atlantic Avenue, 757-425-0612; Barclay Cottage B&B, 400 Sixteenth Street, 757-422-1956; The Capes, 2001 Atlantic Avenue, 800-456-5421.

Area attractions: First, let me explain those signs on Atlantic Avenue, before you do like I did, stepping out of your car and saying, "What the %$*@ does that mean?" The "%$*@" signs with the red circle and slash mean that Atlantic Avenue is a "no profanity zone." Virginia Beach wants to preserve its family appeal, and local police will issue citations for swearing on the avenue. Apparently the ACLU hasn't gotten wind of this yet. There's no drinking or "throwing" allowed on the beaches, either, so leave the Frisbees at home. But you can certainly swim, sun, and sample the joys of the **Boardwalk,** which is really what Virginia Beach is here for. The surfing's not bad either, for the East Coast.

That's not only what Virginia Beach is all about, though. The **Virginia Marine Science Museum** (717 General Booth Boulevard, 757-425-FISH) has eight hundred thousand gallons worth of aquariums, including the Atlantic Ocean Pavilion, a seal tank right at the entrance, a stingray tank, and a salt marsh tank with otters and an aviary overhead that holds beautiful ospreys. There is also a large IMAX theater that features a trip through a kelp forest.

The **Old Coast Guard Station Museum** (Twenty-fourth Street and Atlantic Avenue, 757-422-1587) is in one of the old lifesaving stations that used to dot these shores. See the equipment of the Surfmen, the brave souls who would venture out in waves wild enough to have foundered a ship, to try to save the souls on board. There is also a video link to spot ships along the coast, and a computer system to identify them.

The **Association for Research and Enlightment** (Sixty-seventh Street and Atlantic Avenue, 757-428-3588) is a center for psychic research founded by famed psychic Edgar Cayce. There are daily activities, including ESP classes; call for a schedule or check www.edgarcayce.org.

BEERWEBS

The Web has become a great place to share beer and bar information. But as with anything else on the Web, you have to use a little wisdom. Websites can be out of date, intensely subjective, poorly edited, and just plain wrong. Let the reader beware.

Here are some websites you can use to find beers, bars, breweries, and beer geeks in the Mid-Atlantic, New York, Pennsylvania, and across the country. If I have any reservations about them, I've stated them.

www.lewbryson.com This is my own website, which includes frequent online updates to this book and my previous books, *New York Breweries* and *Pennsylvania Breweries*, plus news on future guides in the series, notes on what I've been drinking, travel notes on my research trips, links to some of my other writing, and other things I find interesting.

www.pubcrawler.com Pubcrawler is simply the best brewery and bar locator website in the world. No other site has its combination of completeness, search tools, longevity, and objectivity. You can search more than five thousand North American breweries, brewpubs, and bars by name, city, state, zip code, or area code, and every entry has a map link for directions. The entries have phone numbers, addresses, links, logos, and, most important, years of patron reviews. You can leave your own as well; you'll find quite a few of mine. My only reservations here are that some of the reviewers are obviously biased, and that sometimes Pubcrawler is not as complete as it could be. I do my best to keep it up-to-date in New York, Pennsylvania, Virginia, Delaware, D.C., and Maryland.

www.citysearch.com CitySearch is a national search site for entertainment, dining, nightlife, shopping, attractions . . . and bars. The site is not anywhere near as beer-aware as it could be, but I've gotten quite a few good leads here. The patron reviews aren't as good as those at Pubcrawler, but the editorial reviews are quite good.

www.BeerAdvocate.com BeerAdvocate is mostly about rating beers and talking about beers and talking about rating beers . . . but it is also an online community of people who really care about the beer they drink *and the beer you drink*. So the BeerAdvocate forums are a great place to get inside scoops on what's going on in bars. The site's online directory, BeerFly, has a wide range of listings for breweries, bars, and beer stores. Useful site.

GLOSSARY

ABV, ABW. Alcohol by volume, alcohol by weight. These are two slightly different ways of measuring the alcohol content of beverages, as a percentage of either the beverage's total volume or its weight. For example, if you have 1 liter of 4 percent ABV beer, 4 percent of that liter (40 milliliters) is alcohol. However, because alcohol weighs only 79.6 percent as much as water, that same beer is only 3.18 percent ABW. This may seem like a dry exercise in mathematics, but it is at the heart of the common misconception that Canadian beer is stronger than American beer. Canadian brewers generally use ABV figures, whereas American brewers have historically used the lower ABW figures. Mainstream Canadian and American lagers are approximately equal in strength. Just to confuse the issue further, most American microbreweries use ABV figures. This is very important if you're trying to keep a handle on how much alcohol you're consuming. If you know how much Bud (at roughly 5 percent ABV) you can safely consume, you can extrapolate from there. Learn your limits . . . before you hit them.

Adjunct. Any non–barley malt source of sugars for fermentation. This can be candy sugar, corn grits, molasses or other nonstandard sugar, corn or rice syrup, or one of any number of specialty grains. Wheat, rye, and specialty sugars are considered by beer geeks to be "politically correct" adjuncts; corn and rice are generally taken as signs of swill. However, small amounts of corn used as a brewing ingredient for certain styles of beer is slowly gaining acceptance in craft-brewing circles, and Dogfish Head deliberately socked the corn to their whimsical, delicious Liquor de Malt. So keep an open mind.

Ale. The generic term for warm-fermented beers. (See "A word about . . . Ales and Lagers" on page 151.)

Alefruit. My own invention, so far as I know. I use this term to signify the juicy esters produced by some yeasts, aromas and flavors of a variety of fruits: pear, melon, plum, peach, lemon drop, pineapple. I use "alefruit" when I can't tease out the exact fruits (or when I can but don't want to sound pretentious).

ATTTB. The federal Alcohol and Tobacco Tax and Trade Bureau, formerly part of the ATF, a branch of the Treasury Department. The ATTTB is the federal regulatory arm for the brewing industry. The ATTTB has to inspect every brewery before it opens, approve every label before it is used, approve all packaging. The ATTTB is also the body responsible for the fact that while every food, even bottled water, *must* have a nutritional information label, beer (and wine and cider and spirits) is *not allowed* to have one, even though it is a significant source of calories, carbohydrates, and in the case of unfiltered beers, B vitamins and protein. The problem is that sometimes every ATTTB agent and bureaucrat seems to have a different interpretation of the regulations, and some have a very negative attitude toward the beverages they're regulating. As a brewer once told me, "I'd enjoy this a lot more if the [agency] didn't make me feel like I was dealing in controlled substances." Note that the various state alcohol control agencies range from relatively strict (Maryland) to reasonable (Delaware) to pretty darned loose (D.C.). Perhaps the most strict alcohol regulation agency in the country is in Montgomery County, Maryland, the country's only "control" county, where all alcohol beverages are sold in county-owned stores.

Barley. A wonderfully apt grain for brewing beer. Barley grows well in relatively marginal soil and climate. It has no significant gluten content, which makes it largely unsuitable for baking bread and thereby limits market competition for brewers buying the grain. Its husk serves as a very efficient filter at the end of the mashing process. And it makes beer that tastes really, really good. Barley comes in two types: two-row and six-row, named for the rows of kernels on the heads of the grain. In days past, two-row barley was plumper and considered finer. Six-row barley was easier to grow, had a better yield per acre and higher enzymatic power, but had a somewhat astringent character. These differences have been lessened by cross-breeding. Most barley grown in North America is six-row, for reasons of soil and climate. (Incidentally, the grain's kernels, or corns, are the source of the name "John Barleycorn," a traditional personification of barley or beer.)

Barrel. A traditional measure of beer volume equal to 31 U.S. gallons. The most common containers of draft beer in the United States are half and quarter barrels, or kegs, at 15.5 gallons and 7.75 gallons, respectively, though the one-sixth-barrel kegs (about 5.2 gallons), known as sixtels, are becoming popular with microbrewers. See also *hectoliter*.

Beer. A fermented beverage brewed from grain, generally malted barley. "Beer" covers a variety of beverages, including ales and lagers, stouts and bocks, porters and pilsners, lambics and altbiers, cream ale, Kölsch, wheat beer, and a whole lot more.

Beer geek. A person who takes beer a little more seriously than does the average person. I've been chided for using the term "geek" here, but haven't found another one I like, so my apologies to those who object. I call myself a beer geek, if that's any consolation. Often homebrewers, beer geeks love to argue with other beer geeks about what makes exceptional beers exceptional. That is, if they've been able to agree on which beers are exceptional in the first place. A beer geek is the kind of person who would buy a book about traveling to breweries . . . the kind of person who would read the glossary of a beer book. Hey, hi there!

BOP. See *brew-on-premise*.

Bottle-conditioned beer. A beer that has been bottled with an added dose of live yeast. This living yeast causes the beer to mature and change as it ages over periods of one to thirty years or more. It will also "eat" any oxygen that may have been sealed in at bottling and keep the beer from oxidizing, a staling process that leads to sherryish and "wet cardboard" aromas in beer. Bottle-conditioned beer qualifies as "real ale."

Brewer. One who brews beer for commercial sale.

Breweriana. Brewery and beer memorabilia, such as trays, coasters, neon signs, steins, mirrors, and so on, including the objects of desire of the beer can and bottle collectors. Most collectors do this for fun, a few do it for money (breweriana is starting to command some big prices; just check eBay), but the weird thing about this for me is the number of breweriana collectors—about a third, from my experience—who don't drink beer.

Brewhouse. The vessels used to mash the malt and grains and boil the wort. The malt and grains are mashed in a vessel called a *mash tun*. Brewhouse size is generally given in terms of the capacity of the brewkettle, where the wort is boiled. A brewery's annual capacity is a function of brewhouse size, fermentation and aging tank capacity, and the length of the fermentation and aging cycle for the brewery's beers.

Brew-on-premise (BOP). A brew-on-premise brewery is a middle ground between homebrewing and commercial brewing. In essence, it is a place where small brewkettles are available for use by customers, along with a variety of malts and extracts, adjuncts, hops, flavorings, and yeasts. The BOP sells the use of the kettles and the ingredients to customers, who brew beer and leave it at the BOP to ferment; they return to package it when it is complete. Some, but not all, BOPs also brew their own beers for small-scale commercial sale. They once were extremely popular in Canada as a way to avoid scurrilously high beer taxes, but law changes have led to a decline in BOPs.

Brewpub. A brewery that sells the majority of its output on draft, on the premises, or a tavern that brews its own beer. Either of these may sell other brewers' beers, and often do. In my opinion, it would be a good thing for the industry in general if more brewpubs had a guest tap or two from other small breweries.

CAMRA. The CAMpaign for Real Ale. A British beer drinkers' consumer group formed in the early 1970s by beer drinkers irate over the disappearance of cask-conditioned ale. They have been very vocal and successful in bringing this traditional drink back to a place of importance in the United Kingdom. CAMRA sets high standards for cask-conditioned ale which only a few brewers in the United States match.

Carbonation. The fizzy effects of carbon dioxide (CO_2) in solution in a liquid (e.g., beer). Carbonation can be accomplished artificially by injecting the beer with the gas or naturally by trapping the CO_2, which is a by-product of fermentation. There is no intrinsic qualitative difference between beers carbonated by these two methods. Brewer's choice, essentially. Low carbonation will allow a broader array of flavors to come through, whereas high carbonation can result in a perceived bitterness. Most American drinkers prefer a higher carbonation.

Cask. A keg designed to serve cask-conditioned beer by gravity feed or by handpump, not by gas pressure. These casks may be made of wood, but most are steel with special plumbing.

Cask-conditioned beer. An unfiltered beer that is put in a cask before it is completely ready to serve. The yeast still in the beer continues to work and ideally brings the beer to perfection at the point of sale, resulting in a beautifully fresh beer that has a "soft" natural carbonation and beautiful array of aromas. The flip side to achieving this supreme freshness is that as the beer is poured, air replaces the beer in the cask, and the beer will become sour within five days. Bars should sell the cask out before then or remove it from sale. If you are served sour cask-conditioned beer, send it back. Better yet, ask politely for a taste before ordering. Cask-conditioned beer is generally served at cellar temperature (55 to 60 degrees Fahrenheit) and is lightly carbonated. Cask-conditioned beers are almost always ales, but some American brewers are experimenting with cask-conditioned lagers.

Cold-filtering. The practice of passing finished beer through progressively finer filters (usually cellulose or ceramic) to strip out microorganisms that can spoil the beer when it is stored. Brewers like Coors and Miller, and also some smaller brewers, use cold-filtering as an alternative to pasteurization (see below). Some beer geeks complain that this "strip-filtering" robs beers of their more subtle complexities and some of their body. I'm not sure about that, but I do know that unfiltered beer right from the brewery tank almost always tastes more intense than the filtered, packaged beer.

Contract brewer. A brewer who hires an existing brewery to brew beer on contract. Contract brewers range from those who simply have a different label put on one of the brewery's existing brands to those who maintain a separate on-site staff to actually brew the beer at the brewery. Some brewers and beer geeks feel contract-brewed beer is inherently inferior. This is strictly a moral and business issue; some of the best beers on the market are contract-brewed.

Craft brewer. The new term for microbrewer. Craft brewer, like microbrewer before it, is really a code word for any brewer producing beers other than mainstream American lagers like Budweiser and Miller Lite. (See "A word about . . . Micros, Brewpubs, and Craft Brewers" on page 33.)

Decoction. The type of mashing often used by lager brewers to wring the full character from the malt. In a decoction mash, a portion of the hot mash is taken to another vessel, brought to boiling, and returned to the mash, thus raising the temperature. See also *infusion*.

Dry-hopping. Adding hops to the beer in postfermentation stages, often in porous bags to allow easy removal. This results in a greater hop aroma in the finished beer. A few brewers put a small bag of hop cones in each cask of their cask-conditioned beers, resulting in a particularly intense hop aroma in a glass of the draft beer.

ESB. Extra Special Bitter, an ale style with a rich malt character and full body, perhaps some butter or butterscotch aromas, and an understated hop bitterness. An ESB is noticeably bitter only in comparison to a mild ale, a style not often found in America.

Esters. Aroma compounds produced by fermentation that gives some ales lightly fruity aromas: banana, pear, and grapefruit, among others. The aromas produced are tightly linked to the yeast strain used. Ester-based aromas should not be confused with the less subtle fruit aromas of a beer to which fruit or fruit essences have been added.

Extract. More specifically, malt extract. Malt extract is almost like concentrated wort (see below). Malt is mashed and the resulting sweet, unhopped wort is reduced to a syrup, which is packaged and sold to brewers. In extract brewing, the extract is mixed with water and boiled. Specialty grains (such as black patent or chocolate malts, wheat, roasted barley) and hops can be added for flavor notes and nuances. It is actually more expensive to brew with extract, but you need less equipment, which can be crucial in cramped brewing areas, and less training, which makes it a lot easier. But the quality of the beer may suffer. Some people claim to be able to pick out an extract brew blindfolded. I've had extract brews that had a common taste—a kind of thin, vegetal sharpness—but I have also had some excellent extract brews at various breweries. My advice is to try it yourself.

Fermentation. The miracle of yeast; the heart of making beer. Fermentation is the process in which yeast turns sugar and water into alcohol, heat, carbon dioxide, esters, and traces of other compounds.

Final gravity. See *gravity.*

Firkin. A cask or keg holding 9 gallons of beer, specially plumbed for gravity or handpump dispense.

Geekerie. The collective of beer geeks, particularly the beer-oriented, beer-fascinated, beer-above-all beer geeks. They sometimes can fall victim to group thinking and a herd mentality, but they are generally good people, if a bit hopheaded and malt-maniacal. If you're not a member of the geekerie, you might want to consider getting to know them: They usually know where all the best bars and beer stores are in their town, and they're more than happy to share the knowledge and even go along with you to share the fun. All you have to do is ask. See the Beerwebs section for links to the better beer pages, a good way to hook up with them.

Gravity. The specific gravity of wort (original gravity) or finished beer (terminal gravity). The ratio of dissolved sugars to water determines the gravity of the wort. If there are more dissolved sugars, the original gravity and the potential alcohol are higher. The sugar that is converted to alcohol by the yeast lowers the terminal gravity, and makes the beer drier, just like wine. A brewer can determine the alcohol content of a beer by mathematical comparison of its original gravity and terminal gravity.

Great American Beer Festival (GABF). Since 1982, America's breweries have been invited each year to bring their best beer to the GABF in Denver to showcase what America can brew. Since 1987, the GABF has awarded medals for various styles of beer; fifty-five styles were judged in

2001, three medals for each style. To ensure impartiality, the beers are tasted blind, their identities hidden from the judges. GABF medals are the most prestigious awards in American brewing because of the festival's longevity and reputation for fairness.

Growler. A jug or bottle used to take home draft beer. These are usually either simple half-gallon glass jugs with screwtops or more elaborate molded glass containers with swingtop seals. I have traced the origin of the term *growler* back to a cheap, four-wheeled horse cab in use in Victorian London. These cabs would travel a circuit of pubs in the evenings, and riding from pub to pub was known as "working the growler." To bring a pail of beer home to have with dinner was to anticipate the night's work of drinking and became known as "rushing the growler." When the growler cabs disappeared from the scene, we were left with only the phrase, and "rushing the growler" was assumed to mean hurrying home with the bucket. When Ed Otto revived the practice by selling jugs of Otto Brothers beer at his Jackson Hole brewery in the mid-1980s, he called them growlers. Now you know where the term really came from.

Guest taps/guest beers. Beers made by other brewers that are offered at brewpubs.

Handpump. A hand-powered pump for dispensing beer from a keg. Either a handpump or a gravity tap is always used for dispensing cask-conditioned beer; however, the presence of a handpump does not guarantee that the beer being dispensed is cask-conditioned.

Hectoliter. A hectoliter (hl) is 100 liters, a metric measure of volume used by some brewers with European- or Canadian-manufactured brewing systems. One hectoliter is approximately 0.85 barrels; 27 hectoliters is just about exactly 23 barrels. There are also "half-hec" kegs that hold 50 liters, or about 13.3 gallons, compared with the 15.5 gallons in a half keg.

Homebrewing. Making honest-to-goodness beer at home for personal consumption. Homebrewing is where many American craft brewers got their start.

Hops. The spice of beer. Hops plants (*Humulus lupus*) are vines whose flowers have a remarkable effect on beer. The flowers' resins and oils add bitterness and a variety of aromas (spicy, piney, citrus, and others) to the finished beer. Beer without hops would be more like a fizzy, sweet "alco-soda."

IBU. International bittering unit, a measure of a beer's bitterness (may also be seen as BU, bittering unit). Humans can first perceive bitterness at levels between 8 and 12 IBU. Budweiser has 11.5 IBU, Heineken 18, Sierra Nevada Pale Ale 32, Pilsner Urquell 43, and a monster like Sierra Nevada Bigfoot clocks in at 98 IBU. Equivalent amounts of bitterness will seem greater in a lighter-bodied beer, whereas a heavier, maltier beer like Bigfoot needs lots of bitterness to be perceived as balanced.

"Imperial." A beer style intensifier, indicating a beer that is hoppier and stronger. Once there was an imperial court in St. Petersburg, Russia, the court of the czars. They supported a trade with England in strong, heavy, black beers, massive versions of the popular English porters that became known as imperial porters, and somewhat later as imperial stouts. Then in the late 1990s, American brewers started brewing IPAs with even more hops than the ridiculous amounts they were already using, at a gravity that led to beers of 7.5 percent ABV and up. What to call them? They looked at the imperial stouts and grabbed the apparent intensifier; "Imperial" IPA was born. Though this is still the most common usage, this shorthand for "hoppier and stronger" has been applied to pilsner and, amusingly, porter. Where it will stop, no one knows, as brewers joke about brewing "imperial mild" and "imperial helles."

Infusion. The mashing method generally used by ale brewers. Infusion entails heating the mash in a single vessel until the starches have been converted to sugar. There is single infusion, in which the crushed malt (grist) is mixed with hot water and steeped without further heating, and step infusion, in which the mash is held for short periods at rising temperature points. Infusion mashing is simpler than decoction mashing and works well with most types of malt.

IPA. India pale ale, a British ale style that has been almost completely co-opted by American brewers, characterized in this country by intense hops bitterness, accompanied in better examples of the style by a full-malt body. The name derives from the style's origin as a beer brewed for export to British beer drinkers in India. The beer was strong and heavily laced with hops—a natural preservative—to better endure the long sea voyage. Some British brewers claim that the beer was brewed that way in order to be diluted upon arrival in India, a kind of "beer concentrate" that saved on shipping costs.

Kräusening. The practice of carbonating beer by a second fermentation. After the main fermentation has taken place and its vigorous blowoff of carbon dioxide has been allowed to escape, a small amount of fresh wort is added to the tank. A second fermentation takes place, and the carbon dioxide is captured in solution. General opinion is that there is little sensory difference between kräusened beer and beer carbonated by injection, but some brewers hold that this more traditional method produces a "softer" beer.

Lager. The generic term for all cold-fermented beers. Lager has also been appropriated as a name for the lightly hopped pilsners that have become the world's most popular beers, such as Budweiser, Castle, Brahma, Heineken, and Asahi. Many people speak of pilsners and lagers as if they are two different styles of beer, which is incorrect. All pilsners are lagers, but not all lagers are pilsners. Some are bocks, hellesbiers, and märzens.

Malt. Generally this refers to malted barley, although other grains can be malted and used in brewing. Barley is wetted and allowed to sprout, which causes the hard, stable starches in the grain to convert to soluble starches (and small amounts of sugars). The grains, now called malt, are kiln-dried to kill the sprouts and conserve the starches. Malt is responsible for the color of beer. The kilned malt can be roasted, which will darken its color and intensify its flavors like a French roast coffee.

Mash. A mixture of cracked kernels of malt and water that has been heated. Heating causes starches in the malt to convert to sugars, which will be consumed by the yeast in fermentation. The length of time the mash is heated, temperatures, and techniques used are crucial to the character of the finished beer. Two mashing techniques are infusion and decoction.

Megabrewer. A mainstream brewer, generally producing 5 million or more barrels of American-style pilsner beer annually. Anheuser-Busch, Miller, and Coors are the best-known megabrewers.

Microbrewer. A somewhat dated term, originally defined as a brewer producing less than fifteen thousand barrels of beer in a year. Microbrewer, like craft brewer, is generally applied to any brewer producing beers other than mainstream American lagers. (See "A word about . . . Micros, Brewpubs, and Craft Brewers" on page 33.)

Original gravity. See *gravity.*

Party Pig. You'll see this term crop up when homebrewers are around, or at one of the Mid-Atlantic's BOPs. The Party Pig is a kind of cross between a growler and a keg. It's a plastic beer container with a soft CO_2-filled bladder inside and a tap on the front, er . . . where the pig's mouth would be. As beer is dispensed, the bladder expands to fill the space, keeping pressure on the beer. It's a popular, simple alternative to kegging small amounts of home- or BOP-brewed beer.

Pasteurization. A process named for its inventor, Louis Pasteur, the famed French microbiologist. Pasteurization involves heating beer to kill the microorganisms in it. This keeps beer fresh longer, but unfortunately it also changes the flavor because the beer is essentially cooked. "Flash pasteurization" sends fresh beer through a heated pipe where most of the microorganisms are killed; here the beer is hot for only a few seconds, as opposed to the twenty to thirty minutes of regular "tunnel" pasteurization. (See also *cold-filtering.*)

Pilsner. The Beer That Conquered the World. Developed in 1842 in Pilsen (now Plzen, in the Czech Republic), it is a hoppy pale lager that quickly became known as *pilsner* or *pilsener,* a German word meaning simply "from Pilsen." Pilsner rapidly became the most popular beer in the world and now accounts for more than 80 percent of all beer consumed worldwide. A less hoppy, more delicate version of pilsner, called budweiser, was developed in the Czech town of Ceske-Budejovice, formerly known as Budweis. Anheuser-Busch's Budweiser, the world's best-selling beer, is quite a different animal.

Pitching. The technical term for adding yeast to wort.

Prohibition. The period from January 1919 to December 1933, when the sale, manufacture, or transportation of alcoholic beverages was illegal in the United States, thanks to the Eighteenth Amendment and the Volstead Act. Prohibition had a disastrous effect on American brewing and brought about a huge growth in organized crime and government corruption. Repeal of Prohibition came with ratification of the Twenty-first Amendment in December 1933. Beer drinkers, however, had gotten an eight-month head start when the Volstead Act, the enforcement legislation of

Prohibition, was amended to allow sales of 3.2 percent ABW beer. The amendment took effect at midnight, April 7. According to Will Anderson's *From Beer to Eternity*, more than 1 million barrels of beer were consumed on April 7: 2,323,000 six-packs each hour of that one day.

Real ale. See *cask-conditioned beer* and *bottle-conditioned beer*.

Real Ale Festival (RAF). An annual Chicago beer festival that celebrates "real ale." Medals are awarded to the best bottle- and cask-conditioned beers in a variety of styles. The medals from the RAF are quite prestigious and are of particular significance to brewers.

Regional brewery. Somewhere between a micro- and a megabrewer. Annual production by regional breweries ranges from thirty-five thousand to 2 million barrels. They generally brew mainstream American lagers. However, some microbrewers—Boston Beer Company, New Belgium, and Sierra Nevada, for instance—have climbed to this production level, and some regional brewers, like Anchor, Matt's, and August Schell, have reinvented themselves and now produce craft-brewed beer. (See "A word about . . . Micros, Brewpubs, and Craft Brewers" on page 33.)

Reinheitsgebot. The German beer purity law, which has its roots in a 1516 Bavarian statute limiting the ingredients in beer to barley malt, hops, and water. The law evolved into an inch-thick book and was the cornerstone of high-quality German brewing. It was deemed anticompetitive by the European Community courts and overturned in 1988. Most German brewers, however, continue to brew by its standards; tradition and the demands of their customers ensure it.

Repeal. See *prohibition*.

Ringwood. The house yeast of Peter Austin and Pugsley System breweries. A very particular yeast that requires an open fermenter, it is mostly found in the northeastern United States. Some well-known examples of Ringwood-brewed beers are Geary's, Shipyard, and Magic Hat; examples in the Mid-Atlantic include Red Brick Station and the Wharf Rat. Ringwood beers are often easily identifiable by a certain nuttiness to their flavor. A brewer who isn't careful will find that Ringwood has created an undesirably high level of diacetyl, a compound that gives a beer a buttery or butterscotch aroma. Note that smaller amounts of diacetyl are perfectly normal and desirable in some types of beer.

Swill. A derogatory term used by beer geeks for American mainstream beers. The beers do not really deserve the name, since they are made with pure ingredients under conditions of quality control and sanitation some micros only wish they could achieve.

Terminal gravity. See *gravity*.

Three-tier system. A holdover from before Prohibition, the three-tier system requires brewers, wholesalers, and retailers to be separate entities. The system was put in place to curtail financial abuses that were common when the three were mingled. Owning both wholesale and retail outlets gave unscrupulous brewers the power to rake off huge amounts of money, which all too often was used to finance political graft and police corruption. The three-tier system keeps the wholesaler insulated from pressure from the brewer and puts a layer of separation between brewer and retailer. Recent court rulings have put the future of the regulated three-tier system in serious doubt, however, which may spell paradise or disaster for beer drinkers.

Wort. The prebeer grain broth of sugars, proteins, hop oils and alpha acids, and whatever else was added or developed during the mashing process. Once the yeast has been pitched and starts its jolly work, wort becomes beer.

Yeast. A miraculous fungus that, among other things, converts sugar into alcohol and carbon dioxide. The particular yeast strain used in brewing beer greatly influences the aroma and flavor of the beer. An Anheuser-Busch brewmaster recently told me that the yeast strain used there is the major factor in the flavor and aroma of Budweiser. Yeast is the sole source of the clovey, banana-rama aroma and the taste of Bavarian-style wheat beers. The original Reinheitsgebot of 1516 made no mention of yeast. It hadn't been discovered yet. Early brewing depended on a variety of sources for yeast: adding a starter from the previous batch of beer; exposing the wort to the wild yeasts carried on the open air (a method still used for Belgian lambic beers); always using the same vats for fermentation (yeast would cling to cracks and pores in the wood); or using a "magic stick" to stir the beer. At the time, the brewers did not realize that the dormant yeast from the previous batch was dried on its surface. British brewers called the turbulent, billowing foam on fermenting beer goddesgood—"God is good"—because the foam meant that the predictable magic of the yeast was making beer. And beer, as Ben Franklin said, is proof that God loves us and wants us to be happy. Amen.

Zwickel. A zwickel ("tzVICK-el") is a little spout coming off the side of a beer tank that allows the brewer to sample the maturing beer in small amounts. If you're lucky, your tour will include an unfiltered sample of beer tapped directly from the tank through this little spout. Most brewers are touchy about this, as the zwickel is a potential site for infection, but with proper care, it's perfectly harmless to "tickle the zwickel." It's delicious, too; unfiltered beer is the hot ticket.

INDEX